Money and Sustainability

The Missing Link

A REPORT FROM

THE CLUB OF ROME - EU CHAPTER
to
Finance Watch and the *World Business Academy*

Bernard Lietaer
Christian Arnsperger ~ Sally Goerner ~ Stefan Brunnhuber

Published in this first edition in 2012 by:
Triarchy Press
Station Offices
Axminster
Devon. EX13 5PF
United Kingdom

+44 (0)1297 631456
info@triarchypress.com
www.triarchypress.com

A catalogue record for this book is available from the British Library.

Print ISBN: 978-1-908009-7-53

Contents

THE CLUB OF ROME: EU CHAPTER - CoR-EU
Honorary President HRH Prince Philip of Belgium

Telling the Truth about Money

Introductory remarks to the Report to *Finance Watch* and the *World Business Academy*

We are not telling the truth about money. Yet money is at the core of the economy. And economy is ruling the world. It dominates human welfare from cradle to grave. It rules the use of the planet's natural resources and the quality of the environment. Today it is generally admitted that many limits of the Earth's ecosystem have been overshot. There is evidence that the present course is not sustainable.

Governments, media and most leaders make every possible effort to convince public opinion to stick to mainstream thinking. If society wishes to be or to become successful, they say, we have to keep faith in the current paradigm. The gospel still is that everything has to be expressed in monetary terms. And that there is no salvation outside the dominant financial systems and banking practices, a monopoly and a major power instrument. Closed systems are preferred to open ones. Complexity is avoided. Indeed a shortsighted vision on sustainable solutions…

There is, though, a lot of thinking and doing 'out-of-the-box' around the world. At conferences, in publications and increasingly through the Web, many authoritative voices are denouncing the blind spots of the present paradigm, inviting us to act without waiting any longer. Yet, their messages are not relayed by the mass media. They are ignored by most political leaders. They don't reach the public at large. At the same time, people are crying out for a radical change, not the least in the European Union.

The Club of Rome EU Chapter (CoR-EU), located in Brussels, aims to build bridges between the institutions of the European Union, their constituencies and the international Club of Rome, which has been a leading think-tank at world level for more than 40 years. The CoR-EU is acting as a catalyst of reflection on sustainable development in Europe. Its strategic aims for the next few years focus on the issues of money and governance. This includes initiating and facilitating cutting-edge research on ground-breaking concepts in these domains.

We asked our fellow Board member Bernard Lietaer to prepare a Report on money and sustainability that could contribute to a societal discourse on the implementation of EU policies for development in a wider global context, involving key public authorities and private sector decision-makers, the media as well as the public at large. With co-authors Christian Arnsperger, Stefan Brunnhuber and Sally Goerner he produced the present Report, which is fully endorsed by the EU Chapter of the Club of Rome.

While the issue is by definition global, the CoR-EU felt the Report should primarily be addressed on its behalf to a recognised, authoritative and independent European body. The most appropriate choice seemed to be *Finance Watch,* a public interest association, recently created on the initiative of members of the European Parliament. It is dedicated to making finance work for the good of society, strengthening the voice of society in financial regulation reforms by conducting citizen advocacy and presenting public interest arguments to lawmakers as a counterweight to private interest lobbying by the financial industry.

It made sense also to address the business community at large. We are delighted that the *World Business Academy*, a non-profit think-tank and network of business leaders, agreed to be a second recipient of our Report. Its mission is to inspire and help business assume responsibility for the whole of society, exploring its role in relation to critical moral, environmental and social dilemmas. Its objectives are to change business leaders' consciousness from self-service to servant leadership as well as to change the behaviour of the public at large, so it spends its money where its values are.

These objectives are close to the Club of Rome's heart.

***

At the time of writing these remarks we witness the dismantling of the state as guarantor of public good. Almost everything is for sale in most EU countries. Austerity is imposed at all levels. Public unrest will continue to grow unless new governance structures replace the obsolete ones.

There is a great challenge here for the European Union. We dare hope that the publication of *Money and Sustainability: The Missing Link* will inspire many a decision maker and opinion leader to change course now, choosing new, creative approaches in monetary issues. We urgently need an increased moral consciousness at all levels.

The CoR-EU is indebted to the World Academy of Art and Science, represented by Ivo Šlaus, President, and Garry Jacobs, Chair of the Board and CEO, as well as to Felix Unger, President of the European Academy of Sciences and Arts for supporting this Report by co-signing these brief preliminary remarks.

Mark DUBRULLE
Member of the Club of Rome
President of the CoR-EU Chapter

Felix UNGER
President of the European Academy
of Sciences and Arts

Ivo ŠLAUS
President of the World Academy
of Art and Science

Message from the Secretary General of the Club of Rome

Is Money the Evil?

Money, so we are told, is the root of all evil; it makes the world go round; but can't buy us love. The truth is money has become a central feature of our existence. It measures our economic growth, our social status and our consumption habits. Two billion of us on planet Earth have nowhere near enough to live on; yet one percent of our population has more than it can ever use and flaunts it in a manner that frequently appalls many of us.

How could this have come about? How could a simple invention which had, at its heart, such a laudable goal – to help people trade their commodities easily and effectively – go so wrong? Why have we this rift between finance and economy, between financial markets and the real economy they were meant to serve? The consequences of this rift have been growing for decades. Over the past forty years, the world has been wracked by over 400 financial crises; they have destabilised economies, impoverished people around the world and wreaked havoc with the planet's natural capital. Money and financial markets have become ends in themselves.

Lietaer and his colleagues have embarked on an ambitious yet timely investigation into the role of money and its effects on sustainability. He takes us on an incredible journey, which places money in its rightful context as a means to a sustainable future. He analyses the emergence of a speculation society where money floats around our global casino and where only 2% of the $4 trillion a day traded in foreign exchange transactions actually makes it way into the real economy. But now, imagine the tables were turned, and we could squeeze 98% into the real economy. What might this mean for jobs or for reducing poverty? For sustainability?

The book contains powerful arguments that need to be listened to, digested and acted upon. The section on how money affects sustainability makes the key point that the global crises we face are interconnected. The financial crisis is but one dimension of a multi-dimensional puzzle. However, the book is more than a diagnosis of the ills and travails of our monetary system; it also points to new ways of reforming our financial system, to pioneering ideas and to potential solutions. The call for alternative thinking and innovative strategies is timely and necessary.

The Club of Rome congratulates the authors. Their book articulates many of the concerns that the Club of Rome has articulated over the years. Let there be no doubt that our financial system is in urgent need of major overhaul. We tamper with it at the margin at our own peril. Without a well functioning financial market we will not see the progress necessary to protect our natural capital base and secure meaningful work for those who need it. We will pay a high price. The authors understand this and have put before us a reasoned and important book.

Ian JOHNSON
Secretary General – The Club of Rome

Before joining the Club of Rome in 2010, Ian Johnson spent 26 years at the World Bank, where he became Vice President for Sustainable Development and, for five years, Chairman of the Consultative Group on International Agricultural Research (CGIAR).

The World Academy of Art and Science

The current economic, political and moral crises cannot be solved, cannot even be reduced, by applying more of the same approaches that generated them in the first place. New ideas, out-of-the-box thinking, and paradigmatic changes are required. Many prevailing concepts currently taken for granted have to be freshly studied and challenged. Money is such a concept.

WAAS endorses and strongly supports the initiative of the Club of Rome-EU Chapter and thanks WAAS fellow Bernard Lietaer who initiated this important and original line of research more than a decade ago and has presented it at meetings of the World Academy. Lietaer and his collaborators, Christian Arnsperger, Sally Goerner and Stefan Brunnhuber, have produced a remarkable study, *Money & Sustainability: the Missing Link*, which merits serious attention from leaders, policy-makers, theorists and others trying to understand the roots of the current monetary crisis and measures for addressing it.

This study complements other endeavours of WAAS stressing the essential value and role of human capital. The Report reminds us that money is a man-made instrument intended to help society optimise human welfare. The prevailing monetary system encourages the multiplication of money for destabilising speculative investment rather than for productive investment that creates jobs, raises real incomes and promotes social equity. The Report examines alternative monetary strategies that can help mobilise under-utilised social resources, especially the huge number of unemployed and underemployed young people and adults whose human potential is ignored and squandered by the current system. This Report is a call for prompt political and economic action.

We wish to express our appreciation to the authors and to the Club of Rome EU-Chapter for this important initiative.

Ivo ŠLAUS
President

Garry JACOBS
Chair of the Board and CEO

4

WORLD BUSINESS ACADEMY
Taking responsibility for the whole

"War is too important to be left to generals," as the old adage goes. Likewise, monetary policy is too important to be left to monetary theorists. The brilliance of this Report is that it captures and maps – with crystal clarity – the fundamental connection between climate change, the cyclical boom and bust of our current monetary system, the fragility of the global economy, the political instability of most of the Western democracies, and the unsustainable overhang over it all of vast pools of international capital in the form of gambling receipts which we euphemistically call "derivatives".

The capacity to report succinctly and in an informative way on the interrelationship of these dynamic pieces is itself a credit to Bernard Lietaer and his associates. Even more important, the Report is so lucid and readable that the average executive can understand the extraordinary issues it presents in a way seldom possible with monetary theorists' articles.

The Report has illuminated essential questions usually left in the dusty corners of academia's ivory towers and brought them into full focus in the hurly burly of the market place. The Report conveys what we must do individually and collectively if we choose to have business enterprises grow in healthy and sustainable ways.

From the business viewpoint, monetary policy isn't an academic exercise:

• In normal times, the pro-cyclical amplification of the money creation process is extremely expensive for the business world; businesses tend to be always under- or over-staffed, under- or over-invested, at both ends of this amplified cycle.

• In times of crisis, when banks misstep they are in fact holding hostage the entire business world and increasing the risk for all businesses, big or small, from Main Street to Wall Street.

• The solutions presented in chapter VII show what businesses can and should do themselves to systematically avoid these problems.

• The full Report is an invaluable tool that enables C-Suite executives and their Boards to understand what they need to know and to do to lead their enterprises and maximize stakeholder value.

The World Business Academy has long been committed to advancing cutting-edge business information among business executives charged with navigating their businesses through the challenging times we live in. The Academy thanks Bernard Lietaer and his associates for presenting this Report to us, and encourages all levels of government and private enterprises to use the Report to begin a serious conversation on the critical issues the Report illuminates – while there is still time.

Rinaldo S. BRUTOCO
President

Foreword by Dennis Meadows

Arsenic was used as a medicine for thousands of years. It is a deadly poison, of course. But its ability to alleviate the short-term symptoms of distress led many sufferers to use it anyway. Only in the past century has it been mainly replaced by less deadly alternatives.

Fiat currency issued by private institutions through the creation of debt has been used by nations for centuries. Its deadly effects are becoming apparent. But its ability to alleviate the symptoms of distress has led to its use anyway. We can only hope that in this century we will begin to use less deadly alternatives.

I have been reading the literature on sustainability for 40 years. I have attended hundreds of conferences on the same theme over that period. However, before I first encountered Bernard's work, I had never heard anyone describe the financial system as a cause of our society's headlong rush to collapse. Quite the contrary: there is a widespread effort to identify how minor changes in the financial system could move global society over to a path that leads to sustainability.

A fish will never create fire while immersed in water. We will never create sustainability while immersed in the present financial system. There is no tax, or interest rate, or disclosure requirement that can overcome the many ways the current money system blocks sustainability.

I used not to think this. Indeed, I did not think about the money system at all. I took it for granted as a neutral and inevitable aspect of human society. But since beginning to read Bernard's analyses I have a very different view. He is not alone. For example Thomas Greco has written on this topic. But the depth of Bernard's practical experience, theoretical understanding, and historical perspectives on the financial system leave him without peer.

I now understand, as proven clearly in this text, that the prevailing financial system is incompatible with sustainability in five ways:

- it causes boom and bust cycles in the economy
- it produces short-term thinking
- it requires unending growth
- it concentrates wealth
- it destroys social capital

Any one of these is probably enough to derail the most carefully considered plan for a transition to sustainability. Together they are a prescription for disaster, which is precisely what they are giving us. The instability of the financial system should be enough to cause alarm, as the authors point out:

"According to the IMF, between 1970 and 2010 there were 145 banking crises, 208 monetary crashes and 72 sovereign-debt crises-in other words, a staggering total of 425 systemic crises. An average of more than 10 per year! These crises have hit more than three-quarters of the 180 countries that are members of the IMF, many of them being hit several times."

Informed observers of the 2008 crisis, by far the most serious so far, believe that the causes of instability have not been changed. Indeed many of them have grown worse. There will certainly be another global financial disaster.

A common English idiom is, 'Like a fish out of water'. It refers to someone or something in a very unaccustomed and awkward situation. But unless the fish does move out of water, its experiments will never lead to fire. We are going to have to go through an awkward period, experimenting with new currency systems, if we are to have any chance of our efforts leading to sustainability.

Viable complementary currency systems are not alone sufficient to halt our headlong drive towards disaster. But we have no chance of avoiding collapse without them.

This text is a rich source of information. It has material for four different books:

- a devastating critique of traditional economic thinking
- an excellent discussion of the mechanisms through which money is created in modern society
- a description of the many problems we may expect from climate change and future collapses of the financial system
- proposals for nine different pragmatic monetary complements to the current financial system

The book is therefore a useful starting point for people with very different goals.

Our earliest ancestors finally did manage to develop a technology based on fire. But they had to emerge from the ocean to do it. Our descendants will no doubt develop a technology based on sustainability. But they will have to emerge from the current financial system to do it. This book gives the motivation and some preliminary directions for doing that.

Em. Prof. Dennis Meadows
New Hampshire, February 2012

Dealing with the Eurozone Crisis... Another Way?

As we go to press, the Greek electorate – after two years of drastic austerity measures – has voted clearly against the cuts, the bailout and the political mainstream. Chaos in the eurozone seems one step closer. So we take this opportunity to outline how just one of the proposals from this book can be applied now, in Greece, Spain or any other country facing this kind of crisis. It's a solution that mainstream financiers and media avoid discussing, but it's elegant and simple. It would work, and the necessary (Open Source) software is available now.

Current monetary orthodoxy says that 100% of the Greek (or any other) economy must be either 'in' or 'out' of the eurozone. Everybody knows that either option will entail even higher unemployment and yet more misery. But it doesn't have to be that way! The core principle of complementary currencies, as set out here, is that they run alongside the main currency, increasing resilience and flexibility for the entire socio-economic system. Here's our systemic solution in a nutshell:

- Greece continues to use the euro for all international business: tourism, shipping, exports and imports, etc. Taxes are levied in euros on profits made in these activities, and used to service the country's national debt.

- In addition, any Greek city/region wanting to participate can issue its own local currency (generically called 'Civics' in the case study in chapter VIII). Civics are used to pay for important local, social and environmental programmes. In our example, 1 Civic is issued to anyone who completes 1 hour of approved service to the community. Projects for which Civics are paid should be decided democratically and locally.

- The issuing city/region requires payment from each household of, say, 10 Civics/quarter.

- Households that have not earned enough Civics can use an online (eBay-style) market to buy them with euros – or any other agreed good or service – from those that have earned more than they need.

- Civics exist only in electronic form, issued by the city/region, using mobile phones as a payment mechanism (as happens in Indonesia, S. Africa and Kenya now). So Civics are 100% traceable and their use is transparent.

- A new type of non-profit organisation audits the validity of the Civics in circulation.

- There is no fixed Civic:euro exchange rate. This is determined in the online market. To increase the value of its Civic, a city simply requires more of them from each household. As the local economy recovers, this number can be reduced, and could even drop back to zero when full employment is reached.

This approach allows the Greek economy to retain the benefits of the euro, while the Civic helps each community solve its own social and environmental problems, while mobilising every household (with appropriate exceptions for disability, etc.) to participate.

(A business-to-business currency called C3 – see chapter VII – could also inject working capital into small businesses and accelerate the recovery of mainstream jobs paid in euros. Similar approaches could be used in other European countries struggling with the consequences of current austerity programmes.)

Bernard Lietaer, Christian Arnsperger, Sally Goerner, Stefan Brunnhuber

May, 2012

Executive Summary

Peple concerned with sustainability in general – with issues like climate change, environmental degradation, food and water shortages, population growth and energy use – tend not to worry about the money system. Nor do they tend to look for solutions that involve monetary innovations. Even those economists who are also concerned about sustainability in principle are seldom aware that our money system systematically encourages unsustainable behaviour patterns that may end up threatening human survival on this planet. In fact, this Report shows that the current money system is both a crucial part of the overall sustainability 'problem' and a vital part of any solution. It makes clear that awareness of this 'Missing Link' is an absolute imperative for economists, environmentalists and anyone else trying to address sustainability at a , national, regional or global level. Aiming for sustainability without restructuring our money system is a naïve approach, doomed to failure.

So the money system is bad for social and environmental sustainability. But this Report also proves – perhaps more surprisingly – that the money system is bad for the money system itself. Unless we fundamentally restructure it, we cannot achieve monetary stability. Indeed, this Report also demonstrates that monetary stability itself is possible if, and only if, we apply systemic biomimicry – that is to say, if we complement the prevailing monetary monopoly with what we call a 'monetary ecosystem'.

Finally, the good news is that the information and communication revolution which we are living today is already pushing us in precisely the right direction.

Let's look at this idea of the money system as the 'Missing Link' in more detail. Our world is facing the immense challenges of a two-fold sustainability crisis. On one hand, climate change, rising greenhouse gas emissions and spikes in food and energy prices signal that our ways of producing and consuming goods and services have become unsustainable. On the other, repeated financial and monetary crises remind us that our money system has its own problems. The efforts to prop up and 'save' this money system during the 2007-2008 banking crash, followed by unsuccessful attempts to contain the toxic economic fallout with a 'Keynesian stimulus', have given rise to stark increases in government indebtedness. In the wake of the sovereign-debt and euro crisis, both the United States and the EU governments are currently being driven to financial extremes. Pensions, unemployment benefits and other social safety nets as well as investment in a post-carbon economy are all in jeopardy at precisely the time when they are most needed. In parallel, many public assets are in the process of being privatised.

Environmentalists often try to address the ecological crisis by thinking up new monetary incentives, creating 'green' taxes or encouraging banks to finance sustainable investment. Economists, in turn, tend to believe the financial crisis can be 'fixed' and kept from recurring with better regulation and a strict, prolonged reduction in public spending. But, whether they are advocating greener taxes, leaner government budgets, greener euros or dollars or pounds, could both camps be barking up the wrong tree?

It is our contention that the 'Missing Link' between finance and the environment, between money and sustainability, lies elsewhere. What this Report demonstrates beyond doubt is a structural monetary flaw – a flaw in the very manner in which we create money – that is generating our disconcerting problems. The inescapable conclusion? That, in order to face the challenges of the 21st century, we need to rethink and overhaul our entire monetary system.

CHAPTER I — Why this Report, Now?

This Report has three objectives:

- To provide evidence that the financial and monetary instabilities plaguing Europe and the rest of the world have a *structural cause* that has been largely overlooked. Addressing this structural cause is a necessary (but not a sufficient) condition for dealing with today's challenges.

- To place the monetary problem, and solutions to it, in the context of two global issues: climate change and population ageing. Indeed it makes clear that, in order to avoid the worst scenarios of climate change, massive investment is needed *now*: investment that will require governmental leadership and funding. Concurrently, the retirement of baby boomers reduces government revenues while adding pressure to already severely strained social programmes. Both issues will reach their peak during this decade, and neither is compatible with austerity measures. Continuing to follow the current monetary paradigm will render governments powerless to address these social and environmental challenges.

- To propose pragmatic solutions that can be implemented cost-effectively by citizens, non-profits, businesses or governments: solutions which would resolve *at a structural level* several critical sustainability issues currently facing many countries.

History will probably see the period 2007-2020 as one of financial turmoil and gradual monetary breakdown. History has also shown that systemic changes in the monetary domain happen only after a crash. Therefore, the time to wake up to monetary issues is now.

CHAPTER II — Making Economic Paradigms Explicit

Debates about economic issues rarely reveal the paradigm from which an economist is speaking. We start by making explicit the conceptual framework that underlies our approach, and compare it with other paradigms currently in use. Rather than defining environmental and social issues as 'externalities', our approach sees economic activities as a subset of the social realm, which, in turn, is a subset of the biosphere. This view provides the basis for the emergence of a new set of pragmatic tools, flexible enough to address many of our economic, social and environmental challenges.

We suffer from a three-layered collective 'blind spot' with regard to our money system. The first blind spot relates to the hegemony of the idea of a single, central currency. It is widely believed that societies have always, and must always, impose, as a monopoly, a single, centrally-issued currency, on which interest is charged. In fact, several interesting societies, such as Dynastic Egypt and Europe during the Central Middle Ages (from the 10th to the 13th century), have encouraged multiple parallel currencies. This latter approach has resulted in greater economic stability, equitable prosperity and an economy in which people naturally tend to consider the longer term more than we do.

The second layer of our collective 'blind spot' is a result of the ideological warfare between capitalism and communism in the 20th century. Although minute differences between these two systems have been studied *ad nauseam*, what they have in common has remained less scrutinised: particularly the fact that both impose a single national currency monopoly that is created through bank debt. The only significant difference between the two is that, in the Soviet system, the state owned the banks, whereas, in the capitalist system, this occurs only periodically (usually after banks 'too big to fail' experience serious difficulties).

From the 18th century onwards, the systemic *status quo* was institutionalised through the creation of central banks as enforcers of the monetary monopoly. This institutional framework spins the final layer of the 'blind spot'.

These three layers explain why there is such powerful and enduring resistance to reconsidering the paradigm of a single, monopolistically produced currency.

CHAPTER III — Monetary and Banking Instability

Today's foreign exchange and financial derivatives markets dwarf anything else on our planet. In 2010, the volume of foreign exchange transactions reached $4 trillion *per day*. One day's exports or imports of *all* goods and services in the world amount to about 2% of that figure. Which means that 98% of transactions on these markets are purely speculative. This foreign exchange figure does not include derivatives, whose notional volume was $600 trillion – or eight times the entire world's *annual* GDP in 2010.

It was in this colossal market that the 2007 banking crisis broke out. As with every previous banking crash, governments felt they had no choice but to rescue the banking system, at whatever cost to the taxpayer. While this is clearly the biggest crisis we have experienced since the 1930s, it is not the first one. According to IMF data, 145 countries experienced banking crises. In addition, there were 208 monetary crashes and 72 sovereign debt crises between 1970 and 2010. That brings the grand total of 425 systemic crises, i.e. an average of more than ten countries in crisis every year!

The consequences in terms of unemployment, lost economic output, societal disruption and widespread human suffering are dramatic. The full financial costs of the 2007-2008 crisis are unprecedented. In the United States for instance, the $700 billion Troubled Asset Relief Program (TARP) is often talked about, although it is only the first slice of the rescue operation. Mention of this programme is usually followed by the comment: "most of that money has by now been reimbursed". The US case is of interest because it is the only country where both the government and the central bank have been forced by the courts to reveal the total costs of the rescue programmes related to the 2007-8 crisis. In addition to TARP, forty-nine other programmes have been involved in the US rescue at a total cost of $14.4 trillion. In comparison, the total US GDP in 2007 was $16 trillion.

The bailouts, followed by a large-scale Keynesian stimulus plan to avoid a deflationary depression, have resulted in enormous budget deficits and additional public debt. In the twenty-three countries most directly affected by the banking crash, government debt jumped by an average of 24% of GDP. Some European countries such as Iceland, Ireland, Latvia, Denmark and Spain fared worse, with increases in national debt between 30% and 80% of GDP.

The timing could not possibly have been worse. The tidal wave of baby boomers retiring over the next decade will make for huge additional pressures on public debt. A 2010 study by the Bank for International Settlements (BIS) estimated that, by 2020, age-related deficits will increase government debt to more than 200% of GDP in the UK and to 150% in France, Ireland, Italy, Greece, Belgium and the United States. This forecast is still optimistic because it rests on the assumption of low interest rates. By 2040, projected age-related expenses will propel the debt/GDP ratios for all these countries to somewhere in the range of 300% to 600%.

The solutions recommended by the financial sector are a package of immediate, coercive austerity measures and a call for governments to privatise *everything*. In countries where the list of targeted government assets is known, this includes all public roads, tunnels, bridges, parking meters, airports, all government-owned office buildings, as well as water and sewerage systems. For the US, where data are available, this amounts to $9.3 trillion of federal, state and city assets. One assessment of the US situation by the financial sector is as follows: "As soon as the political pain from cutting public services becomes greater than the cost in terms of votes lost due to selling assets, this market will take off. At the grass-roots level, this critical political pain threshold has now been reached."[1]

Similarly in Europe, the UK has announced a £16 billion privatisation programme; in Italy, 9,000 publicly owned properties were put up for sale by the Berlusconi government; France's Sarkozy government sold all the country's toll roads for €5 billion; the conditions attached to the Greek rescue package included a €50 billion privatisation; and the list goes on. These pressures will remain pervasive for a long time. But what happens afterwards? Why would governments become more credit-worthy once they have to pay rent for their offices, and have to pay tolls for their employees to drive to work on roads that were once publicly owned?

Before proceeding blindly on this course, would it not be useful to determine whether, far from the current crisis being merely another case of gross financial mismanagement, there is an underlying systemic cause common to all financial and monetary instabilities?

CHAPTER IV — Instabilities Explained: The Physics of Complex Flow Networks

Since the 19th century, mainstream economics has classified the economic system as a closed one. Closed systems have relatively little interaction with other systems or with the outside environment, while open systems do. An intellectually convenient feature of closed systems is that they reach static equilibrium when left undisturbed.

This report proposes that we view the economy as an open system consisting of complex flow networks in which money circulates between and among various economic agents. It has recently become possible to measure with a single metric the sustainability of any complex flow network on the basis of its structural diversity and its interconnectivity. A key finding is that any complex flow system is sustainable if, and only if, it maintains a crucial balance between two equally essential but complementary properties: its efficiency and its resilience. When too much emphasis is put on efficiency at the cost of resilience, diversity is sacrificed. This will automatically result in sudden systemic collapses.

We have a worldwide monetary monoculture in which the same type of exchange medium is put into circulation in every country: a single national currency created through bank debt. Such a monoculture tends to spawn a brittle and unsustainable system. The structural solution needed to give sustainability a chance, albeit totally

---

1   *Euromoney*, April 2010, p.85.

unorthodox, is to diversify the available exchange media and the agents that create them. In short, in place of a monetary monoculture, we need a *monetary ecosystem.*

CHAPTER V — The Effects of Today's Money System on Sustainability

Monetary or financial crises can be highly destructive and are obviously not compatible with sustainability. What can be more difficult to perceive is how some mechanisms built into our current money system shape individual and collective behaviours, even when it is not in crisis. On the positive side, modern money should be credited with triggering an explosion of entrepreneurial and scientific innovation without historical precedent. However, there are also five other mechanisms that turn out to be directly incompatible with sustainability. They are:

- *Amplification of boom and bust cycles:* Banks provide or withhold funding to the same sectors or countries at the same time, thus amplifying the business cycle towards boom or bust. Such amplification is detrimental for everyone, including the banking sector itself. In the worst-case scenario, we end up where we are now: when banks stop trusting each other.

- *Short-term thinking:* 'Discounted cash flow' is standard practice in any investment evaluation. Because bank-debt money carries interest, the discounting of all future costs or incomes inevitably tends to lead to short-term thinking.

- *Compulsory growth:* The process of compound interest or interest on interest imposes exponential growth on the economy. Yet exponential growth is, by definition, unsustainable in a finite world.

- *Concentration of wealth:* The middle class is disappearing worldwide, with most of the wealth flowing to the top and increasing rates of poverty at the bottom. Such inequalities generate a broad range of social problems and are also detrimental to economic growth. Beyond the economic issue, the very survival of democracy may be at stake.

- *Devaluation of social capital:* Social capital which is built on mutual trust and results in collaborative action has always been difficult to measure. Nevertheless, whenever measurements have been made, they reveal a tendency for social capital to be eroded, particularly in industrialised countries. Recent scientific studies show that money tends to promote selfish and non-collaborative behaviours. These behaviours are not compatible with long-term sustainability.

Far from being a behaviourally neutral and passive medium of exchange, as generally assumed, conventional money deeply shapes a range of behaviour patterns, of which the five listed above are incompatible with sustainability. The continual imposition of a monopoly of this type of currency thus directly affects the future of humanity on our planet.

CHAPTER VI — The Institutional Framework of Power

The history of money is intimately entwined with power. Historian Niall Ferguson shows how the modern monetary framework evolved to finance wars through the emergence of four key institutions: parliaments, a professional tax bureaucracy, national debt and central banks. This 'Square of Power' was first optimised in 18th century Britain to give birth to industrialisation and to an global empire. These same monetary arrangements spread around the world to become the fundamental structure in place practically everywhere today.

It is often assumed that the relationship between the banking system and governments has remained unchanged for centuries. A case study of France shows that this is not necessarily the case. Indeed, since 1973, the French government has been forced to borrow exclusively from the private sector and therefore pay interest on new debt. Without this change, French government debt would now be at 8.6% of GDP instead of the current 78%. Furthermore, the Maastricht and Lisbon Treaties have generalised this same process to all signatory countries.

One radical solution would be for government itself to issue a currency that it later collects in the form of tax payments. This solution was known in the 1930s as the 'Chicago Plan'. Nationalising the monetary creation process confines banks to the role of mere money brokers. Although the Chicago Plan dramatically reduces the possibility of future banking crashes and instantly resolves all sovereign debt crises, it merely replaces a private monopoly with a public one. This does not get us any closer to the monetary ecosystem which is called for.

The 'official story' is that governments, just like any household, must raise the money needed to pay for their activities. This is done either through income (by taxation) or through debt (by issuing bonds). In this story, banks simply act as intermediaries collecting deposits and lending parts of that money to creditworthy individuals and institutions, including governments. However, since 1971, when fiat currency – that is, money created out of nothing – became universal, this story has been a complete fiction.

The Fiat Currency Paradigm provides an alternative interpretation of this story. With fiat currency, the primary purpose of taxation is to create demand for a currency that has otherwise no intrinsic value. The obligation of paying taxes only in the chosen currency is what gives the currency its value. A sovereign government can therefore choose what it wants to attribute value to by requiring it in the form of tax payments. Governments can thus determine the kind of efforts its citizens must make to obtain this chosen currency. Although this interpretation has impressive academic backing, it is being ignored in favour of the 'official story'.

In the 'official story', governments are completely powerless in the face of an anonymous and all-powerful 'financial market'. In the Fiat Currency Paradigm, given the nature of fiat currency, governments could conceivably choose to give value to other currencies in parallel to bank-debt money. We propose that meeting the challenges of the 21ˢᵗ century will require them to do so.

CHAPTER VII — Examples of Private Initiative Solutions

Nine examples of innovative motivation systems are presented in this and the next chapter. They can all work in parallel with conventional bank-debt money, use cost-effective electronic media, and should be as transparent as possible to their users. By making these systems more self-policing, such transparency could go a long way towards reducing potential fraud. The systems are presented in order, starting with the easiest and least controversial and ending with the most complex and revolutionary. The first five can be started privately, either by NGOs or businesses. They are:

- *Doraland*: a system proposed for Lithuania, with the purpose of creating a 'Learning Country'. In such a system everybody can volunteer to learn and/or teach, and be rewarded in Doras, a currency whose purpose is to help people realise their dreams. This would best be implemented by an NGO.

- *Wellness Tokens*: an NGO initiative working in cooperation with preventive health care providers to deal with issues even before they arise. Wellness Tokens reward and encourage healthy behaviours and thereby reduce long-term medical expenses for society.

- *Natural Savings*: a financial savings product that is fully backed by living trees. It would be a savings currency with inflation protection superior to that of any national currency, while simultaneously providing an incentive to reforest areas and thereby creating long-term carbon sinks. Another of its qualities: it works well for micro-savings.

- *C3*: a Business-to-Business (B2B) system that reduces unemployment by providing working capital to small and medium-sized businesses. The network's clearing currency would be fully backed by high-quality invoices and convertible into conventional money on demand. The insurance industry and banks both play critical and profitable roles in this system. C3s are working today in Brazil and Uruguay, and the latter country accepts C3s in payment of all taxes.

- *TRC*: the Trade Reference Currency is a global B2B currency proposal that would make it profitable for multinational companies to think long-term, thereby resolving the conflict between short-term financial corporate priorities and long-term social and environmental needs. It would be an inflation-proof and crash-proof global currency fully backed by a basket of commodities and services relevant to the global economy. The TRC would be a global currency distinct from any existing national currency, thus reducing the risk of geopolitical tensions around monetary zones of influence.

CHAPTER VIII — Examples of Governmental Initiatives

The next four examples of innovative motivation systems are governmental initiatives started at a city, regional or country level. They are:

- *Torekes*: a city-based initiative to encourage volunteering while promoting green behaviour and social cohesion in a poor neighbourhood. It has been running since 2010 in the city of Ghent, Belgium.
- *Biwa Kippu*: a proposal for the Biwa Prefecture in Japan to fund the labour components of the ecological restoration and maintenance of Lake Biwa, the oldest and largest lake in Japan. It could be either voluntary or obligatory for households in the area.
- *Civics*: a proposal empowering a city or region to fund civic activities without burdening their budgets. These activities could provide the labour component for social, educational and/or ecological projects. Such a system could also take the form of a compulsory contribution.
- *ECOs*: a national or Europe-wide system making it possible to fund critical components of large-scale ecological projects, such as climate change prevention and adaptation projects. It would be an interest-free currency issued by governments. Governments would require businesses to make a contribution proportional to their total sales, payable only in ECOs. This is the most controversial of the nine proposals, because it would be seen as a new type of corporate tax on the largest corporations. Such an initiative may require governments to 'declare war' on run-away climate change.

Not all nine systems – five private and four public – have to be implemented before the benefits of different monetary ecosystems start to become visible. Each community, city, region or country can pick and choose which kinds of system it implements. Together with a dozen other designs already in operation around the world, each combination of new exchange media would give an appropriate monetary ecosystem a chance to emerge. Some of these systems will fail. However, just like in a forest, the most successful types will spontaneously tend to spread. We still have much to learn, particularly about which governance structures are most appropriate for each type of system.

CHAPTER IX — Beyond the Limits to Growth?

H.G. Wells claimed: "History is a race between education and catastrophe". The stakes in this particular race have never been as high as they are today. Learning will be needed on everyone's part:

For today's elites, particularly the financial elites, perusing the classic works of economic historian Arnold Toynbee or more recently of Jared Diamond[2], might be relevant. Toynbee attributed the collapse of twenty-one different civilisations to just two causes: too much concentration of wealth, and an elite unwilling until too late to shift priorities in response to changing circumstances. Diamond focuses on environmental degradation as a proximate cause for civilisation collapses. Currently, we are simultaneously pushing the limits on all three of these causes. History teaches that even elites are not spared in a collapsing civilisation.

For those trained in economics, the necessary mental switch required is to look at the paradigm implicit in the teachings they received, and compare it to the approach used in this report.

For the population at large, perhaps the most important learning needed is to understand non-linearity, specifically the difference between linear and exponential growth. We are now dealing with an increasingly non-linear world. Grasping these different dynamics will be useful in understanding what is happening to us, and what to do about it.

In closing, it would be naïve to think of complementary currencies as a magic bullet to solve all our current and future problems. However, rethinking our money is a necessary ingredient in any effective solution. We can no longer afford to overlook complementary currencies as the 'Missing Link' that can deliver a money system which promotes sustainability rather than undermining it at every turn.

---

2   Jared Diamond, *Collapse: How Societies Choose to Fail or Succeed* (2005).

Chapter I

Why this Report, Now?

"My heart is moved by all I cannot save.
So much has been destroyed.
I have cast my lot with those who, age after age, perversely,
with no extraordinary power, reconstitute the world."

Adrienne Rich[1]

Humanity – and Western civilisation in particular – are on an untenable course. Climate change and species extinctions, an ageing population, high levels of joblessness and unsustainable energy consumption patterns are all issues needing urgent attention. There is a political consensus from the right to the left that, over the next decade, widespread and rapid changes in behaviour will be required. Governments and businesses have traditionally used monetary incentives as the primary motivational tool to induce non-spontaneous behaviour patterns. However, our monetary system is now itself in serious trouble. Because of the mounting challenges we face, the manner in which money shapes our motivations and actions has become part of the problem rather than part of the solution.

Our current monetary system – the specific manner in which money is created, circulated and managed in our society – is taken for granted by just about everyone. This includes not only the general public, the business community and non-governmental organisations, but also policy makers and a majority of academics. Consequently, after the massive 2008 financial crisis – the biggest systemic financial failure in history so far – the only option considered was to bail out the banking system at whatever cost to taxpayers, in order to return as quickly as possible to business as usual. This scenario has been repeated for every one of the large-scale banking crises and monetary meltdowns of our times.[2]

---

1 ˙ Adrienne Rich, 'Natural Resources', *The Dream of a Common Language – Poems* (1993), p.60.

2 Details of 425 systemic crises that have occurred since 1970 are given in Chapter III.

19

1. Identifying Structural Issues

The first purpose of this Report is to provide evidence that the instability of our monetary and banking system is due to a *structural* reason. As a result, the regulatory changes and capital requirements being debated and implemented within the existing framework will not succeed in avoiding future crashes, precisely because they all leave the actual structure of the monetary system intact. These structural features include the notion that money should be monopolistically created by a banking system, in exchange for debt.[3] We claim that reconsidering this monopoly is essential if sustainability is to have a chance to prevail during the 21st century. This does *not* mean that such a change will be sufficient to resolve all these problems automatically. Several other dimensions are clearly also relevant – education and governance, to name but two – but these other dimensions will not be the focus of this Report. Instead, we intend to show that if the monetary structure issue is not dealt with, all the other policies will prove fruitless.

A monetary system is a form of operating system for human activities. What is urgently needed, we argue, is an upgrade of our collective operating system to one with greater robustness and flexibility that will allow us to deal successfully with the numerous large-scale challenges of the 21st century. Changing our assumptions about how money is created and circulated could move us towards a sustainable world, one that includes humanity as well as the planet's biosphere, for which humanity has now collectively, and unwittingly, become responsible. Far from being a neutral tool facilitating exchanges, our current monetary system plays a key role in shaping human incentives and decisions at all levels: from small-scale local exchanges, to multi-billion dollar decisions by global corporations.

However, what we are proposing will require a paradigm shift in the monetary domain. Paradigm shifts are controversial because they challenge ideas held as self-evident truths, which in this case have prevailed for centuries. But the challenge is worth taking because it leads to a path where economics could become a genuinely emancipating social science. Even sustainable abundance could become a realistic possibility...

2. Offering Pragmatic Solutions

The second purpose of this report is to provide pragmatic suggestions for what can be done now. We will propose several examples of monetary innovations that increase the policy options available to governments, as well as pragmatic financial strategies for businesses, NGOs and citizens at large. Taken together, the synergies between

---

3 A layperson's 'Primer', which explains this process in simple language, appears in Appendix A (online). The respective roles of central banks, the International Monetary Fund and other monetary firemen are discussed.

such innovations would generate a radically different human incentive system for living both collectively and individually on our planet.

In practice, the new system we describe provides ordinary people with more freedom to live a life that honours more of their humanity, *it gives them choice from a wider spectrum of activities to meet their needs, and increases their chances of expressing their gifts and developing their creative passions.* For members of today's wealthy elite, the proposed approach makes it possible *to remain financially wealthy, and to do so without this being at the expense of the rest of humanity.*

Such possibilities may currently sound completely utopian and, as long as we stay caught in the conventional monetary paradigm, they will remain so. The highest cost we are paying for the maintenance of today's monetary paradigm is the limitation it imposes on what we believe is possible.

The response of governments to our current monetary predicaments brings to mind a statement by Winston Churchill about the United States during World War II: "You can always count on the Americans to do the right thing... after they have tried everything else!" Since the great banking meltdown of 2008, policy makers have indeed been trying everything possible to resolve the financial crisis except addressing the structure of the monetary system itself.

We review recent past events in Europe in order to illustrate this point. As of early 2012, all those countries involved in the 2008 crisis have become massively indebted in the process of saving their banking systems from bankruptcy. The financial system has 'reciprocated' by observing that these countries have now become too highly indebted, and by demanding the dismantling of Europe's social safety nets, which have taken centuries to build.

Austerity programmes are being imposed simultaneously everywhere, guaranteeing that the economic downturn will last longer than customary. Violent social unrest and the serial stepping-down of governments, as well as authoritarian and nationalistic reflexes, are highly likely to occur in the near future.

Even if the euro collapses, the only alternative being considered is a return to a system of national monopolies, each with one national currency, created through bank debt. In the hope of escaping the constraints of the euro by reverting to a currency it can devalue, each European country would still remain locked into the old straightjacket of trying to solve all its problems via the mechanism of a single currency.

3. The Importance of Timing

Perhaps the most important factor of all is timing. 2012 is the year of Rio+20, the twentieth anniversary of the first United Nations Conference on Sustainable Development, for which many organisations are arranging special events.[4] It is also the fortieth anniversary of *The Limits to Growth,* the first Report for the Club of Rome.[5]

The coming decade also happens to be an unusually critical one in two even more important respects. First, this decade will see the 'baby boomers' retire, triggering massive unresolved financial problems concerning pensions and increased health care costs. The Bank for International Settlements (BIS) forecasts that by 2020, on the basis of these extra age-related expenses alone, debt/GDP ratios will rise to more than 300% in Japan, 200% in the United Kingdom, and more than 150% in Belgium, France, Ireland, Greece, Italy and the United States.[6]

Second, the consensus in scientific and business circles is that to avoid the worst climate change scenarios[7], unprecedented investment is necessary within this same period to move to a post-carbon economy. Such a rapid introduction of the necessary technologies will require government leadership and subsidies *en masse.*

Both these issues are time-bound: we cannot afford to wait to address them until after public finances have improved. Missing this decade's deadline will have dire consequences: the promises made to a whole generation of people who faithfully contributed for their entire working lives to pension funds and health care insurance may be sacrificed. The potential damage to the planet's biosphere is even more critical, and its effects are expected to last more than 1,000 years! Indeed, the journal *Nature* recently published warnings about the implications of even moderate climate change.[8]

---

4   *www.uncsd2012.org ~ bit.ly/TPlink14* (As here, all references to online sources show first the root url, followed by an easy-to-use direct link to the source. In some browsers, it may be necessary to type www. first.)

5   Donella H. Meadows, Dennis L. Meadows, Jorgen Randers and William W. Behrens III, *The Limits to Growth* (1972). The validity of many of the forecasts made in that Report has been documented in Donella H. Meadows *et al. Limits to Growth: the 30-Year Update* (2004).

6   Stephen G. Cecchetti, Madhusudan S. Mohanty and Fabrizio Zampolli, 'The Future of Public Debt: Prospects and Implications', BIS Working Paper #300 (2010). See also Chapter III for a more detailed analysis of the impact of age-related expenses on governmental indebtedness.

7   That humans are causing global warming is the position of the Academies of Science from 19 countries plus many scientific organisations that study climate science. A survey of 3,146 earth scientists asked the question "Do you think human activity is a significant contributing factor in changing mean global temperatures?". 97.5% of climatologists who actively publish research on climate change responded "yes". (Doran, 2009)

8   Joseph Romm, 'Desertification: the Next Dustbowl', *Nature* 478 (27 October, 2011), pp.450–451.

Here are some excerpts from that paper:

"A basic prediction of climate science is that many parts of the world will experience longer and deeper droughts, thanks to the synergistic effects of drying, warming and the melting of snow and ice.

Precipitation patterns are expected to shift, expanding the dry subtropics. What precipitation there is will probably come in extreme deluges, resulting in runoff rather than drought alleviation. Warming causes greater evaporation and, once the ground is dry, the Sun's energy goes into baking the soil, leading to a further increase in air temperature. That is why, for instance, so many temperature records were set for the United States in the 1930s Dust Bowl; and why, in 2011, drought-stricken Texas saw the hottest summer ever recorded for a US state. Finally, many regions are expected to see earlier snowmelt, so less water will be stored on mountaintops for the summer dry season...

The paleoclimate record dating back to the medieval period reveals droughts lasting many decades. But the extreme droughts that will be faced this century will be far hotter than the worst of those: recent decades have been warmer than the driest decade of the worst drought in the past 1,200 years...

Most pressingly, what will happen to global food security if dust-bowl conditions become the norm for both food-importing and food-exporting countries? Extreme, widespread droughts will be happening at the same time as sea level rise and salt-water intrusion threaten some of the richest agricultural deltas in the world, such as those of the Nile and the Ganges. Meanwhile, ocean acidification, warming and overfishing may severely deplete the food available from the sea...

Human adaptation to prolonged, extreme drought is difficult or impossible. Historically, the primary adaptation to dust-bowlification has been abandonment... Feeding some 9 billion people by mid-century in the face of a rapidly worsening climate may well be the greatest challenge the human race has ever faced."

Figure 1.1 illustrates the effects of this 'dust-bowlification' on a global level in the decade of the 2060s, assuming a scenario of *moderate* climate change. The figure's author emphasises that "these predictions are not worst-case scenarios: they assume business-as-usual greenhouse-gas emissions. We can hope that the models are too pessimistic, but some changes, such as the expansion of the subtropics, already seem to be occurring faster than models have projected."

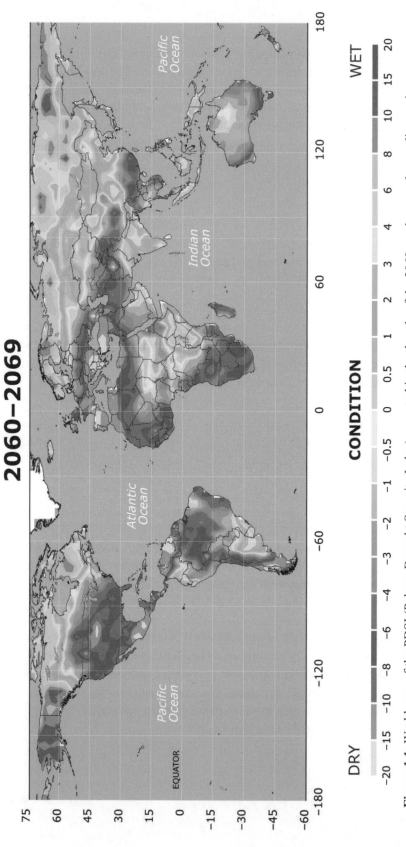

Figure 1.1: World map of the PDSI (Palmer Drought Severity Index) expected in the decade of the 2060s under a moderate climate change scenario. By comparison, in the US Great Plains during the Dust Bowl of the 1930s, the PDSI spiked very briefly to -6, but otherwise rarely exceeded -3 for the decade. This was sufficient to provoke abandonment of agricultural land on a large scale.
Source: Aiguo Dai, 'Drought under Global Warming: A Review', *Climate Change*, Volume 2, Issue 1 (Jan/Feb 2011), pp.45–65.

This map gives those who believe there is no need to tackle climate change head-on some food for thought. Climate change will affect not only all of Mediterranean Europe, but also much of France, Southern Germany, England and almost all of the USA (except Alaska), Brazil, half of Africa and China, and inhabited Australia. Imagine drought conditions similar to those prevailing in Northern Africa today, worse than the Dust Bowl of the 1930s, as far north as Paris, London, Berlin, Beijing or San Francisco… These dust-bowl conditions are projected to worsen for many decades and to be "largely irreversible for 1,000 years after emissions stopped".[9] When these drought conditions are combined with rising sea levels from melting ice in Greenland and the poles, much of Earth's biosphere and many of the places where humans have lived from time immemorial are at stake. Appendix B provides further evidence about climate change and its planetary consequences.[10]

If we remain trapped inside today's monetary paradigm, governmental austerity will need to prevail during the decade ahead, precisely the decade when investment in a post-carbon economy needs to take place. The monetary system is maintained thanks to a powerful and sophisticated banking lobby which logically prefers the structural *status quo*. However, does it make sense to keep accumulating financial wealth? What is the point of owning even half of Manhattan, London or Shanghai, if it is three feet under water or in the middle of a vast dustbowl?

Finally, the dollar and the euro, the world's first and second most important currencies, are now both wobbly for different reasons. If and when a euro or a dollar crisis breaks out, we should again expect a new round of bank emergencies. However, as the 2010 sovereign debt crisis demonstrated, the majority of governments are no longer creditworthy enough to bail out the financial system once more. What then? Just as we no longer have time to wait for further deterioration of the climate, we do not seem to have time for a new monetary and banking crash.

Five thousand years of monetary history reveals that significant changes in the monetary domain take place only when the previous system has collapsed. The most critical time for rethinking the monetary system will therefore be just after a big turmoil.

In short, we will be forced to consider stepping out into totally unorthodox monetary terrain – a terrain of the kind that this Report explores. When assailed by qualms as to how heterodox some of this sounds, please remember that it is orthodoxy that led us to our current predicaments…

---

9   Romm (2011)

10 This and the other appendices can be seen online at *www.money-sustainability.net* and
    www.triarchypress.com/missinglink

Finally, a clarification about the style of this document. Because this is a report and not a treatise, emphasis has been placed on succinctness and clarity rather than on exhaustive demonstration or academic references. In some cases, specialised appendices are provided to develop an argument or provide more evidence for the claims made. However, we are fully aware that what is proposed in this text cannot provide all the answers. It is rather an invitation to consider a new approach offering options that have not been sufficiently explored until now. That is why we are inviting readers to question and debate the topics we survey here.

The website *www.money-sustainability.net* is part of this Report. It provides some extracts from this text and some updates, as well as all the appendices. It also makes available ways to communicate about these ideas. The extracts and appendices are also available at *www.triarchypress.com/missinglink.*

Chapter II

Making Economic Paradigms Explicit

"Your paradigm is so intrinsic to your mental process that you are hardly aware of its existence, until you try to communicate with someone with a different paradigm."
Donella Meadows

A paradigm is the conceptual framework from which reality is perceived, evaluated, or acted upon.[1] In economics, such a framework or paradigm often remains unspoken and hidden. This has the disturbing implication that sometimes economics is presented as neutral and objective, an incontrovertible 'hard science'. Paul Samuelson, who received the Nobel memorial price in economics in 1970, is reported to have said late in his life that, "Economics has never been a science. And it is even less now than a few years ago".

What often remains unclear is the particular epistemic orientation that economists speak from. "Paradigms are inevitable. Therefore, no economist can speak from anywhere but from inside a paradigm. He can change paradigms, but he can never proceed without any paradigm at all, because that would mean having no structuring theoretical conceptions, no formal toolbox, and no empirically oriented techniques".[2]

---

1   The canonical definition was provided by the philosopher of science Thomas Kuhn in *The Structure of Scientific Revolutions* (1965). He defines a scientific paradigm as an epistemological pattern, a mental framework that specifies a series of what's and how-to's: *what* is to be observed and scrutinised, and by implication what is to be overlooked; the kind of *questions* that are supposed to be asked or ignored; *how* these questions are to be structured; *how* the results of scientific investigations should be interpreted. A paradigm, according to Kuhn, adjusts over time to the everyday requirements of what he calls 'normal science', i.e., the business of tinkering with models and making them fit empirical data as well as possible, for as long as possible. The period of normal science is sometimes ended, more or less abruptly, by a 'scientific revolution'.

2   Christian Arnsperger, *Full-Spectrum Economics: Towards an Inclusive and Emancipatory Social Science* (2010a), p.25.

We will focus here on two specific dimensions of economic paradigms:

- how a paradigm deals with the natural world, specifically with the environment and the planetary ecosystem
- how a paradigm deals with the monetary system

1. Dealing with the natural world

Conceptual relationships between the field of economics and the natural world can be described in three different ways. The most conventional view is to treat anything that is not dealt with unambiguously within one's own theoretical framework as an 'externality' (see Figure 2.1). This economic view defines its own field as completely self-contained and excludes any other consideration as irrelevant. For instance, in such a view, the natural world is reduced to a resource, an input that is considered to be cost-free – to the extent that no money is exchanged to acquire it. Similarly, humans are reduced to their productive labour input, and their interactions are relevant only if they qualify as 'services'. As a consequence, work performed by a stay-at-home carer for an elderly relative or a child are not counted in a nation's GDP, because they do not get paid for it. Therefore even though this represents a valuable contribution to society, it simply doesn't exist in this view.

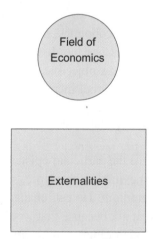

Figure 2.1: The Traditional Economics Paradigm: Complete disconnection between economics and its 'externalities'.

We will use the term 'Traditional Economics' to describe this particular approach to economics. It is the dominant economic paradigm currently still being taught at most universities and implicitly used by the media and in many corporate boardrooms. This view is quite reductionist and a movement of professional economists have labelled it as "autistic".[3]

Others define it as "a fantasy world":

"Why do I say today's economics portrays a fantasy world? Is that unnecessarily offensive to all those earnest individuals labouring with a demanding discipline? In a sense, it is, and I would apologize if it were not for the fact that these same individuals usually denounce interior-oriented work [such as individual or collective values and psychology] as fantasy; and that, to say the least, is offensive, too. True enough, the more sophisticated among them do not outright denounce hermeneutic-cultural work. They simply claim it can ultimately be reduced to brain-and-system categories – if not, that will just show it was not much use as far as scientific work goes. So we should not be too courteous vis-à-vis those hard-labouring individuals, because they harbour an intellectually and politically dangerous agenda. They would devise macro- or micro-policies – to be implemented on us – subject to the 'working assumption' that our interiors do not really matter at all."[4]

The mainstream paradigm harbours the notion that economic agents themselves do not have the capacity to interpret reality, do not care for cultural or spiritual traditions,[5] and have no non-materialistic values or deep-lying psychological structures (such as archetypes or an unconscious mind). Such a view has contributed to what Karl Marx and Karl Polanyi a century later saw as the 'disembedding' of the economy from the rest of society and from nature or an autonomisation of narrowly economic matters, linked to production and circulation, with respect to the broader contexts of social and environmental issues.[6]

---

3   In opposition to the Traditional Economic paradigm, a movement that initially called itself 'Post-Autistic Economics' (PAE) was born at the Sorbonne in Paris in 2000 and was endorsed by a group of Cambridge PhD students in 2001 with the publication of 'Opening Up Economics: A Proposal by Cambridge Students'. (See *The Cambridge 27*, July 2001, and *Post-Autistic Economics Newsletter,* issue 7, article 1.) This declaration was later signed by 797 other PhDs in economics. For a detailed compendium of the documents that launched the 'Post-Autism' movement, see Edward Fullbrook (ed.), *The Crisis in Economics: The Post-Autistic Economics Movement – The First 600 Days* (2003). For a follow-up with more reflective, in-depth contributions, see Edward Fullbrook (ed.), *A Guide to What's Wrong With Economics* (2004).

4   Arnsperger (2010a) p.9.

5   In fact, they *should* not, because that might contradict instrumental rationality, such as in the case where respect for a 'Mother Earth' tradition leads some people to renounce exploitation of some natural resource. American Indians have been denounced as anti-progressive because they give the sacredness of their land priority over marketable coal, ores or petroleum.

6   See Karl Polanyi, *The Great Transformation: The Political and Economic Origins of Our Time* (1944).

To address this problem, the OECD[7] proposed, for over a decade, a framework with three partially overlapping fields: the economic, the social and the environmental (see Figure 2.2). It considers the area where the three fields overlap as relevant, but also sees a substantial domain where economics operates independently of the other two. This is an improvement over the previous case, as it acknowledges some interaction between economic activities, other human endeavours and the rest of the biosphere. However, it still retains the idea that the economy is a domain partly abstracted and autonomous from cultural, social and environmental issues.

In this framework it remains possible, therefore, for mainstream economists to claim that introducing psychological, cultural and/or environmental dimensions detracts from what is 'really economic' and to see only economics as the discipline that studies all 'pure' phenomena 'disembedded' from the two other spheres.

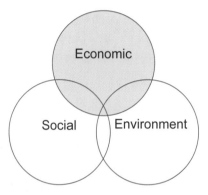

Figure 2.2: Overlap between the economics, the social and the environmental (OECD approach).

The economic paradigm underlying our own view is linked to what is now sometimes called 'Ecological Economics' inspired by Nicholas Georgescu-Roegen, Kenneth Boulding, Herman Daly, René Passet, and Robert Costanza.[8] In this paradigm, the field of economics is *fully embedded* as a subsystem within the social – and the latter, in turn, is a subsystem of the biosphere (see Figure 2.3).[9]

---

7   *Towards Sustainable Development* (Paris: OECD, 2000).

8   See e.g. Nicholas Georgescu-Roegen (1971); René Passet (1979); Herman Daly (1996); Robert Costanza (2003) pp.237-246; John Gowdy & Jon D. Erikson (2005). For a general but exhaustive treatment, see e.g. Molly Scott Cato (2009) and Herman Daly & Joshua Farley (2011). Ecological economics should not be confused with 'environmental economics', which was initially part of the Traditional Economics approach and has been a driving force behind the OECD approach shown in Figure 2.2.

9   In this statement, we extend ecological economics into what might be called 'political ecology', since traditionally ecological economists emphasise more the embeddedness of the economic within the environmental, and less its embeddedness within the social. However, political ecology and ecological economics are very closely linked, and most ecological economists will have no objection to our graph here.

This 'nested hierarchy' of the environment, the social and the economic has been called a *growth hierarchy* as opposed to an 'oppression hierarchy'.[10] In a growth hierarchy, each successive level includes and transcends its predecessor – the latter, therefore, acts as a condition of possibility for the former to exist. The economy exists only thanks to its social infrastructure and human society exists only because a sufficiently healthy biosphere sustains it. Thus, while in some cases it may be possible to study economic phenomena such as financial flows without *explicitly* modelling all components of the underlying social and environmental contexts, the contexts can never be *assumed away*. The extent to which an economic event or institution influences social organisation, human motivation and/or the environment must be taken into account in this paradigm. Otherwise, the economy risks sawing off the tree branches that it rests on.

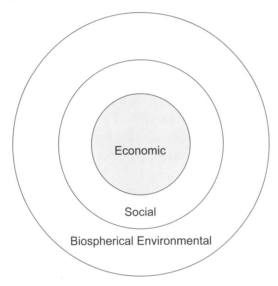

Figure 2.3: The economic as a subset of the social and the social, in turn, as a subset of the biosphere.

The clear difference between Figures 2.1 and 2.3 is that the latter contains *no* 'externalities'. What was considered an externality in Figure 2.1 is the context in which economic activities take place. This context contains overarching rules such as entropy that must be taken into account by economics to avoid getting lost in an 'autistic' or 'fantasy' world.

The difference between Figures 2.2 and 2.3 is that, in the OECD approach, substitutability between natural, social and economic capital is assumed. This conjecture pervades the influential approach of 'endogenous growth' in mainstream economics.[11] In contrast, there is no substitutability between these three forms of

---

10 See, amongst others, Ken Wilber, *Sex, Ecology, Spirituality: The Spirit of Evolution* (1995).

11 An approach that has led mainstream economists to reason as if, with good enough economic and 'human' capital in the form of extremely high-grade technologies and an extremely well-trained workforce, the whole world's production might be manufactured with virtually no natural capital, e.g., with just a few grains of matter...

capital in the Ecological Economics approach. Here, natural and social capital can be replaced by economic capital only to a limited extent. This limit is the threshold beyond which the conditions of economic sustenance from social and/or natural networks start being destroyed. This occurs in the form of *social and ecological 'debts'* often invisible in the short term but with destructive potential in the longer run.[12]

This Ecological Economics paradigm, which takes into account human values and well-established laws of nature, is not new to 21st-century economics. From the basic sciences viewpoint, there have been brilliant contributions that explicitly incorporate the constraints of the physical world into economics. However they have not been integrated into the mainstream economic paradigm. The pioneering theoretical work of Nicholas Georgescu-Roegen, which provides a valid framework to address today's major concerns, is one example.[13]

For more than half a century now, mainstream economics has been unable to integrate sustainability constraints, even those that are unquestioned in 'hard' sciences like physics or thermodynamics. There are, of course, some exceptions. Orio Giarini, for instance, has been dealing explicitly with entropy and uncertainty, as well as monetised and the unmonetised activities with economic value.[14] Hazel Henderson used the metaphor of a four-layered cake to make this same point: the private sector economy resting on the goods and services provided by the public sector, which in turn rests on non-monetised social economy, which finally rests on 'Mother Nature'.[15]

---

12 This idea – and especially the notion of 'ecological debt' – is a major theme in the influential book of Tim Jackson, *Prosperity Without Growth: Economics For a Finite Planet* (2009).

13 Nicholas Georgescu-Roegen (1906-1994) was born in Romania but did most of his academic work at Vanderbilt University in the USA, where he was acknowledged as Distinguished Fellow of the American Economic Association. He made significant contributions in both conventional economics (utility theory, input-output analysis, production theory) and in paradigm-shifting economics – what along the lines of Thomas Kuhn might be labelled 'revolutionary' economics. He applied rigorous systemic thinking on how to link economics to the physical laws of sustainability in *Analytical Economics* (1966). Paul Samuelson said in the Preface that he considered Georgescu-Roegen to be "a scholar's scholar, and an economist's economist". He added: "I defy any informed economist to remain complacent after meditating over this essay". Nevertheless, complacency is what has greeted that book and its successor, *The Entropy Law and the Economic Process*. Ecological economist Herman Daly concludes in his 'Obituary Essay on Georgescu-Roegen': "One does not expect fundamental change to occur overnight. But twenty-five years is a reasonable time over which to hope for progress. What is the matter with our discipline?" (Daly [1996] p.192 and p.198). Even Samuelson himself, for all his professed lack of complacency, never updated his bestselling economics textbooks to integrate Georgescu-Roegen's findings. Even 30 years before Georgescu-Roegen, Frederick Soddy, a Nobel laureate in Chemistry, had drawn the attention of economists to their ignorance of entropy and the unsustainability of compound interest, all without success.

14 Orio Giarini 'Science and Economy: The Case of Uncertainty and Disequilibrium' *Cadmus,* Vol I, No.2 (April 2011) pp.25-34.

15 Hazel Henderson: *Paradigms in Progress: Life beyond Economics* (1991). See also Hazel Henderson: *Creating Alternative Futures* (1996) p.xii.

But the problem is that such bridges between 21st century science and economics remain an exception.

The standard measurement of economic progress thus remains the Gross National Product (GNP) per capita, which captures neither the depletion of natural resources, nor the quality of growth, nor the distribution of its benefits. Furthermore, market prices rarely reveal the real costs of a product or service. Their production and disposal can create damage that remains ignored in the conventional accounting system.[16] Sufficient evidence now exists for a fundamental rethinking to take place if sustainability is taken seriously. If humanity's decisions continue to be made on the basis of the Traditional Economics paradigm (Figure 2.1) or even the OECD paradigm (Figure 2.2), all signs point to a bleak future for our human condition and our planet. Indeed, humanity's unsustainable behaviour is provoking the sixth great mass extinction of the geological record at a rate of 30,000 species per year or three species per hour. Having a greater awareness of the limitations of the dominant economic paradigms is therefore not merely of academic relevance.

But what exactly is meant by sustainability in this context?

Defining Sustainability

There are currently over a hundred definitions of sustainability, of which we list only a very small sample.

"The World Commission on the Environment and Development defined a sustainable society as one which 'satisfies its needs without limiting the prospects of future generations' Moreover, 'Sustainable development is growth in well-being without physical growth. It is a process and not a state, and therefore does not necessarily imply that the population or the economy are static or stagnant.'"
—Brundtland Report: *Our Common Future*[17]

"Sustainability is a rallying cry for hope. It postulates that there can be a future design of society in which environmental degradation and extremes of social inequity are avoided on an ongoing basis. As an agenda, it implicitly calls for a sense of responsibility and action sincerely aimed at improving or changing our current way of living, and averting what many feel is a looming social, ecological and economic crisis."
—Global Business Network: *Report on Sustainability*[18]

---

16 E. U. von Weizsäcker, A. B. Lovins and L. H. Lovins, *Factor Four: Doubling Wealth – Halving Resource Use* (1997).

17 World Commission on the Environment and Development, *Our Common Future* (1989), p.200.

18 Harding Tibbs, 'Sustainability", *The Deeper News,* Vol. 3, no.1, Jan. 1999, p.5.

Former World Bank economist Herman Daly[19] proposes three conditions for a society to be physically sustainable:

1. The rates of use of renewable resources do not exceed their rates of regeneration.

2. Its rates of use of non-renewable resources do not exceed the rate at which sustainable renewable substitutes are developed.

3. The rates of pollution emissions do not exceed the assimilative capacity of the environment.

As we see in many of these definitions, the first dimension of sustainability deals with the environmental impact of an economy.

Environmental Sustainability

We previously stated that the world is currently undergoing a powerful set of shifting conditions including large-scale biodiversity extinction, climate change in the form of extreme weather conditions (including higher frequency of extreme floods and droughts), deterioration of arable soil through salination, pollutants and organic exhaustion as well as fresh water shortages. If not properly addressed, these shifting conditions will threaten the survival of the biosphere, which business, the economy, and all other human activities depend on. The following figure provides a summary of the most important threats to long-term ecological sustainability if we continue along our current economic path.

Biodiversity	Every hour, three species become extinct. The loss of biodiversity is now 50-100 times higher than under natural conditions, without human intervention.[20]
Water	1.1 billion people have no direct access to drinking water. An additional 2.5 billion live without sanitary facilities. Every year, 2.4 million children die as a result of diseases transmitted via contaminated water.
Soil depletion	17% of the area that was formerly fertile soil is showing evidence of significant depletion.
Climate	The average surface temperature of the Earth is expected to rise between 1.4°C and 5.6°C by the year 2100. Already, significant changes in weather patterns have occurred worldwide. The melting of polar and Greenland ice is well under way and, if not reversed, could raise sea levels to flood coastal lands where 1/3 of humanity currently lives.

Figure 2.4: Some unresolved environmental problems on our current economic path.[21]

---

19 Herman E. Daly and John B. Cobb, *For the Common Good: Redirecting the Economy Toward Community, the Environment, and a Sustainable Future* (1989).

20 The rate of species extinctions at present is estimated at 100 to 1,000 times 'background' or average extinction rates in the evolutionary time scale of the Earth. J. H. Lawton and R. M. May, *Extinction Rates* (1995).

21 Figures according to: FAO; CBD Secretariat; World Bank; IPCC.

In some circles, the word 'sustainability' has become synonymous with constraints, heavy-handed governmental regulations, or even a leftist conspiracy. This perception has been amplified by well-funded disinformation campaigns underwritten by various vested business interests, in particular from the carbon energy industries.[22] As will be seen in Chapter V, such campaigns are an example of the systematic short-term thinking automatically generated by our monetary system and the manner in which it 'programs' our behaviour.

Contrary to this view, we see the 'sustainability sector' as one of the most promising business opportunities of the 21ˢᵗ century. During the first ten years of this century, sustainable economic, social and ecological development has become strategically important for business. Corporations with serious environmental and social governance strategies and integrated policies are performing better than the average.[23]

There is greater demand for products and services that impose lower burdens on ecosystems. This not only relates to *new* products and services such as renewable energy, but also to 'redefining business' such as, cradle-to-cradle or bio-mimicry industries.[24] Among the pioneers of such new business models, Interface carpets and Herman Miller office furniture are examples of long-existing corporations that have transformed themselves into different and more sustainable entities. Many more examples of such transformations exist and their numbers continue to increase rapidly.[25] Corporations and countries providing these new goods and services will be better prepared than those that only retain industrial-age ideas, processes and markets.

The future relevance of environmental sustainability is voiced by many leaders without any leftist political leanings. Below are a few observations from such leading figures:

"It's good business to anticipate the inevitable, and it seems to me inevitable, whether we like it or not, that we are moving toward an economy which must be limited and selective in its growth pattern. The earth has finite limits – a difficult idea for Americans to adjust to."

—John D. Rockefeller III

---

22 For a detailed analysis of these campaigns see, for instance, Naomi Oreskes and Erik M. Conway, *Merchants of Doubt: How a Handful of Scientists Obscured the Truth On Issues From Tobacco Smoke to Global Warming* (2010).

23 "… companies with superior performance and positioning on 'sustainability' (i.e., environmental and social) issues achieved, on average, superior financial returns" – Matthew J. Kiernan, *Investing in a Sustainable World* (2009), p.xiii.

24 See, e.g., Michael Baumgart and William McDonough, *Cradle to Cradle: Re-Making the Way We Make Things* (2002).

25 See Peter M. Senge, *The Necessary Revolution: How Individuals and Organizations Are Working Together to Create a Sustainable World* (2008).

"Socialism collapsed because it did not allow prices to tell the economic truth. Capitalism may collapse because it does not allow prices to tell the ecological truth."

—Øystein Dahle, former vice-president of Exxon for Norway and the North Sea

"Human beings and the natural world are on a collision course. Human activities inflict harsh and often irreversible damage on the environment and on critical resources. If not checked, many of our current practices put at serious risk the future that we wish for human society and the plant and animal kingdoms, and may so alter the living world that it will be unable to sustain life in the manner that we know. Fundamental changes are urgent if we are to avoid the collision our present course will bring about."[26]

—Declaration of 1700 leading scientists from 70 countries, including 102 Nobel laureates in the sciences, with endorsements from the science academies of the USA, the UK, Brazil, Canada, China, France, Germany, India, Italy, Japan and Russia (June 5, 2005)

"Business is a large vessel; it will require great common effort and planning to overcome the inertia of the present destructive course, and to create a new momentum towards sustainable development..."

—"Changing Course", World Business Council for Sustainable Development (Geneva, 1992)

"In our view as Philips, sustainability is no longer an option but an imperative. Over the past five years, we have seen more and more institutional and individual investors equating sustainability with good management and good long-term prospects. And so they should."

—Gerard Kleisterlee, CEO of Royal Philips Electronics[27]

"As far as [the Dutch specialised chemical company] DSM is concerned, the need for sustainable development is beyond debate. Sustainable entrepreneurship involves the simultaneous pursuit of profitable economic growth, further development of our employees, good corporate citizenship and sustainable use of natural resources."

—Peter Elverding, CEO of Royal DSM (Triple P Report, 2005)

"All our efforts to defeat poverty and pursue sustainable development will be in vain if environmental degradation and natural resource depletion continue unabated."

—Kofi Annan, former UN Secretary-General[28]

---

26 The *World Scientists' Warning to Humanity* was spearheaded by the late Henry Kendall, former chair of the Union of Concerned Scientists' board of directors (*www.ucsusa.org ~ bit.ly/TPlink15*).

27 At the 'Captains of Industry' conference in Singapore on September 27th, 2005.

28 In *Larger Freedom: Towards Development, Security and Human Rights for All*, 2005 report for the United Nations 60th-anniversary summit.

However, the ecological crisis is only one of the issues threatening sustainability today. The human dimension is just as relevant.

Human Development

We define *human development* as an increase in the capacity for a human being to choose.[29] The choices being referred to here involve life choices such as careers, lifestyles or locations to live. On that basis, *sustainable development can be defined as augmenting man's capacity for choice now, while preserving the options available for future generations.* In such an interpretation, the 'prospects of future generations' involve not only the ecological aspects, but also the social, economic, cultural and governance underpinnings necessary for a good quality of life.

Our Own Framework for Sustainability

In this Report, we use the definition of sustainability developed as an outcome of the 1992 Rio Earth Summit as our reference. During this summit, an 'Earth Charter' was drafted, headed by Maurice Strong of Canada, Mikhail Gorbachev of Russia and Steven Rockefeller of the United States. Along with various stakeholders, they developed a set of principles necessary to achieve a just and sustainable world. These principles can be found at *www.earthcharter.org* and fall into four key categories:

1. Respect and care for the whole community of life
2. Ecological integrity
3. Social and economic justice
4. Democracy, non-violence and peace

The reference material for our analysis in this Report also includes the work known as 'The Natural Step', by Karl-Henrik Robert, a physician from Sweden who started by researching the systemic reasons for the escalating cancer rates in his medical practice. The Natural Step offers four system conditions that must be met for a sustainable world:

1. Eliminate our contribution to the progressive build-up of substances extracted from the Earth's crust (for example, heavy metals and fossil fuels)
2. Eliminate our contribution to the progressive build-up of chemicals and compounds produced by society (for example, dioxins, PCBs and DDT)
3. Eliminate our contribution to the progressive physical degradation and destruction of nature and natural processes (for example, over-harvesting forests and the paving-over of critical wildlife habitat)

---

29 Jamshid Gharajedaghi, *Systems Thinking: Managing Chaos and Complexity* (1999), p.xvi.

4. Eliminate our contribution to conditions that undermine people's capacity to meet their basic human needs (for example, unsafe working conditions and insufficient pay to live on)[30]

Understanding the community systems that are capable of satisfying a fuller range of human needs is a cornerstone of environmental and human sustainability. The Earth Charter Commission, working with the World Resources Institute and Global Community Initiatives, developed a comprehensive methodology for communities to evaluate their own sustainability and plan for a more sustainable future.[31]

2. Dealing with the Monetary System

In order to spell out the economic paradigm in which we operate, the monetary dimension of the economy must explicitly be explored. Not all paradigms do this – some, and most notably the dominant Traditional Economics approach, view money as a passive element not affecting the way that individuals and collectives choose to act. The Ecological Economics paradigm, in the way we conceive it here, takes the monetary dimension much more seriously. How so? This is what we intend to explain in the remainder of this chapter. The exploration of this feature is what most sets this study apart from other economic texts and studies on sustainability.[32]

The modern monetary system has played a positive role in the achievements of the Industrial Age. For better and for worse, it has made a human population explosion possible, from 250 million in 1750 to over seven billion today. The production of goods over time follows a similar curve to that of population growth: between 1800

---

30 See Sarah James and Tobjörn Lahti, *The Natural Step for Communities: How Cities and Towns Can Change to Sustainable Practices* (2004).

31 See Gwendolyn Hallsmith, *The Key to Sustainable Cities: Meeting Human Needs, Transforming Community Systems* (2004) and The Earth Charter Community Action Tool *www.earthcat.org*.

32 Indeed, the monetary dimension has not been very much at the centre of many of the most recognised and widely cited contributions to the sustainability debate, such as David Pearce and Edward Barbier's *Blueprint For a Sustainable Economy* (2000), Daly (1996) or Jackson (2009). (For a critical assessment of Jackson's book from the monetary angle, see Christian Arnsperger, 'Monnaie, dette et croissance sans prospérité: Portée et limites du "tournant jacksonnien"', *Etopia*, No. 8, December 2010, pp.109-116.) Edward Barbier's momentous study on *A Global Green New Deal: Rethinking Economic Recovery* (2010) deals extensively with the crucial issue of 'green' investment but does so without questioning the structural properties of the current monetary system. In her influential book *Plenitude: The New Economics of True Wealth* (2010), Juliet B. Schor at least mentions the problem of how money is created and is circulated – but she does not place structural financial and monetary issues at the centre of her proposal, even though she fully realises that growth as ever-increasing material throughput cannot continue. The veil of monetary denial seems to have been torn very recently in two sustainability studies destined to have a wide readership: Charles Eisenstein's *Sacred Economics: Money, Gift, and Society in the Age of Transition* (2011) and Richard Heinberg, *The End of Growth: Adapting to Our New Economic Reality* (2011) – the former offers a whole chapter on non-monopolistic, non-debt money alternatives, and the latter has a section called 'Post-Growth Money' where structural reform towards non-monopolistic, non-debt money is explicitly cited and discussed sympathetically.

and the present, GDP per capita in the developed world multiplied by a factor of at least twenty. China, India and Brazil are in the process of reproducing this process as we write. As a result of industrialisation, many people in Europe, North America and parts of Asia have seen their standard of living soar from subsistence to what our ancestors would have considered extraordinary affluence. These are immense accomplishments, which, irrespective of their drawbacks, should be recognised and honoured.

But what of the other side of this balance sheet? Based on past evidence, what is the effect of the current architecture of money, banking and financial markets on sustainability? The focus here is not on the obvious effects of policy decisions – such as the shaping of Third-World policies by the IMF[33] – but rather on the effects that systematically arise from the architecture of the monetary and financial systems themselves.

The 'Service Function' Paradigm: Money as an Innocuous Facilitator

According to the dominant view of economics, the monetary and financial system is merely a coordinating mechanism. It is a service function supporting the 'real' economy where physical goods and services are produced and exchanged. Money is assumed to play a role analogous to that of an engine lubricant, acting as an auxiliary to smooth the way the motor runs without altering the engine itself.

All schools of economic thinking view the monopolistic creation and circulation of a single currency as a given. It is no more questioned than the fact of having one moon rotating around the Earth. There is wide assumption that all advanced civilisations have used a monopolistic, centrally issued fiat currency because it is the most efficient arrangement. Therefore, the overwhelming majority of economists whether of classical, neoclassical, Austrian, Keynesian or neoliberal persuasion, whether they are 'Chartalist' post-Keynesians or complexity-oriented 'emergentists', do not see the need to question the currently established monetary *modus operandi*. This notion even extends to the Marxist paradigm: the Soviet system imposed the same monopoly of a single currency created through bank debt. The only significant difference in the Soviet system is that the government owned the banks, while in capitalist societies bank ownership has traditionally been private. Even adherents of the Ecological Economics paradigm – the one espoused in this Report – are frequently unaware of how central the assumption of a single, all-purpose, bank-debt-driven currency is when it comes to the very problems they seek to address.

For a more detailed discussion of how different paradigms are mapped, and some of their consequences, please see Appendix C.

---

33 On the so-called 'Washington consensus' and its deleterious effects, which are well documented, see e.g. Joseph Stiglitz, *Globalization and Its Discontents* (2002).

Why do practically all economic paradigms share the belief that the only way to operate a national economy is through a monopoly of a single type of currency?

The Monetary 'Blind Spot'

The human eye possesses a biological blind spot where the optical nerve enters the eye. This is an area without vision. Humanity appears to suffer from a similar blind spot when it comes to the way money enters the economy and the social system. There are at least three layers to this phenomenon which include:

- the hegemony of single-currency thinking
- the 'capitalist versus communist' ideological war
- an institutionalised *status quo*

Our objective in studying this 'blind spot' is to identify our underlying assumptions; rather than to criticise them. Rather than being 'natural' or 'objective' descriptions of a given reality, they form part of specific *paradigms*. The sets of assumptions and specific world-views that relate to monopolistic money are deeply ingrained in our thinking and lead to this partial blindness. However, like any paradigmatic option, these assumptions and world-views are not laws of nature: we made them up and we can change them.

The hegemony of single-currency thinking

Many societies have imposed a single, monopolistic, hierarchically-issued currency, naturally or artificially kept scarce, and associated with positive interest rates. This was true in Sumer and in Babylon, in Ancient Greece and in the Roman Empire, as well as from the Renaissance onwards in all Modern societies. The form of these currencies has varied widely, from standardised commodities, precious metals and natural objects such as shells, to paper or electronic bits. But they have had three crucial properties in common: in all cases, only *that* specific currency was accepted for the *payment of taxes*; the currency could be stored and accumulated, i.e. *hoarded*; and borrowing such currencies implied the *payment of interest*. So widespread has been this approach that we tend to think that it is the only option, leading to the hegemony of single-currency thinking.

In fact, many societies have use a dual-currency or multi-currency system. In those societies, the monopolistic currency described above was then used for long-distance trading with foreigners or with people whom one didn't know personally. The second type of currency was used for exchanges within the local community, and was of a very different nature. This second currency was usually created locally by its users. It was issued in sufficient amounts and did not bear interest. In the most sophisticated cases, this second currency even carried a demurrage fee – i.e. a negative interest on money – which discouraged its accumulation. In short, this other currency would be used as a *pure medium of exchange* not as a store of value. This was the case with the wheat-backed currencies that lasted for well over a millennium in Dynastic Egypt, and with local and regional currencies in Western Europe, during almost three centuries of the Central Middle Ages (10ᵗʰ-13ᵗʰ centuries). These dual systems provide some of the best explanations for the unusual economic well-being of these ancient societies.[34] Societies in which such dual-currency or multi-currency systems have prevailed have often been matrifocal ones – not to be confused with matriarchal ones. There is no evidence that genuinely matriarchal societies have ever existed. By contrast, there is widespread evidence that advanced matrifocal societies, loosely defined here as those *where feminine values are honoured*, have existed in various parts of the world, though less frequently than patriarchal ones.[35]

The ideological warfare between capitalism and communism

The second layer of the blind spot is more recent. During most of the 20ᵗʰ century, an intense ideological war was waged worldwide between communism and capitalism. This affected all social and political sciences, including the science of economics with its different schools of thought and particular views on the corresponding ideology (see Figure 2.5). Strenuous debates between the different schools of economic thought have resulted in the publication of thousands of books describing the most minute differences between the multifarious ideologies both within and across 'camps'.

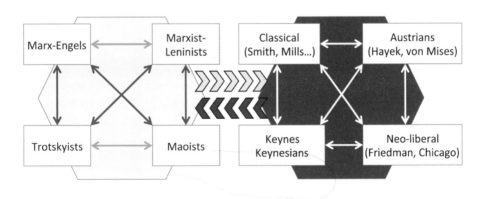

Figure 2.5: Ideological polarisation between communism and capitalism.

34 See Friedrich Preisigke, *Girowesen im Griechischen Ägypten, enthaltend Korngiro, Geldgiro, Girobanknotariat mit Einschluß des Archivwesens* (1910; reprinted 1971); and Bernard Lietaer, *Mysterium Geld: Emotionale Bedeutung und Wirkungsweise eines Tabus* (2000); *Au Coeur de la Monnaie* (2011).

35 Much more detail on these claims about matrifocal societies is given in Lietaer (2000). See also Bernard Lietaer and Stephen Belgin, *New Money for a New World* (2011), also available on *www.newmoneyforanewworld.com*.

What these ideologies all have in common, however, is almost completely overlooked: they all take for granted the monopoly of a centralised currency. Could the reason for this be that both communism and capitalism emerged during a period where patriarchal ideologies were dominant, sprouting two distinct and rival ways of organising an Industrial Age? Their disagreement was not on whether monopolistic money and material growth are beneficial, but rather on what organisational principles, social mechanisms and political means were best suited to building an efficient industrial growth economy. By bringing the focus of attention onto everything *except the common monetary aspect of the two competing ideologies*, this ideological split substantially reinforced the monetary 'blind spot'.

An institutionalised *status quo*

At some point during the 18th and 19th centuries, the use of a single currency issued through bank debt was institutionalised. This institutionalisation generates the third layer of the 'blind spot'. This role is now still played by central banks in every country and/or monetary union. With the 1930 Copenhagen agreements, the Bank for International Settlements (BIS) was created, and with the Bretton Woods agreements of 1944, the International Monetary Fund (IMF) and the World Bank came into existence. More recently, the Treaty of Amsterdam in 1998 led to the establishment of the European Central Bank.

While these institutions obviously fulfil important and useful tasks in terms of preserving the integrity of the system, they have also become the guardians of a monetary orthodoxy, which reigns almost universally today. And this orthodoxy shapes academic thinking. For instance, is it a coincidence that none of the 69 Nobel laureates in economics to date have made the mistake of questioning the prevailing money paradigm? While two Nobel laureates ended up suggesting monetary reforms, they only did so *after* they had received the prize. One of them was Friedrich von Hayek with his proposal for the privatisation of money emission (still within the banking sector, however); the other was Maurice Allais with his scathing criticism of fractional-reserve banking, which he likened to counterfeiting.

What is colloquially called the 'Nobel prize for economics' has as official title the 'Sveriges Riksbank Prize in Economic Sciences in Memory of Alfred Nobel' (Swedish: *Sveriges riksbanks pris i ekonomisk vetenskap till Alfred Nobels minne*). This prize happens to be funded by a central bank, actually the oldest central bank in existence, also called today the Bank of Sweden. Does this reinforce some biases within academia? Peter Nobel, the great-great nephew of Alfred Nobel, seems to think so.

"'Unlike the Nobel Prizes for Medicine, Chemistry, Physics, Literature and Peace, which were created by Nobel in his 1896 will and first awarded in 1901, the Economics Prize was conceived by Sweden's central bank in 1968 to mark its

tricentenary and first awarded a year later. 'There is nothing to indicate that he would have wanted such a prize.'[says the great great nephew of Alfred Nobel]

"The Economics Prize has over the years been criticised as not being a 'real' Nobel, and a newspaper article Peter Nobel wrote in 2010 refuelled the debate. 'The Economics Prize has nestled itself in and is awarded as if it were a Nobel Prize. But it's a PR coup by economists to improve their reputation', he bristles."[36]

Central banks remain attached to the notion that a monopoly of a single national, bank-debt-based currency must be enforced in each country or group of countries. They do so despite the poor track record of repeated banking and monetary collapses, crowned by the massive collapse of 2008. Even a shock of this scale originating in the country at the core of power, the United States, has not been sufficient to shake the belief that only a single currency per country is required. We can predict with 100% certainty that additional, even bigger crashes will occur again and it is only a question of when, not of whether. The next chapter explores what such crashes mean in practice today.

---

36 'Nobel Descendant Slams Economics Prize', *The Local*, 28 September, 2010 (*www.thelocal.se ~ bit.ly/TPlink16*).

Chapter III

Monetary and Banking Instability

"Of all the many ways of organising banking, the worst is the one we have today. Change is, I believe, inevitable. The question is only whether we can think our way through to a better outcome before the next generation is damaged by a future and bigger crisis."

Sir Mervyn King, Governor of the Bank of England[1]

The global monetary system seems to run on automatic pilot. What's more, the current global foreign exchange market dwarfs all other markets in history. By 2010, foreign exchange volumes had routinely reached the equivalent of $4 trillion *every working day.*

1. The Emergence of a 'Global Casino'

The real economy consists of goods and services being produced and traded. When these exchanges take place internationally, one of the parties must exchange the corresponding currency. For example, if someone buys a car imported from Japan in the UK, someone along the supply chain will have to exchange the corresponding pounds for yen. Out of the $4 trillion of daily foreign exchange transactions only about 2% are associated with the real economy; the other 98% are purely speculative. The sole purpose of a speculative transaction is to buy or sell a foreign currency to make money on the change in value between currencies. Using the proverbial metaphor of the tail wagging the dog, if a dog were to consist of 98% tail and have just 2% available for the rest of its body, visualise what would happen to the dog when the tail moved.

---

1   Source:Speech made in New York 25 October 2010 See:*www.qfinance.com ~ bit.ly/TPlink17*

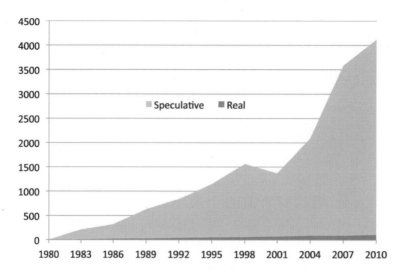

Figure 3.1: Daily volume of foreign exchange transactions as reported by the Bank for International Settlements (BIS) in April each year *versus* foreign exchange transactions based on 'real' economic exchanges (1980-2010). The temporary dip in 2004 was due to the replacement of 12 European currencies with the euro.

Such daily volumes of speculative currency transactions are thousands of times larger than the daily trading volumes of all stock markets worldwide. One day's currency speculation represents more than the *annual* economic output of Germany or China changing hands.[2] Even these figures may be an underestimate given that hedge funds can trade directly with each other, and those transactions are not registered in the BIS's survey. Another way to measure the scale of this market is the notional amount of currency derivatives, which rose from approximately $100 trillion at the end of the year 2000 to more than $700 trillion today. Currency derivatives by themselves represent therefore almost nine times the entire global annual GDP![3]

In short, a 'global casino' on an unprecedented scale has established itself in our midst. John Maynard Keynes, one of the most prominent economists of the 20th century, correctly identified the implications as follows: "Speculators may do no harm as bubbles on a steady stream of enterprise. But the position is serious when enterprise becomes the bubble on a whirlpool of speculation. When the capital development of a country becomes the product of the activities of a casino, the job is likely to be ill-done."[4]

The only effective solution when an asset bubble is bursting, and thereby threatens the financial system, is to create a new bubble in another asset class. This is what has repeatedly happened over the past decades. For instance, after the 'dot-com' bubble

---

2   'The Global Currency Game is Exploding', *The Wall Street Journal*, 26 September 2007, pp.C1 and C3.

3   *The CIA Factbook 2012* estimates global GDP at purchasing power parity at US$78.98 trillion.

4   John Maynard Keynes, *The General Theory of Employment, Interest and Money* (1936), p.159.

imploded at the end of the 1990s in the USA, a real-estate bubble was created. When the real-estate bubble collapsed in 2007, the quantitative easing programmes that ensued started an emerging market bubble. The implications of such bubble strategies are summarised by Ludwig von Mises, one of the founders of the Austrian school of economics: "There is no means of avoiding the final collapse of a boom brought about by credit expansion. The alternative is only whether the crisis should come sooner as the result of voluntary abandonment of further credit expansion, or later as a final and total catastrophe of the monetary system involved."[5]

A Scary Banking Season

The consequences of the 2007-2008 crisis will be felt for the next decade and dozens of studies have been published on the 'causes' of this banking system meltdown. Among the more thorough analyses is the official probe by the US Financial Crisis Inquiry Commission (FCIC).[6] Also worthy of mention is Andrew Ross Sorkin's *Too Big to Fail*, the detective story narrating hour-by-hour who talked to whom about what during the critical days in New York when a global banking meltdown was averted in extremis.[7] Detailed case studies for specific banks or countries include one by Anton Valukas, the court-appointed examiner who produced a 2,200-page analysis of the Lehman bankruptcy and failures in risk management and governance.[8] The governor of Ireland's central bank, Patrick Honohan, mined the depths of Ireland's financial and regulatory failures.[9] The University of Iceland produced a general systems model to explain the political, social and economic feedback loops leading to the Icelandic banking system meltdown. This last model seems equally applicable to Wall Street or the City of London.[10]

These reports all suggest at least one common culprit: the financial innovations that had been welcomed for over a decade as ways of spreading risk more efficiently – including the now infamous credit default swaps (CDS) and 'derivatives' in general.[11] As transactions became more complex and opaque, these innovations resulted in no-

---

5   Ludwig von Mises, *Human Action: A Treatise on Economics* (1949).

6   *The Financial Crisis Inquiry Report: Final Report of the National Commission of the Financial and Economic Crisis in the United States* (2011).

7   Andrew Ross Sorkin, *Too Big to Fail* (2010).

8   Anton R. Valukas, Lehman Brothers Inc. Chapter 11 Proceedings Examiner's Report (2010), downloadable from *http://lehmanreport.jenner.com* ~ *bit.ly/TPlink18* (visited: 8 January 2012).

9   'Restoring Ireland's Credit by Reducing Uncertainty', Remarks by Mr Patrick Honohan, Governor of the Central Bank of Ireland, at the Institute of International and European Affairs, Dublin, 7 January 2011, downloadable from *www.bis.org* ~ *bit.ly/TPlink19* (visited: 8 January 2012).

10 Máni Arnarson, Þorbjörn Kristjánsson, Atli Bjarnason, Harald Sverdrup and Kristín Vala Ragnarsdóttir, *Icelandic Economic Collapse: A Systems Analysis Perspective on Financial, Social and World System Links* (2011), online at *http://skemman.is* ~ *bit.ly/TPlink20* (visited: 8 January 2012).

11 See for instance Adrian Buckley, *Financial Crisis: Causes, Context and Consequences*, (2011), pp.74-88.

one truly knowing who was exposed to what type and scale of risk. Because of this, big banks stopped trusting each other and the inter-bank market abruptly froze. The same happened again in early 2012, but this time mainly involving European banks.

While the above analyses allow us to understand retrospectively what happened, they do not tell us how to avoid them in the future. Policy debates have primarily focused on the 'excesses' of this latest financial crisis. The tendency is to treat each crisis as if it were a unique and isolated case. As a consequence, recommendations remain within the framework of the existing monetary structure. What most analysts fail to realise is that to identify structural problems, one must focus on what is common among all financial and monetary crises rather than on their differences. In metaphorical terms, a view of the entire forest is required, rather than a close-up inspection of any individual tree or of a specific type of tree.

For example, excessive public debt is generally considered to be the problem in the ongoing euro crisis. The large-scale use of derivatives during a US real-estate bubble is seen as the proximate cause of the 2008 crash. The inflexible link between the national currency and the US dollar was determined to be the proximate cause of the 2001 Argentine peso collapse. The 1999 Asian crash, which affected a dozen countries, was blamed on 'crony capitalism'. While such proximate factors may indeed act as triggers, they never reveal structural causes. Even when different breakdowns are analysed in conjunction, they are usually regrouped within specific categories: for example, 'banking crises', 'monetary crises', 'sovereign-debt crises', and so on. Each category is then analysed to understand the common causes associated with it; however, deeper structural issues still tend to be neglected. To use another metaphor, if one is dealing with a proverbial 'house of cards', different triggers can bring about different categories of crashes. What would truly make a difference would be to identify the structural brittleness of the house of cards itself.

What governments have learned from the 1930s is that, if one lets the banking system collapse, the rest of the economy will plunge with it. With the ongoing euro crisis, governments may learn that they can no longer afford to save the banking system. The financial system's own verdict is already clear: the increased public debt burden triggered by the recent banking crisis has led several governments to abruptly lose their creditworthiness. If one wants to remain firmly within the constraints of the Traditional Economy, the only logical solution is for governments, at all levels, to cut budgets in all domains except debt servicing, and privatise everything. This would include privatisation of infrastructural assets traditionally considered normal for governments to own. Examples of this range from city parking meters and streets, to bridges, tunnels and interstate highways, educational facilities, governmental office buildings and water and sewerage systems. Although the privatisation of some assets can be beneficial for society at large, the sudden and forced 'fire sale' of critical infrastructure that has taken decades to build up with taxpayers' money, is not a likely context for fair prices and beneficial outcomes for society. While this new privatisation process is at different stages in different countries, the overall mechanism can be clearly seen – particularly at the US State and city levels, such as in Florida, Illinois or California. Similar privatisation has also started in Europe and is most visible in the UK, Italy and Greece.

To provide more detailed evidence for this argument, we will look at systemic crises, their frequency, types and geographical spreads. We will then probe the consequences of a financial or monetary crisis. Finally, we will take a critical look at privatisation as the solution within the current – and, in our view, defective – monetary paradigm.

2. Systemic Crises: Frequency, Types and Geographical Spread

We need first to clarify what is meant by banking, sovereign-debt and monetary crises, as well as the phenomena that accompany them, such as 'contagion'. A *banking crisis*[12] occurs when a group of banks simultaneously go bankrupt in a country, requiring significant intervention by the authorities to nationalise or bail them out at taxpayers' expense. A *sovereign-debt crisis*[13] occurs when financial markets estimate that a country or group of countries may default on their national debt. Under the prevailing European rules, governments need to raise the money they need either through higher taxes or by borrowing more from the banking system. Sovereign debt is ultimately backed only by the belief in the capacity for a government to impose on its citizens the taxes necessary to service that debt.

---

12 This is the IMF's definition, "in a systemic banking crisis, a country's corporate and financial sectors experience a large number of defaults and financial institutions and corporations face great difficulties repaying contracts on time. As a result, non-performing loans increase sharply and all or most of the aggregate banking system capital is exhausted. This situation may be accompanied by depressed asset prices (such as equity and real estate prices) on the heels of run-ups before the crisis, sharp increases in real interest rates, and a slowdown or reversal in capital flows. In some cases, the crisis is triggered by depositor runs on banks, though in most cases it is a general realisation that systemically important financial institutions are in distress… we exclude banking system distress events that affected isolated banks but were not systemic in nature. As a cross-check on the timing of each crisis, we examine whether the crisis year coincides with deposit runs, the introduction of a deposit freeze or blanket guarantee, or extensive liquidity support or bank interventions. This way we are able to confirm about two-thirds of the crisis dates. Alternatively, we require that it becomes apparent that the banking system has a large proportion of nonperforming loans and that most of its capital has been exhausted." (*www.imf.org ~ bit.ly/TPlink21* p.5)

13 This is the IMF's definition, "We identify and date episodes of sovereign debt default and restructuring by relying on information from Beim and Calomiris (2001), World Bank (2002), Sturzenegger and Zettelmeyer (2006), and IMF Staff reports. The information compiled includes year of sovereign defaults to private lending and year of debt rescheduling. Using this approach, we identify 63 episodes of sovereign debt defaults and restructurings since 1970." (*www.imf.org ~ bit.ly/TPlink21* p.6). More details can be found in Federico Sturzenegger and Jeromin Zettelmeyer, *Debt Defaults and Lessons from a Decade of Crises* (2006), table 1 in Chapter 1.

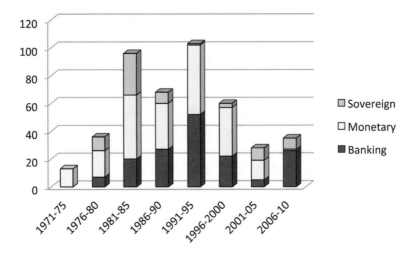

Figure 3.2: Number of systemic crises, with distinctions between the three types: sovereign-debt, monetary and banking crises (1970-2010).[14]

A *monetary (or currency) crisis*[15] takes place when the currency of a country suddenly suffers a substantial drop in value in relation to other currencies. In order to refer to the three types of crises above using a single word, we will define as a *systemic crisis* any large-scale disturbance involving either a sovereign-debt crisis, a monetary crisis and/or a banking crisis or any combination of those three.

A *contagion effect* is defined as "the spread of market disturbances, mostly on the downside, from one country to another, a process observed through co-movements in exchange rates, stock prices, sovereign spreads, and capital flows".[16] In short, it is possible for a crisis in one country to trigger a crisis in an unrelated country, regardless of the differences in economic fundamentals. The 'Tequila effect' of the Mexican crisis in the 1980s on the rest of Latin America was the first large-scale example. The Southeast Asian crisis of the 1990s was another spectacular demonstration of crisis contagion across national borders.

---

14 *Sources*: World Bank, IMF. Graph created by Michelle Bishop using IMF definitions and data from Gerard Caprio & Daniela Klingebiel (1996); J. Frankel and A. Rose (1996); Graziela L. Kaminsky & Carmen M. Reinhart (1999); and, for the data after 2006, Luc Laevan & Fabian Valencia (2010).

15 The more detailed definition of a currency crisis as used by the IMF is "a nominal depreciation of the currency of at least 30% that is also at least a 10% increase in the rate of depreciation compared to the year before. In terms of measurement of the exchange rate depreciation, we use the percentage change of the end-of-period official nominal bilateral dollar exchange rate from the World Economic Outlook (WEO) database of the IMF. For countries that meet the criteria for several continuous years, we use the first year of each 5-year window to identify the crisis. This definition yields 208 currency crises during the period 1970-2007. It should be noted that this list also includes large devaluations by countries that adopt fixed exchange rate regimes." (*www.imf.org ~ bit.ly/TPlink21* p.6).

16 Rüdiger Dornbusch, Yung Chul Park and Stijn Claessens, 'Contagion: How It Spreads and How It Can Be Stopped', *World Bank Research Observer*, Vol. 15, issue 2 (August 2000), pp.177-197.

The contagion effect is a clear symptom of the structural nature of these crises. Even countries or institutions doing everything 'right' according to monetary orthodoxy can be swept into a maelstrom of trouble without much warning. Another sign of the structural nature of these crises is their repetitiveness, independent of the size of, or degree of development in, the countries involved.

The interconnection between these different types of crisis is further justification for looking at what they have in common *systemically*. For example, when one is able to go behind the scenes as a 'country' is being saved from a financial disaster, one can see that it is another country's banking system that is, in reality, being saved. The emergency package put forward at the EU level for Greece in 2010-2011 was thus less about European solidarity than about the German and French banks, which were the biggest holders of Greek sovereign bonds. German and French banks would have needed a new bailout if the Greek government were to have defaulted on its bonds.[17] This is the stark reality behind many historic 'country bailouts', including Mexico's being 'saved' in 1981 and again in 1994. In reality, both cases were about avoiding a banking crisis on Wall Street.

Furthermore, the label 'sovereign debt crisis' can hide the direct consequences of an earlier banking crisis. For instance, the Irish crisis of 2011 is currently referred to as a sovereign-debt crisis. In fact, it is simply the automatic fallout from Ireland's bailout of its banking system in 2008.

According to the IMF data summarised in Figure 3.3, there were 145 banking crises, 208 monetary crashes and 72 sovereign-debt crises between 1970 and 2010. This represents a total of 425 systemic crises, an average of more than 10 countries getting into trouble each year! These crises have hit more than three-quarters of the 180 IMF member countries, many of whom have experienced them several times. However, the decrease in the number of crises since 2000 as shown in Figure 3.3 provides little comfort. This is because the smaller number of countries experiencing a crisis has been counterbalanced by the larger size of the economies involved. The 23 countries involved in the 2007-2008 banking crash – including the USA, the UK and Germany – represent approximately half the world's demand and output.

If a car, a plane or an organisation had such a track record, would there not be a universal outcry to send the designers back to the drawing board? Furthermore, the number of casualties from a defective car, plane or organisation is insignificant when compared with the number of victims of a systemic financial or monetary crisis, which can be counted in the millions, sometimes in the hundreds of millions. Nevertheless, in the case of the monetary system, the organisations in charge (such as banks, central banks or the IMF) not only failed to foresee or to effectively cope with the breakdowns, they have also never considered any alternative to the systemic *status*

---

17 See *www.nytimes.com ~ nyti.ms/TPlink22*

quo. Their solution is invariably to return as quickly as possible to 'normal', without making any significant changes to the system's structure. While it has been officially stated that changes in the "international financial architecture may be necessary to reduce these risks",[18] none of those 'architectural' changes has ever been implemented in the real world. This ensures that more crises will occur in the future.

For those of us who are not bankers, what is meant on a practical level by one of these crises?

The impact on unemployment

There is general awareness of the nefarious impact that these crises have on employment. Notwithstanding stimulus programmes, the number of unemployed since March 2008 has significantly increased in both the euro area (EA-16) and the EU as a whole (EU-27). By the end of 2011, the number of unemployed people in EA-16 went up by 4.4 million to a total of 16 million or a seasonally adjusted unemployment rate of 9.9%. Over the same period, unemployment in EU-27 rose by 6.9 million to reach 23.051 million (9.6%).[19] In the USA, the unemployment rate roughly doubled between 2007 and 2010, with 13.3 million people unemployed in December 2011.

Any downturn in unemployment is being hailed as 'the end of the crisis'. History indicates, however, that the impact of a banking crisis on unemployment rates takes an average of 4.8 years to fully manifest itself and that it can last as long as eleven years (see Figure 3.3). In the case of Europe, the ongoing and simultaneous austerity programs will make this effect last significantly longer than average.

---

18 George Kaufman, 'Banking and Currency Crises and Systemic Risk: Lessons From Recent Events', *Economic Perspectives: A Review from the Federal Reserve Bank of Chicago*, No. 3 (2000), p.1.

19 Source: Eurostat (*http://epp.eurostat.ec ~ bit.ly/TPlink23*, updated with *http://epp.eurostat.ec ~ bit.ly/TPlink24*)

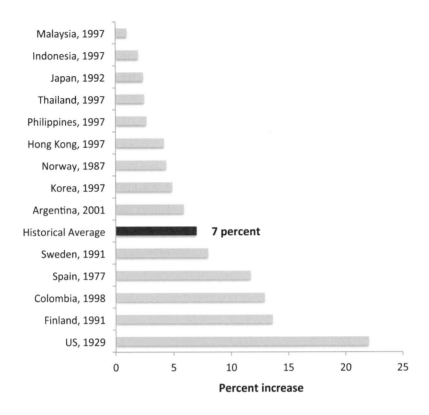

Figure 3.3: Percentage increase in unemployment for selected crises.[20] Each banking crisis episode is identified by the country and by the beginning year of the crisis.

Human and societal costs

The social and environmental consequences of a monetary and/or banking crash are felt far longer than the purely financial ones. A systemic crisis affects not only all aspects of the economy, but also leads to social and political turmoil, creating additional uncertainties for everyone in addition to increasing levels of poverty.

In 2010, the US Census Bureau reported 4 million additional Americans in poverty, making a total of 44 million, or one in every seven residents. The rise was steepest for children, with one in five children affected.[21] Because the crisis started later in Europe than in the USA, the full impact on poverty in Europe has not yet been fully documented.

---

20 Source: Carmen M. Reinhart and Kenneth S. Rogoff, 'The Aftermath of Financial Crises', *American Economic Review*, Vol. 99 (May 2009), pp.466-472. Only major (systemic) banking crises episodes are included, subject to data limitations. The historical average reported does not include ongoing crises..

21 *The New York Times*, 16 September, 2010.

Even countries theoretically immune to the financial side of a crisis end up being hit through unemployment and increases in poverty. For instance, the World Bank estimates that the impact of the 2008 crisis in Poland will result in a 3% increase in the number of people in poverty; in the Philippines and Bangladesh, an additional 5% of the population will be in poverty, and in Mexico an additional 8%.[22]

Output losses

The economic impact of a crisis is broadly measured by the GDP 'output loss', the difference between the actual GDP of a country and the output that had been expected based on the long-term trend before the crisis. It provides an indirect estimate of how non-financial businesses within the country are affected, and the extent to which external trade for other businesses with that country suffers. Here are two recent analyses:

"The economic cost of the 2007-8 crisis is on average much larger than that of past crises, both in terms of output losses and increases in public debt. The median output loss (computed as deviations of actual output from its trend) is 25 percent of GDP in recent crises, compared to a historical median of 20 percent of GDP, while the median increase in public debt (over the three year period following the start of the crisis) is 24 percent of GDP in recent crises, compared to a historical median of 16 percent of GDP." [23]

"In countries that experienced a banking and a monetary crisis simultaneously, the estimated output loss was also substantially greater than when each crisis was experienced separately. The average cumulative output loss was 14.4% in the 32 simultaneous crises and, for the first time in history, was greater for industrial than for emerging economies." [24]

Transfer costs

Another aspect of a banking crisis is the question of who ultimately ends up paying for it. Historically, taxpayers have invariably ended up paying to bail out failing banking systems. The IMF estimates that the transfer payments in support of deposit guarantees during banking crises topped 10% of GDP in many countries. These figures even exceeded 40% in Argentina, Thailand, Korea, Indonesia and Malaysia.

The magnitude of comparable transfer payments in monetary crises from taxpayers to foreign creditors, including the repayment of loans provided by official international institutions, has not been quantified. However, we surmise they must have been

22 Bilal Habib, *et al.* (2010); Anthony B. Atkinson & S. Morelli (2010).
23 Laevan & Valencia (2010).
24 Kaufman (2000) p.24.

similarly sizeable in a number of recent crises. Such crises are typically accompanied by sharp depreciations in exchange rates. These devaluations directly increase the burden of debt denominated in foreign currency to domestic borrowers and, therefore, the probability of default on this debt by governments or local businesses. This, in turn, sets the scene for further rounds of banking problems. Because all IMF data are based on government statistics provided by the countries involved, the comprehensiveness of this data is debatable. One exception is the case study of the 2007-2008 US banking crash.

Evaluating the real costs of the 2007-2008 bailout: The case of the USA

In the United States, successful legal manoeuvres and lawsuits have forced the Federal Reserve and different government agencies to release data that would otherwise remain hidden. Thanks to the unprecedented scale of this 'forced transparency', we can more closely study the 2007-2008 bailout.

Discussion of the cost of the US bailout usually focuses on the $700 billion Troubled Asset Relief Program (TARP) squeezed through Congress during the final months of the Bush administration. This programme was managed by the US Treasury Department. As banks reimbursed these funds over time, the total amount gradually dropped so that by December 2010, the estimated total cost was assessed at "only $25 billion".[25] Public attention has been primarily focused on this programme. However, Neil Barofsky, the Special Inspector-General for the TARP, told lawmakers: "Inadequate oversight and insufficient information about what companies are doing with the [TARP] money leaves the program open to fraud, including conflicts of interest facing fund managers, collusion between participants...".[26]

Bernie Sanders, the independent senator from Vermont, managed to pass an amendment to the Wall Street Reform Act forcing the disclosure by the Federal Reserve of an additional $3.3 trillion in emergency loans and other support to the largest financial institutions. The Center for Media and Democracy identified 34 other programmes besides TARP used to prop up the housing and financial sectors.[27] This includes both the Treasury and the Federal Reserve providing direct loans to Wall Street companies and banks, making purchases of toxic assets, and offering guarantees for the mortgage and mortgage-backed securities markets through federal housing agencies. According to the government's own data for these 35 programmes, the amount disbursed for the bailout is actually $4.7 trillion. This amounts to 30% of the United States' GDP and 130% of the federal budget for the fiscal year 2009.

---

25 See *http://cbo.gov ~ 1.usa.gov/TPlink28* and *www.reuters.com ~ reut.rs/TPlink29*

26 See *www.sigtarp.gov ~ bit.ly/TPlink27*

27 See *www.sourcewatch.org ~ bit.ly/TPlink26*

The Wall Street financial reporting company Bloomberg went to court to extract additional data from the administration. Upon completing their research in March 2009, they claimed: "The U.S. government and the Federal Reserve have spent, lent or committed $12.8 trillion, an amount that approaches the value of everything produced in the country last year. The money works out to $42,105 for every man, woman and child in the U.S. and 14 times the $899.8 billion of currency in circulation. The nation's gross domestic product was $14.2 trillion in 2008".[28]

The most comprehensive estimate has been made by Nomi Prins, an ex-Wall Street insider. Before becoming a journalist, Prins worked as a managing director at Goldman Sachs and ran the international analytics group at Bear Stearns in London. Her estimate includes all the types of supports and guarantees provided by both the US Treasury and the Federal Reserve. She found a total of fifty programmes, several of which were concealed until then, that amounted to a total of $14.4 trillion – a sum greater than the entire US GDP for 2008.[29]

Most of us have trouble grasping what a billion dollars represents, not to speak of a trillion (= 1,000 billion). To put things into perspective, let us look at the lowest of these estimates, the $4.6 trillion disbursed according to publicly available data. Even that amount makes it by far the most expensive programme ever to have been funded by a government. It is more than the entire inflation-adjusted costs of World War II borne by the United States – that is, $288 billion, which, when adjusted for inflation, would amount to $3.6 trillion today. It is more than the inflation-adjusted costs of the Louisiana Purchase, the New Deal, the Marshall Plan, the Korean and Vietnam Wars, the Savings-and-Loan debacle, and the entire NASA budget (including the race to the moon) *combined* – namely, a "mere" $3.91 trillion.[30] And remember that it took two centuries to spend that amount of money on all these programmes, compared to less than two years for the financial bailout.

In countries where there is no independently minded Senator such as Bernie Sanders to force disclosure of central bank data, and no Bloomberg pushing investigative zeal through the courts, such consolidated data are not available. In the eurozone and in Europe in general, no-one has made the effort to consolidate data from the different programmes created to pay for it all or, as far as we know, drawn up an appraisal of the collateral financial damage.

The increase in public debt

One ironic problem, in light of what is currently happening, is the effect of the banking crisis on public finances. "The median debt increase among recent crises is 24% of

---

28 See *www.bloomberg.com* ~ *bloom.bg/TPlink25*

29 Nomi Prins, *It Takes a Pillage* (2009).

30 See *www.ritholtz.com* ~ *bit.ly/TPlink30*

GDP. Thus, public debt burdens have increased significantly as a consequence of policy measures taken during the crisis."[31]

Notice that this impact is completely independent of the quality of any government's own policies, before or during the crisis. While much has been made of the case of Greece where fraud was involved, not much can be blamed on governments or citizens in Iceland, Ireland, Latvia, Denmark or Spain, all hit with sudden increases in their national debt, which reached 35% - 75% of their GDP. The irony is that, as soon as governments borrow these large sums from the financial system to save the system itself from bankruptcy, the financial system concludes that governments are now too indebted and need to be 'disciplined'.

Figure 3.4 brings together the various components of the impact of banking crises on government finances. The direct fiscal cost of bailing out the banking system is added to output losses with an automatic drop in tax income. Governments thus have no other option than to increase their indebtedness. This, in turn, results in the downgrading of the creditworthiness of affected countries and makes their debt more expensive. What does all this lead to?

	Direct Fiscal cost	Increase in Public Debt Medians (% of GDP)	Output Losses
Old crises (1970-2006)			
Advanced economies	3.7	36.2	32.9
Emerging markets	11.5	12.7	29.4
All	10.0	16.3	19.5
New crises (2007-2009)			
Advanced economies	5.9	25.1	24.8
Other economies	4.8	23.9	4.7
All	4.9	23.9	24.5
Note : New crises include Austria, Belgium, Denmark, Germany, Iceland, Ireland, Latvia, Luxembourg, Mongolia, Netherlands, Ukraine, United Kingdom and United States.			

Figure 3.4: Summary of the costs of banking crises[32]

3. The Sovereign Debt Squeeze

The timing of this sudden increase in government debt is particularly unfortunate. The current decade is one in which the OECD countries and their governments have to deal with unprecedented pressures not amenable to being postponed. As mentioned in Chapter I, two critical and predictable challenges during the next decade will be the

31 Laevan & Valencia (2010) p.4.

32 *Source*: Laevan & Valencia (2010) p.24 and the present authors' own calculations.

transition to a post-carbon economy and the sharp increase in financial requirements for retiring baby boomers.

There is currently wide acceptance that massive investments are needed to avoid the worst-case scenarios of global warming. Similarly, there is agreement that will require strong leadership from governmental bodies for such a shift to occur. Because the private sector has invariably required financial incentives to make the necessary commitments, either subsidies or tax deductions are required. After making an inventory of the breakthrough possibilities in current renewable energy technologies, the MIT's *Technology Review* concluded:

> *"None of [these technologies] would have happened without federal support. Although some alternative energy technologies might eventually achieve grid parity, few, if any, can survive without subsidies now, as they improve their cost and efficiency. 'All the darling energy technologies – essentially all the renewables and all the grid-powered electric vehicles – depend on huge subsidies,' says David Victor of UC San Diego, 'and no one really knows what a world of fiscal austerity will look like for these technologies'."*[33]

Postponing the transition to a time when the pressures on government finances are alleviated is not an option: beyond a given level of carbon dioxide in the atmosphere and of higher average temperatures, we truly risk runaway climate change. This would lead to rising sea levels, requiring roughly one third of humanity to move to higher ground. As described in Chapter I, the phenomenon of 'dust-bowlification' would damage the biosphere to a grave extent. Humanity is playing Russian roulette with the global climate and with the biosphere, while breakthrough energy solutions are available, albeit only with massive governmental support. How will we explain to future generations that this support was not forthcoming because we were not able to think outside the box of our monetary arrangements, a legacy system whose main features are centuries old?

The second pressing issue is the impending retirement of baby boomers. This will generate a substantial increase in government spending for pensions and health care – an issue for all OECD countries. The unprecedented 'Age Wave' will transform the economics and politics of the world. One expert's opinion is that "Global ageing will become not just the transcendent economic issue of the 21st century, but the transcendent political issue as well. It will dominate and haunt the public-policy agendas of the developed countries and force renegotiations of their social contracts."[34] There are no historical precedents to help us deal with the Age Wave, and just like with climate change issues, buying time is not an option: all the people involved are alive today,

---

33 David Rotman, 'Praying for Energy Miracle', *Technology Review*, March/April 2011, p.52.
34 Peter G. Petersen, 'Gray Dawn: The Global Aging Crisis', *Foreign Affairs* (January-February 1999), p.43.

and pushing back the age of retirement only postpones the day of reckoning by a few years.

What effects will these two unprecedented challenges now bearing down on us have on government debt, given that they must be dealt with one way or another between now and 2020?

For climate change and the related post-carbon economy issues, no study exists yet about the impact on government finances. In connection with the impact of ageing on public debt, however, the BIS prepared a thorough study entitled *The Future of Public Debt: Prospects and Implications.*[35]

The BIS's baseline scenario assumes that total government revenue and non-age-related spending remain a constant percentage of GDP and that real interest rates remain unchanged from the historically low average levels of the 1998-2007 period. Both these hypotheses should be considered optimistic ones. Nevertheless, in this başeline scenario, debt/GDP ratios rise rapidly in the coming decade, exceeding 300% of GDP in Japan, 200% in the United Kingdom and 150% in Belgium, France, Ireland, Greece, Italy and the United States. In the longer term, the situation grows even more unmanageable: by 2040 the projected debt/GDP ratios for all these countries range from 300% to 600%! Similarly, the fraction absorbed by interest payments in each of these countries points to the same conclusion: from around 5% today, these numbers rise continuously to above 10% in all cases and climb as high as 27% in the United Kingdom. Some fundamental change will obviously happen before these projections become reality. The BIS study says:

> *"Fiscal problems confronting industrial economies are bigger than suggested by official debt figures that show the implications of the financial crisis and recession for fiscal balances. As frightening as it is to consider public debt increasing to more than 100% of GDP, an even greater danger arises from a rapidly ageing population. The related unfunded liabilities are large and growing, and should be a central part of today's long-term fiscal planning. It is essential that governments not be lulled into complacency by the ease with which they have financed their deficits thus far. In the aftermath of the financial crisis, the path of future output is likely to be permanently below where we thought it would be just several years ago. As a result, government revenues will be lower and expenditures higher, making consolidation even more difficult. The recent sharp rise in risk premiums on long-term bonds issued by several industrial countries suggests that markets no longer consider sovereign debt low-risk."*[36]

---

35 Cecchetti *et al.* (2010)

36 *Ibid.*, p.16.

The BIS's conclusion is that "Our projections of public debt ratios lead us to conclude that the path pursued by fiscal authorities in industrial countries is unsustainable". This means that the increase in sovereign debt due to the 2008 banking crisis plus the inevitable financial consequences of an ageing population are sufficient to push most developed countries into an unprecedented fiscal squeeze. Some authors are unambiguously claiming that we are "all going to be bankrupt within ten years".[37]

What solution to these quandaries has the financial system proposed?

4. A Solution: The Privatisation of Everything?

In early 2009, merely months after the bailouts for the 2007-2008 banking crisis, a 'working group' of eighteen banks, investment funds and lawyers[38] released a report entitled *Benefits of Private Investment in Infrastructure*. This strategy is outlined most clearly for the USA, in an article in *Euromoney* by Nick Lord, 'The Road to Wiping Out the US Deficit':

> *There is a perfect mechanism [for governments] to raise that money: the monetization of existing assets. These assets are extremely valuable. In 2008 the total value of US government fixed assets (at a federal, state and local level) was $9.3 trillion. Of this $1.9 trillion is owned by federal government, while $7.4 trillion is held at the state level. If one assumes that the federal government will not be selling the navy or the municipalities their schools, there is still an immense amount of assets that can be sold. For instance, the value of all the highways and roads owned by states and municipalities is $2.4 trillion. There are $550 billion of sewerage assets at state and local levels along with a further $400 billion of water assets. And in the real estate sector, the federal, state and local governments own assets worth $1.09 trillion. The moment the political pain from cutting services is more than the votes lost in selling assets, this market will take off. At grass-root level, that political pain threshold has been reached.* [39]

As of early 2012, forty-four out of the fifty US States face bankruptcy. They are under increasing pressure to start 'Public-Private Partnerships', called P3s in the USA and Private Finance Initiatives (PFI) in the UK. What actually occurs in these benign-sounding partnerships is that governments are obliged to sell off existing infrastructure, built and paid for with taxpayers' money, in order to reduce existing debt or pay for current public expenditures. Once the infrastructure is privatised, new

---

37 This is the title of a book by Jacques Attali, *Tous ruinés dans dix ans? Dette publique: la dernière chance* (2010).

38 Abertis, Allen & Overy LLP, Barclays Capital, Carlyle Infrastructure Partners, Chadbourne & Parke LLP, Citi Infrastructure Investors (CII), Credit Suisse, Debevoise & Plimpton, Freshfields Bruckhaus Deringer, Fulbright & Jaworski, Mayer Brown, McKenna Long & Aldridge LLP, Merrill Lynch, Morgan Stanley, RBC Capital Markets, Scotia Capital and UBS.

39 *Euromoney,* April 2010, p.85.

owners can charge fees for the use of a once free public utility, or increase existing tolls. Thus taxpayers will end up paying twice for the same infrastructure and the second time could be more expensive than the first, given that many infrastructural assets are natural monopolies.

Private investments in public utilities can generate a 'win-win' situation when designed and implemented properly. In several European countries, there is a well-established practice of, for instance, the private sector building new toll-paying highways. When such auctions are well prepared and transparent, the results can be beneficial to all parties. However, the P3s currently being proposed are different from their historical precedents in three ways:

1. The new P3s have a strong preference for buying up existing assets, rather than building new ones, because the time required and the risks involved are much higher in new projects.
2. Today's privatisations are decided under unusually powerful financial pressures, so that a 'crisis' fire sale may well distort the whole deal unfairly against the public interest.
3. Such distortions are more likely to occur now because of the unprecedented concentration in the financial sector, with the overall share of financial assets held by the largest financial institutions increasing sharply. The same institutions are, on the one hand, both the direct or indirect buyers of the infrastructure assets and, on the other, control access to other sources of government funding such as the traditional bond sales.

In other words, the "perfect mechanism" to which Nick Lord refers to in *Euromoney* may be perfect for the financial sector, but not necessarily for the rest of society.

One well-documented example is the sale of the revenue of all 36,000 existing parking meters for a period of 75 years by the city of Chicago for a lump-sum payment of $1.2 billion. This decision was approved on 4 December 2008 by the Chicago city council, by 40 votes to 5. The rates charged by the meters went up immediately by 400 to 500%.[40] A later investigation of this deal by the Chicago Inspector-General's Office includes the following findings:

"The driving force behind the decision to lease the parking meters was the City's short-term budgetary need. While we do not question the seriousness of the City's budget problem that was presented in Fall 2008 because of the recession, the hasty, 'crisis' nature of the decision-making process meant that the short-

---

40 Rates for most city parking meters increased from 25 cents to $1 an hour. The most expensive meters increased in parallel to $3.50 an hour, and will be increased to $6.50 by 2013 (*Chicago Tribune*, 2 December, 2008).

term budget problems and the large upfront payment the City was receiving overshadowed all other legitimate, long-term, public-interest issues. "[41]

It also demonstrates that the city was underpaid by a factor of three! At a discount rate of 5.5% (equivalent to the cost of the city's borrowing), just holding on to the parking meters the city would have received over time $3.51 billion ($2.35 billion more, or 67% more than the sales price). Even using a discount of 7% would have yielded $2.13 billion ($997 million or 45% more than the amount received).

This report shows that the deficit for the years 2008-2009 was only $150 million, and the option of a 20-year lease with a 50% revenue-sharing (on the same terms as in the 75-year lease) would have provided the City with between $302 million and $444 million for immediate use. However, such an arrangement was not proposed during negotiations.

According to Bloomberg,[42] Chicago drivers will pay Morgan Stanley at least $11.6 billion to park at city meters over the next 75 years: ten times what the system was sold for. The next steps are plans to fit more cars into fewer metered spaces by removing marking lines, raising the number of metered slots and expanding the hours requiring fees. "These deals are rarely done under the bright light of public scrutiny", said Richard Little, director of the Keston Institute for Public Finance and Infrastructure Policy at the University of Southern California in Los Angeles. "Often the facts come out long after the deal is done."

All this happened even though the City of Chicago was not an inexperienced apprentice in such privatisation programmes. In 2005, the City leased its Skyway toll road for ninety-nine years for $1.83 billion; and in 2006, its parking garages for ninety-nine years for $563 million. A plan to privatise Midway Airport collapsed in 2009, because the recession drained investors' interest. Nor is Chicago the only US city engaged in such deals. Dana Levenson of the Royal Bank of Scotland and Chicago's chief financial officer from 2004 to 2007, counts about 50 other deals pending in North America, worth between $35 and $40 billion.[43]

Why do we focus on these American examples? The first reason is that, according to John Perkins' disturbing book *Confessions of an Economic Hit Man,* US banks and corporations in Latin America and other developing countries have applied similar policies for many decades.[44] The current privatisation process is the 'economic hit man' coming home. Furthermore, at least in the USA, consolidated data are available.

41 Office of the Inspector-General, City of Chicago, An Analysis of the City's Parking Meter Lease, September 2009 (*http://chicagoinspectorgeneral.org ~ bit.ly/TPlink31*).

42 *www.bloomberg.com ~ bloom.bg/TPlink32*

43 "The Big Sale', *The Economist*, 18 September, 2010, p.51.

44 John Perkins, *Confessions of an Economic Hit Man* (2004).

In Europe, each country is dealing separately with the fallout from the 2007-2008 crisis, without pulling all the pieces of the puzzle together. But there should be no doubt that what is happening in the USA is also taking place in Europe. The same financial institutions are involved in both the USA and Europe; and they are applying the same strategies in Europe, simply with less fanfare and less visibly than in the United States.

For instance, the Berlusconi government started the process of selling an estimated 9,000 publicly owned properties in Italy. They include a former royal palace in Palermo, Sicily, several islands in the Venice lagoon and near Sardinia, former convents, lighthouses and aqueducts, as well as long-term leases on beaches, rivers, lakes and Alpine summits. In Rome, the Etruscan museum at Villa Giulia and the land around the Villa Gregoriana in Tivoli are also being considered. The government expects an income of about €3 billion from these sales, three quarters of which is to be used to reduce the debts of local authorities, and the rest to reduce the national debt.

"Critics have attacked the government for selling off assets that have been public property for centuries, and predicted that local authorities will grant speculators permission to build in previously protected areas. 'What lies behind this transfer of assets is the biggest building and real-estate operation in the history of the republic', said Angelo Bonelli, chairman of the Green party. Salvatore Settis, a leading archaeologist and head of the prestigious Scuola Normale Superiore, a university in Pisa, denounced 'a draining and dismantling of the state just to raise money'. He added: 'The country hasn't realised yet that we are all having our pockets picked'."[45]

The UK government of David Cameron has officially announced a £16 billion privatisation programme, which includes the high-speed rail link from St Pancras to the Channel Tunnel, the Royal Mail, and NATS, the air traffic control service.

Such privatisation policies could be exported to some other European countries forcefully, as part of future IMF support conditions, as was done in the sovereign-debt crises in the Third World during the 1980s and 1990s. As part of the €110 billion EU-IMF package to avoid default on the Greek debt in 2010, Greece was forced to commit to selling approximately €50 billion of public property. A full understanding of what this entails is still unavailable as of this writing. Although two-thirds of the population are strongly opposed to such an approach, Margaret Thatcher's famous expression, "There Is No Alternative" (TINA), is widely considered to be applicable.

But is there *really* no other way?

---

45 John Follain, 'Hard-Up Italy Sells Islands and Palaces', *Sunday Times*, 7 April, 2010, p.24.

5. Conclusion

Surely the monetary system has amply proven its inadequacy in view of the frequency of systemic crises worldwide — averaging ten per year over the past forty years? It may be a banking crisis, a monetary crisis and/or a sovereign-debt crisis, or a combination of them. However, the tendency to consider each systemic crisis separately tends to obscure the common drivers behind all these crises.

The 2007-2008 banking crash has been the worst on record so far. More catastrophic consequences were avoided through massive government support for the financial sector, followed by large-scale Keynesian stimulus programmes to avoid a deflationary depression. This has resulted in significant budget deficits and additional public debt. If we keep within monetary orthodoxy, pressures will continue to mount on governments to reduce their deficits by any means, including the dismantling of government-funded social safety nets. In parallel, the cost of baby boomers retiring and the need for massive support for a post-carbon economy present two unavoidable developments requiring large governmental financial resources. The only solution the financial sector has offered is the privatisation of most significant publicly owned infrastructures. How governments will be better financially positioned to deal with the critical needs of this decade at the end of this process remains unclear. Why would governments be more creditworthy when they have to pay rent for the public offices they once owned, or tolls for the use of highways that were previously free?

Budgetary pressures and the threat of a major monetary crash will continue for many years. The social and political consequences are hard to imagine, but will no doubt include large-scale social unrest in a number of countries, which may favour more nationalistic and extremist political parties. Such movements are already identifiable both in the USA and in Europe even though the big financial squeeze is just beginning. History has shown that it is easier to start extremist movements than to stop them, and that such scenarios often end up being 'resolved' through conflict.

The next chapters will deal with the following questions:

- Beyond the symptoms, is there a systemic mechanism that explains endemic financial and monetary instability? If so, what is it?
- Assuming that the monetary system can be stabilised, are our current monetary arrangements appropriate to deal with the challenges of the 21st century? To be precise, is today's monetary structure compatible or not with the sustainability issues ahead?
- Are changes in the monetary structure possible? If so, what should they be?

Chapter IV

Instabilities Explained:
The Physics of Complex Flow Networks

"One of the beauties of biology is that its facts become our metaphors."
– Kenny Ausubel[1]

"The need for regulation is always the sign of a faulty design."
– William McDonough, architect

The previous chapter discussed how banking and monetary instability have been both recurrent and destructive to society. We will now show that these phenomena are caused not only by imperfect monetary policies, lax regulators or unhealthy banking practices, but rather by a *structural* instability in the monetary and banking system itself. The system's brittleness stems from its very structure, a legacy dating back centuries to the beginning of the industrial age. This structure lacks the agility and adaptability needed to cope with the accelerating changes in the economic and social environment that characterise our post-industrial age.

One trap is attributing the problem to 'human nature'. For instance, the former governor of the Federal Reserve, Alan Greenspan, admitted, after the banking collapse of 2008, that "the world will suffer another financial crisis" and blamed "human nature" for this state of affairs.[2] The most complete quantitative study of financial crises, entitled *This Time Is Different*, similarly explains the systematic repetition of such crises: "Countries, institutions, and financial instruments may change across time, but human nature does not".[3] By doing this, they appear to follow Isaac Newton, who, after the collapse of the South Sea Bubble, allegedly said: "I can calculate the

---

1   Kenny Ausubel, *Nature's Operating Instructions* (2004), p.xiv.

2   Interview on 8 September, 2009 on BBC2. (*bbc.co.uk ~ bbc.in/TPlink33*)

3   Reinhart & Rogoff (2009b) p.xxviii.

motions of heavenly bodies but not the madness of men".[4] While human nature may indeed play a role, the limitation of these interpretations is that changing human nature is not a realistic basis for attaining global financial stability any time soon...

The interpretation that such crashes are simply part of the process of 'creative destruction' is also of limited use. Although this is considered by Schumpeter to be a basic characteristic of capitalism,[5] the examples he uses all refer to the rise and fall of specific products or individual business units rather than entire monetary or financial systems. Furthermore, Schumpeter's notion of destruction is limited to older institutions, unable to compete with the innovations of entrepreneurial newcomers. Unfortunately this does not account for what is currently happening in the financial or monetary domain. After each crash, the banking system is bailed out at government expense, and the old way of doing business is taken up again after fine tuning of the regulatory or managerial environment. The fundamental structure – a monopoly of money created through bank debt – is invariably left intact.

Something else must be quite wrong with our monetary system, something that has been wrong for centuries. Charles Kindleberger identifies financial crashes as "hardy perennials" for a good reason.[6] Similarly, when Carmen Reinhart and Kenneth Rogoff chose the title '*This Time is Different*' for their exhaustive study of financial instabilities, it was meant as a warning of something bad repeating itself. In other words, something has been triggering the same type of problems for centuries. What could it be?

Instability as a Structural Flaw

The difficulties we face can be compared to the difference between a driver and a car designer. A bad driver can wreck any car. However, a bad car design can make a car unsafe at any speed, so that even a superb driver would have difficulty driving it safely. Thus, while monetary policies, appropriate regulation and bank management are important, there exists a flaw in the design of the monetary system which causes it to fail despite appropriate interventions. What we discuss in this chapter is the structural flaw in our modern monetary system: a flaw that is centuries old. This structural flaw was already present in 1637 when the Dutch Tulip bubble burst, and has played an unacknowledged role in every crash since that time, including the current one. Our evidence for this claim comes from the fundamental laws governing all complex flow systems, including natural ecosystems, economies and financial systems.

---

4   This alleged *bon mot* was first put forward by H. R. Fox Bourne in *The Romance of Trade* (1876), p.292. (see *www.archive.org ~ bit.ly/TPlink34*). However, it is unlikely that its attribution to Isaac Newton is valid, because we know that Newton himself lost quite a fortune in the South Sea Bubble.

5   Joseph A. Schumpeter, *Capitalism, Socialism and Democracy* (1942).

6   Charles P. Kindleberger, *Manias, Panics, and Crashes: A History of Financial Crises*, 5th edition (2005).

Our thesis will be presented in six steps. First, we will show that the Traditional Economics paradigm badly misclassifies economic systems. In his remarkable book *The Origin of Wealth: Evolution, Complexity and the Radical Remaking of Economics* (2006), Eric Beinhocker demonstrates how the Traditional Economics paradigm misclassified the economy as a closed system in general equilibrium. This explains the dominant paradigm's empirical failure to deal with several key issues of today. Rather than continuing to describe them with a simple mechanical metaphor in which linear cause-and-effect mechanisms are at play, we need to see economic systems as open systems, which act like complex flow systems with multiple and interrelated causalities.

Second, we will deal with complexity theory. A new set of mathematical tools allows us to deal with complexity and effectively explain a wide range of processes, including economic processes unexplainable using the Traditional Economics paradigm.

The third step will be to examine the theory of complex flow networks, a subset of complexity theory that integrates several recent breakthroughs in theoretical ecology, thermodynamics, information theory and network analysis. These breakthroughs allow us for the first time to quantify with a single metric the sustainability of any complex flow network. Within this framework, sustainability is defined as an optimal trade-off between two variables working in opposite directions: *efficiency* and *resilience.*

The fourth step will consist of testing the 'complex flow network' methodology on real-life natural ecosystems and exposing the structural conditions required for a network to be sustainable. We will demonstrate that these findings are applicable to any complex system possessing a similar structure regardless of what circulates in a given network – biomass in an ecosystem, electrons in an electrical power network or money in an economy.

The fifth step will then consist of applying this methodology to monetary systems. We will clarify how the pressures towards greater efficiency in finance, economics and engineering have often occurred at the expense of resilience. This is the cause of the systemic brittleness of the monetary and banking system. This dynamic is also the key to a solution that offers greater monetary sustainability.

The last step focuses on potential solutions. Greater diversity and interconnectivity is the key to rendering complex flow networks adaptable and resilient. Our monetary system must therefore evolve from being a monopoly of conventional money towards becoming an 'ecosystem' of multiple currencies. We will subsequently describe how this evolution towards greater monetary diversity is already taking place, albeit below the radar screen of officialdom.

1. The Misclassification of Economics

Until the late 19th century, economics was considered a field of applied moral philosophy rather than a science, and even less a mathematical science. For instance, Adam Smith was a Scottish professor of moral philosophy. Similarly, the school of the French Physiocrats (including people like François Quesnay) and Jeremy Bentham in England, saw themselves as philosophers and were considered as such by the wider public. It was not until Léon Walras's *Éléments d'économie pure* (1874) that mathematics was introduced into economics, thus changing economics into a science.

Walras saw a parallel between the idea of balancing points in economic systems and balancing points in nature. He "saw the balance of supply and demand in a market as metaphorically like the balance of forces in a physical equilibrium system. He conjectured that for each commodity traded in a market, there was only one price, one *equilibrium point*, at which traders would be satisfied and the market would clear. Prices in a market would predictably settle to a single equilibrium level, just as a ball would predictably settle into the smooth bottom of a bowl."[7]

By importing the mathematics of equilibrium theory from the mathematician Louis Poinsot, Walras provided the foundation for the Traditional Economics paradigm.[8] This paradigm can be found in all textbooks, most economics journals and implicitly in many corridors of power. Unfortunately, a fundamental misconception occurred during the import from physics into economics and is explained most succinctly by Eric Beinhocker (see box 4.1).

Box 4.1 — Eric Beinhocker and the Misclassification of Economics

Eric Beinhocker is a Senior Advisor to McKinsey & Co and author of the book *The Origin of Wealth*. The magazine *Fortune* named him "Business Leader of the Next Century". What follows are highlights of his reasoning.

"Without realising it and with the best intentions, the late-nineteenth-century economists borrowed from physics a set of ideas that fundamentally misclassified the economy as a closed equilibrium system. Their approach set the framework for the Traditional Economics we see today. Unfortunately, [this] misclassification has acted as a straightjacket, forcing economists to make highly unrealistic assumptions and limiting the field's empirical success."[9] Indeed, Walras and his contemporaries were unaware of the distinction between closed and open systems. A closed system is one in which there are no inputs from, or outputs to, the outside world: all energy originates and remains within the system itself. An open system operates with inputs and outputs. 19th century scientists believed most systems to be closed.

---

7   Eric Beinhocker, *The Origin of Wealth: Evolution, Complexity and the Radical Remaking of Economics* (2006), p.31, italics added.

8   Specifically, Chapter 2 of Louis Poinsot's *Elements of Statics* (1803), entitled 'On Conditions of Equilibrium Expressed by Means of Equations', was the source of Walras's models. Even the title of Walras's *Éléments* found its inspiration in this book. See Ingrao & Israel (1990), p.88 and Mirowski (1989), pp.219-220.

9   Beinhocker (2006) p.74.

We now know that economies function as open systems, absorbing massive amounts of energy from the outside (e.g., solar, mineral, human and animal inputs). They also produce significant amounts of unwanted by-products (e.g., gases, waste, pollution). Even our planet can be classified as an open system, sitting in the middle of a river of energy from the sun that promotes life and evolution at all levels. While closed systems have a predictable end state, open systems do not necessarily. They can remain relatively stable and in relative equilibrium for a period, but also exhibit patterns of exponential growth, radical collapse or cyclical oscillations. These patterns all exist in actual economies and are dismissed as 'anomalies' in the Traditional Economics paradigm.

The second fundamental error in the Traditional Economics paradigm relates to the state of knowledge of thermodynamics until the late 19th century. At that time, scientists only knew about the First Law of thermodynamics, which "states that energy is neither created nor destroyed and is otherwise known as the *Conservation of Energy Principle*. This was developed in the early to mid-nineteenth century and was clearly spelled out in the texts that Walras… and others read."[10] However, "the Second Law, which was missing from the physics Walras and Jevons knew, states that *entropy*, a measure of disorder or randomness in a system, is always increasing (…) Over time all order, structure, and pattern in the universe breaks down, decays and dissipates. Cars rust, buildings crumble, mountains erode, apples rot and cream poured into coffee dissipates until it is evenly mixed." [11]

Entropy is time's arrow. "Without entropy and the inevitable drift from order to disorder there would be no way to tell what the past, present or future is. Since its discovery, entropy has become a central concept in the way physicists view the world. Unfortunately, for Walras, Jevons and the other builders of Traditional Economics, this supreme law of nature was missing from their framework."[12] Among all the laws of physics, this Second Law is not one that can be overlooked. The famous astrophysicist Sir Arthur Eddington[13] showed no mercy for those unwilling to accept the implications of the Second Law of thermodynamics: "If your theory is found to be against the second law of thermodynamics I can give you no hope; there is nothing for it but to collapse in deepest humiliation."[14] Some economists have tried to revise economic theory to include entropy but have had only few followers until recently.[15]

These two foundational errors in the field of Traditional Economics — misclassifying the economy as a closed instead of open system, and ignoring the Second Law of thermodynamics — make a long list of unrealistic assumptions necessary for the equations to function. Among them is the need for humans to be driven only by self-interest and perfect rationality, the idea that all economic agents have access to all relevant information from the present and the future, and that they process all this information perfectly in an instant. In reality, we must

---

10   *Ibid*, p. 66.

11   *Ibid*, p. 67

12   *Ibid*, p. 68.

13   Sir Arthur Stanley Eddington (1882-1944) was one of the most prominent and important astrophysicists of his time. It is often claimed that only Arthur Eddington and Albert Einstein had a full understanding of relativity until the mid-1920s.

14   Arthur S. Eddington, *The Nature of the Physical World* (1928), p.74.

15   The most prominent example is Nicholas Georgescu-Roegen. As we saw earlier, his work remains largely ignored by the dominant Traditional Economics paradigm, while it has deeply and durably influenced the Ecological Economics paradigm we are using here as a basis for our study, and which Beinhocker obviously espouses as well.

often make decisions with incomplete and ambiguous information with finite calculative and cognitive abilities. Furthermore, the world in which these super-humans operate is assumed to be incredibly simple: it does not include any barriers to buying or selling; it involves no transaction costs; all producers are always perfectly efficient; participants interact only through price in perfect markets; all relevant information is available to everyone and resources are either infinite or so abundant that no radical scarcity is ever on the horizon. "This combination of assumptions has caused Axel Leijonhufvud, an economist at the University of California, Los Angeles, to assert that Traditional Economics models 'incredibly smart people in unbelievably simple situations' while the real world is in fact more accurately described as 'believably simple people [coping] with incredibly complex situations'."[16]

Mainstream economics has attempted to deal with some of these limitations. For instance, as early as 1978 the Nobel prize in economics was awarded to Herbert Simon, the father of 'bounded rationality' theory, and the 2007 prize was given to three Americans for their work in 'mechanism design theory', a branch of economics examining situations in which markets work imperfectly, such as when competition is not completely free, consumers are not fully informed or people hold back private information. Similarly, the 2009 award went to Elinor Ostrom "for her analysis of economic governance, especially the commons".

However, ecological economists including Nicholas Georgescu-Roegen, Kenneth Boulding and Herman Daly who question the fundamental premise of an economy as a closed system and stress the need to account for entropy have to this day been ignored by the Swedish Academy of Sciences and by the Bank of Sweden.

Neither Beinhocker nor we are attacking economists, nor are we questioning the legitimacy of the aspirations of economics to become a science nor its use of advanced mathematics. Beinhocker simply asserts that traditional economics has not been using the right conceptual and mathematical tools. In his approach to the economy, as in the Ecological Economics paradigm generally, consumer demand, markets, technologies, business plans and stocks of natural resources are all in evolution. The one critical exception he implicitly makes is that money itself remains unchanged and non-evolving. We will discuss in this chapter why this assumption is not valid; and in subsequent chapters what becomes possible when we let go of this assumption.

Beinhocker proposes 'complexity economics' as his solution for the radical remaking of economics. Regrettably, the words 'complexity theory' and 'chaos theory' have been used, overused and even abused so that their precise meaning has become unclear. We will now define what is meant by complexity and complexity theory.

2. Complexity

As a starting point, let us distinguish between systems according to the characteristics of their causality mechanism. At one end of the spectrum lies simple *linear causality*. This concept dates back to the classical Greeks. Since Newton's time, effective mathematical tools such as mechanics have been available to study processes involving

---

16 Beinhocker (2006) p.52.

linear causality. At the other end of the spectrum, one finds systems with a *lack of causality,* without interaction among variables. This latter realm is best explored with the mathematical tools of statistics. The domain of *complexity* lies between these two extremes; here, there are several causes interacting and there are multiple interactions between variables. Figure 4.1 illustrates this dynamic.

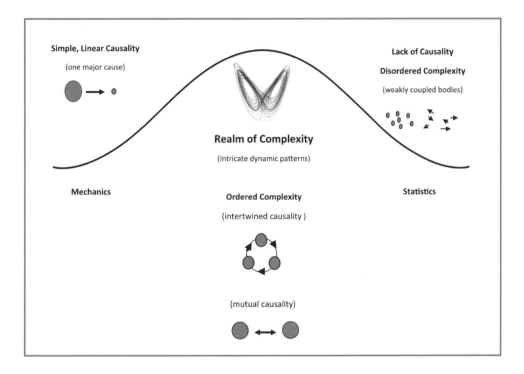

Figure 4.1: The Realm of Complexity.[17] The ability to study the order of intertwined and mutual causality in real-world systems opens up a new scientific realm. This could not be appropriately done using either of today's mainstay approaches: mechanics (simple linear causality) or statistics (weakly connected causality). The vast majority of real-life natural, social and economic phenomena belong to the realm of complexity. Indeed, natural systems, whether physical, social or economic, only rarely exhibit simple causality (one single cause) or weakly connected causality (weakly connected components).

The middle of the spectrum encompasses the majority of real-life systems. This realm of complexity is characterised by intertwined and mutual causality,[18] and dynamic feedback loops between a system's multiple components. From this form of causality emerges 'ordered complexity'. The simplest physical example of this can be observed when one brings a liquid, such as water, to a boil (Figure 4.2).

---

17 Figure adapted from Sally J. Goerner, *After the Clockwork Universe: The Emerging Science and Culture of Integral Society* (1999).

18 A good summary of intertwined causality is provided by Erwin Laszlo, *The Systems View of the World: A Holistic Vision for our Time* (1996). For the definition and implications of mutual causality, see Joanna Macy, *The Dharma of Natural Systems: Mutual Causality in Buddhism and General Systems Theory* (1991).

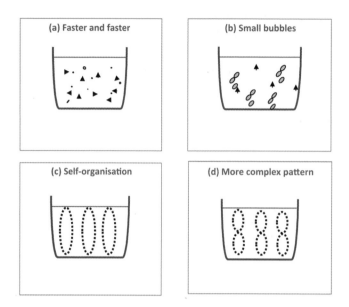

Figure 4.2 (a-d): From random collisions to self-organisation.[19] When one applies heat to water, a predictable sequence occurs in distinct stages, each with its own specific characteristics. Before applying any heat, the water molecules randomly move and collide with one another. When heat is applied, the molecules continue to move in the same fashion at a higher speed (figure a). This continues until bubbles appear in the liquid, the first organisational change or 'phase change' (figure b). As the temperature increases further, self-organising loops emerge (figure c). As even greater energy is applied, the structure of the loops changes to a more complex, tightly interconnected pattern (figure d). These patterns of increasingly intricate orders spontaneously emerge from the very structure of a system. In an apparent paradox, a local reduction of entropy (i.e. more intricate local order) makes it possible for the broader system and the universe to produce more entropy. The resulting self-organisation process has been described as the driving force behind evolution, including the evolution from atoms to more complex molecules, the origins of life and the evolution of all the different life forms on Earth.

Each successive phase is characterised by higher complexity, and the self-organising order also produces higher entropy.[20] For example, a life form is clearly more organised than its surroundings (i.e. reduces entropy locally). However, any living being feeds on elements of its surroundings and produces waste (i.e. increases entropy in its surroundings). The life forms that will be successful are those whose internal capacity to circulate energy is the highest, something that will also tend to increase the total entropy of the universe.

---

19 Figure taken from Goerner (1999).

20 See Robert Ulanowicz and B. M. Hannon, 'Life and the Production of Entropy', *Proceedings of the Royal Society of London B*, Vol. 232, pp.181-192. See also Sally J. Goerner, Robert G. Dyck and Dorothy Lagerroos, *The New Science of Sustainability: Building a Foundation for Great Change*, (2008).

This phenomenon of *ordered complexity* does not occur in systems ruled by simple linear causality, nor does it arise when the components are only weakly coupled. It is the key attribute of the realm of complexity. A system can therefore be labelled complex if, and only if, it has two characteristics: a high diversity of components and a dense network of interactions between these components. As Beinhocker and others[21] have shown, this is certainly the case with economic processes.

The classical mathematical tools used by economists, typically involving linear regressions and general statistics, assume linear causality and independent variables and therefore cannot capture this type of complexity. Traditional Economics must oversimplify economic reality in order to 'make the equations work'. One consequence of this over-simplification is the failure of economics to deal with the issue of resilience and sustainability.

It is only recently, as more powerful and inexpensive computing power has become available, that a new set of mathematical tools dealing with ordered complexity has emerged. These new tools developed for complexity theory include agent-based modelling (promoted by the Santa Fe Institute); and those that emerged from network and information theories and thermodynamics (which will be our approach). Complexity theory has already revolutionised a wide range of fields including geophysics, demography, ethology, biology, medicine, acoustics, electronics and finance.

As stated earlier, almost all real-life natural systems lie in the realm of ordered complexity. Because this is the case, complexity laws may even be more important to understanding real-world systems than the law of gravity itself. In particular, recent findings in thermodynamics unite long-standing observations about universal patterns of growth and development into a law of physics with profound implications for our understanding of developmental change and evolution itself, as astrophysicist François Roddier claims, along with many others (see Box 4.2).

---

21 See, e.g., Paul Ormerod (1994); Sunny J. Auyang (1998); and Robert Axelrod & Michael D. Cohen (2000).

Box 4.2 – François Roddier and Dewar's law

François Roddier is considered to be one of the most brilliant astrophysicists of our times. He is the inventor of an atomic spectrometer used to study the internal workings of the sun, and he has developed the field of adaptive optics that corrects astronomical observations for atmospheric turbulences. Since his retirement in 2000, he has been focusing on the impact of recent thermodynamics findings on evolution. What follows are some extracts from his latest work:[22]

"A new law of physics has recently been proven. It is an abstract theorem that was published in 2003 in a top European journal of mathematical physics.[23] No mainstream newspaper mentioned this breakthrough. The importance of this discovery is nevertheless equivalent to the law of gravity by Newton or Darwin's theory of evolution. This new law even conditions the latter two, as will be shown. Many scientists themselves apparently have not yet realised its relevance.

"The proof is due to Roderick Dewar, a physicist of Scottish origin who works in the National Institute of Agronomic Research in Bordeaux, France. Why in an agronomic institute? This law of physics has fundamental implications for the entire field of biology. It also applies to humankind and evolution of human societies.

"From its very beginning, the universe evolves by creating more and more complex material structures capable of dissipating energy ever more efficiently. The stars, the planets, plants, animals and finally mankind are a sequence of such structures. Dewar's law explains why. A Belgian physicist of Russian origin, Ilya Prigogine, first studied this process of energy dissipation in detail. His work earned him the Nobel Prize in physics in 1977. Stars, planets, plants, animals, humans, human societies are all 'dissipative structures' as defined by Prigogine. ...Energy dissipation produces disorder or degradation of energy, called entropy in physics. That is why the dissipation of energy is also called 'entropy production'. Dewar's law is abbreviated as MEP (Maximum Entropy Production): a dissipative structure reduces its internal entropy – i.e. gets more organised internally – to maximise total energy dissipation...

"For plants and animals, information about the environment is stored in genes. Plants and animals have adapted to a specific environment. This adaptation takes place through natural selection. The plants and animals selected are those capable of most rapidly and effectively dissipating energy. By doing this, a living being changes its environment. As the environment changes, its genes are no longer adapted. This living being needs to evolve again. To remain in harmony with the environment which it is making evolve, a living being needs to adapt with greater speed. After atoms and molecules, living beings increase in complexity. Those most adept at dissipating energy are the ones that invariably win.

---

22 François Roddier, *Le pain, le levain et les gènes* (2009), excerpts translated from pp.55-58 and 61-72.

23 Roderick Dewar, 'Information Theory Explanation of the Fluctuation Theorem, Maximum Entropy Production and Self-Organized Criticality in Non-Equilibrium Stationary States', *Journal of Physics A: Math. Gen. 36 #3* (2003), pp.631-641.

"Geothermal energy dissipates not gradually but suddenly, in the form of earthquakes. The same is true with life. Plant and animal ecosystems develop quickly and collapse suddenly, to be replaced by more evolved populations that can better dissipate energy. The Australopithecus species disappeared along with all other humanoid species except for our own, initially because of the domestication of fire and the cooking of food.

"From the Neolithic onwards, information about the environment previously only stored in genes started to be stored in the human brain. From this point on, the human brain controls the evolution of humanity. The English zoologist Richard Dawkins has proposed to call 'memes' information stored in human brains, by analogy to 'genes'. For humanity, memes replace genes with notable consequences. Humans start sharing the same memes thereby creating a new type of dissipative structure. Different human societies emerge. …The development of economies is nothing more than the elaboration of the dissipation of energies through structures that have become human societies.

"I am convinced that Dewar's results will become the pillar of a new economic science once economists become aware of its implications. During the 17th century, England, as the most advanced mimetic society of the time, was the first to limit the powers of monarchy. France followed suit during the eighteenth century. Because absolutist monarchy limited the development of economies, it was doomed to disappear. During the nineteenth century, European nations - at that time still different mimetic societies - entered into competition with one another. The consequences of this during the twentieth century included two world wars and a Great Depression.

"At the end of the second war, two big ideologies, capitalism and communism, remained and entered into conflict. The memes of the free economy eventually ended up spreading into the USSR. Because the Soviet economy was developing more slowly, it collapsed. Humanity as a whole now dissipates 2kW/kg per person. An average Frenchman dissipates 6kW/kg/person, an average American 10kW/kg/person. By dissipating energy in this way, the economy is rapidly modifying its environment (exhaustion of oil reserves, pollution, etc.), and social inequalities are being exacerbated.

"Physics and biology show us where this leads: the extinction of species and the end of civilisations. Biology has demonstrated how our genes are continuously forced to evolve. We now realise that the same is true with our memes. They, too, have to evolve. No isolated individual can unilaterally reduce its energy dissipation without taking the risk of being eliminated by natural selection. Similarly, no country or isolated civilisation can unilaterally limit its economic development.

"The only hope is a change of consciousness on a global level – the realisation of the need for a new meme: the need to reduce our energy consumption on a planetary scale. Such a change is starting to occur because, for the very first time, the degradation of the environment is visible within the time span of one generation – the sign of a seismic environmental shift on a global level. Hence the urgent call for sustainable development. While trying to save a planet which could not care less, we may be able to save humanity."

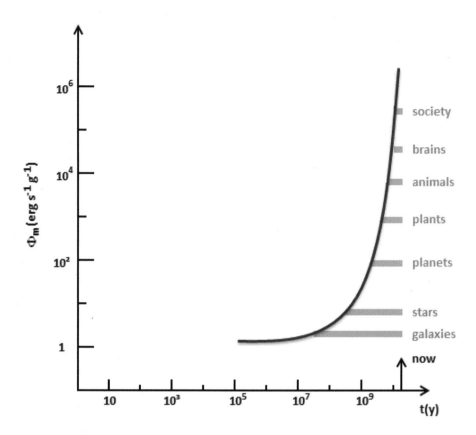

Figure 4.3: Growth of dissipated energy as a function of the age and the evolution of the universe (from Eric Chaisson[24]).

Figure 4.3 shows the evolution of the efficiency of dissipated energy over time. Energy can be measured in watts. The efficiency of dissipated energy is then measured in watts per kilogram of matter. Everything starts with the 'Big Bang' some 13.7 billion years ago. Matter starts condensing almost immediately. Under the force of gravity, galaxies slowly start forming, hydrogen is transformed into helium, and heat dissipates at the rhythm of one tenth of a mW/kg (milliwatt per kilogram of matter). Further condensation creates stars for which the rhythm of dissipation is measured in tens of mW/kg. As stars age and become super-giants, they form atoms of increasing complexity, and agglomerations form to become planets. Planets absorb the light emitted by the stars and reemit it in the infrared, dissipating energy at the rhythm of one mW/kg. On some planets, under the right conditions, life emerges. Even the most primitive forms of life – cyanobacteria – already dissipate 10 mW/kg, and over a time span of a few billion years they have produced all the oxygen we are currently breathing. Plants develop and dissipate about 100 mW/kg. In the Cambrian period,

24 Eric Chaisson, 'Non-equilibrium Thermodynamics in an Energy-Rich Universe', in A. Kleidon and R.D. Lorenz (eds), *Non-Equilibrium Thermodynamics and the Production of Entropy: Life, Earth, and Beyond* (2005), pp.21-33.

animals appear and dissipate more than one W/kg. Finally, humans appear. A human at rest dissipates a minimum of 3W/kg. During an effort the amount of energy dissipated increases ten-fold. The evolution of human societies and their economies is currently driving humanity's capacity to dissipate energy at an average rate of 2000W/kg – and this in an exponential manner.

Roddier reveals the scale and scope of forces driving evolutionary change at an exponentially accelerating rhythm. Could the same law by which dinosaurs had to give way to smaller and more agile mammals, by which absolute monarchies became irrelevant, or by which communism collapsed also apply to our money system? Could it be that the prevailing meme of a monoculture of money is strangling human evolution and creativity at a critical juncture of our collective journey? If Roddier's claims and Dewar's law are valid, they force upon us the realisation that we must unlock this monetary stranglehold or become extinct as a species. The next two sections provide the evidence for such a claim.

3. The Physics of Complex Flow Networks

The same approach to thermodynamics that Roddier describes has also been applied to the study of complex *flow networks* such as living organisms, river systems, ecosystems, urban networks, social systems and business networks.[25] The result of an integration of a large body of existing work in various fields, this Energy Network Analysis research on the physics of flow networks is also the natural extension of the results of Nobel Prize-winning chemist Illya Prigogine and Club of Rome co-founder Erich Jantsch's work on self-organising energy-flow systems. In fact, according to ecological economist Kenneth Boulding, many early economists held views that took energy into account. This changed when those who favoured Newtonian mechanics imposed on economics the Traditional Economics paradigm with its now familiar views on the mechanics of 'rational actors' and the reliable self-restraint of general equilibrium theory.

The particular synthesis we present here is the contribution of four people: the physicist and quantitative ecologist Robert Ulanowicz,[26] the nonlinear dynamist Sally Goerner, the professor of Architecture and Urban Planning Robert G. Dyck, and the professor of Government and Environmental Management Dorothy Lagerroos.[27]

This new approach provides a concise explanation of why we need to use new tools to understand monetary and economic dynamics as they are actually manifesting in the

---

25 See, for example, Sally Goerner, Bernard Lietaer and Robert Ulanowicz, 'Quantifying economic sustainability: Implications for free-enterprise theory, policy and practice'. *Ecological Economics*, 2009, Vol. 69(1), pp.76-81.

26 See, *among others*, Robert Ulanowicz, *A Third Window: Natural Foundations for Life* (2008).

27 Goerner, Dyck & Lagerroos (2008)

real world. In this approach, complex systems such as ecosystems, living organisms and economies are all seen as matter-flow, energy-flow and information-flow systems. For example, the famous 'food chain' is actually a matter/energy-flow network built out of complex relationships between organisms. Plants capture the sun's energy with photosynthesis; animals eat the plants; species then eat each other in a chain leading all the way to the top predator, only to have all organisms die and decompose, and their energy/matter be recycled by bacteria.

One peer-reviewed paper[28] gathered extensive research on real-life ecosystems and generalised these findings to the sustainability of any complex flow network. We will provide here only a summary of its findings. Readers interested in the complete technical and mathematical proofs should refer to the original published paper.[29]

Decades of studying natural ecosystems have led to a sophisticated mathematical understanding of how a network structure affects an ecosystem's long-term viability. This depends on a balance between *efficiency* and *resilience*. Efficiency, also called throughput efficiency, measures the ability of a system to process volumes of the relevant matter-flow, energy-flow and/or information-flow. Resilience measures the ability of a system to recover from a disturbance, an attack or a change in the environment. With these definitions in mind, we can now define and precisely quantify a complex flow system's sustainability using a single metric.

In general, a system's resilience is enhanced by higher diversity and by more pathways (or connections) because there are numerous channels of interaction to fall back on in times of trouble or change. For example, a predator fish may 'connect' to – i.e., acquire energy and resources, usually by eating from – three or four other species (e.g. turtles and snakes) or it may link to only one (e.g. prawns). A fish depending on a single other species for its food supply will have difficulty adapting when that one species gets into difficulty. Researchers have therefore been able to use the amount of diversity and connectivity to quantify a system's resilience.

Diversity and connectivity also play an important role in throughput efficiency, but in the opposite direction: *efficiency increases* as diversity and connectivity *decreases*. Furthermore, as a flow system becomes more efficient, it tends to build up a kind of self-fuelling momentum (technically called 'autocatalysis') that eliminates diversity as it gradually streamlines the process. In general, increasingly efficient systems tend to become more directed, less diverse and, consequently, more brittle.

28 Robert E. Ulanowicz, Sally J. Goerner, Bernard Lietaer and Rocio Gomez, 'Quantifying Sustainability: Resilience, Efficiency and the Return of Information Theory', *Ecological Complexity*, Vol. 6 (2009), pp.27-36.

29 Appendix D has a synthesis of this paper with a more detailed graphic analysis than the one displayed here. For anyone interested in traditional Chinese philosophy, Appendix E shows some parallels between our framework and the Taoist view of yin-yang polarities as a universal dynamic.

The point being made here is profound and has wide-reaching implications for all complex flow systems, including our worldwide economy. Since resilience and efficiency are both necessary but pull in opposite directions, nature tends to select those systems which have an optimal balance of the two. The exact balance varies depending on the system. Therefore, we propose the working definition of sustainability as *the optimal balance between efficiency and resilience*. A system is maximally sustainable when that balance attains its optimal mix. In Appendix D1, a concrete example is provided of how this methodology applies to the three channels of carbon flow leading from freshwater prawns to the American alligator, via three intermediate predators: turtles, large fish and snakes, located in the Cypress wetlands of South Florida.

When we want to express sustainability graphically, three variables are involved: diversity, interconnectivity and the relative weight put on efficiency *vs.* resilience. We are thus dealing with a four-dimensional object, which is difficult to render in a two-dimensional graph. In Appendix D2, a one-minute animation movie presents all four dimensions. In the same section a sequence of three-dimensional graphs gives an idea of what shape we are dealing with.

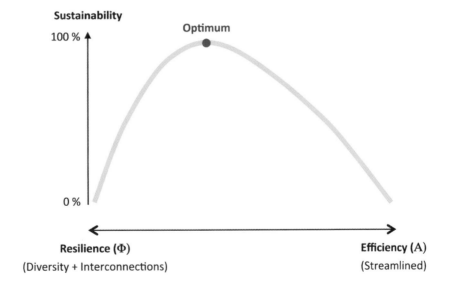

Figure 4.4: Sustainability curve mapped between the two polarities of efficiency and resilience. In nature, resilience is given more importance than efficiency and the curve is steeper on that side of the graph. Notice that this two-dimensional graph is a didactic simplification of a four-dimensional object. More complete explanations and a 3-D graphic analysis are available in Appendix D.

Of perhaps even greater importance, the physics of flow networks also explains why excessively large and efficient organisations may pull the whole system toward collapse. In essence, large, highly efficient organisations in the network 'out compete' the smaller organisations for resources, drawing ever more energy, information and resources into the big, and away from the smaller participants. This, of course, causes the big organisations to get bigger still, and the smaller ones to die off, just as Schumpeter's classical 'creative destruction' theory predicts. Unfortunately, killing off large numbers of smaller organisations reduces resilience, increases instability and steadily moves the whole system towards collapse (i.e., sustainability = 0). Common examples include: large, unrestrained predators killing off all their prey causing an ecosystem to collapse; digging large canals in the New Orleans delta, which drained soil from the wetlands, causing the city to sink and the wetlands to die; and monopolies of commerce which kill off so many small competitors that a positive feedback cycle of 'the more you have, the more you get' locks into a 'winner takes all' game. This can lead to an economic 'bubble', a shimmering bubble of wealth over a feeble, eviscerated real economy. This law of physics explains why we once introduced anti-trust laws.

In conclusion: "Life tends to optimise, rather than maximise. Maximisation is another word for addiction."[30] Indeed, in the real world, all networks corresponding to natural ecosystems operate around the optimal point, within a specific range called the 'window of viability', [31] which lies on either side of this optimum, as can be seen in Figure 4.5.

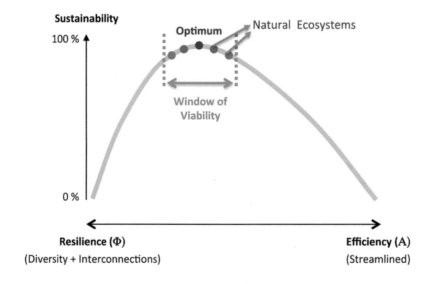

Figure 4.5: All natural ecosystems operate within a 'window of viability' around the optimal point.

What can we learn from this exploration of sustainability, combining network and information theory with data from real-life ecosystems?

---

30 Paul Hawken, *Blessed Unrest* (2007), p.183.

31 This is also called "window of vitality" in the ecological literature. See Ulanowicz (2008).

4. Lessons from Nature

The main point is that nature does not select for maximum efficiency but for an optimal balance between the two opposing poles of throughput efficiency and resilience. In other words, sustainability requires just enough, and not too much, of both efficiency and resilience. In most human-designed systems, and certainly in the monetary domain, we have been concerned only with efficiency, and have therefore tended to unduly sacrifice resilience.

Until recently, total throughput and efficiency were assumed to be the main measures of system health, whether in natural science or in economics. Now, however, we can distinguish whether a particular increase in organisational size and/or efficiency is truly a sign of healthy growth, or the beginnings of a short-term bubble doomed to collapse.

Finally, we can assume that nature has solved many of the developmental problems in ecosystems over time. Otherwise, these ecosystems would no longer exist today. These are the same type of problems with which humanity is still struggling in economic terms. Also of interest is that all ecosystems have their most critical structural parameters such as diversity and interconnectivity within a very specific narrow range or what we have called the window of viability.

Sally Goerner points out, "All systems, no matter how complex, fall into one of a few classes. All members of a class share certain common patterns of behaviour."[32] Similarly, complexity theorist Predrag Cvitanovic states, "The wonderful thing about this universality is that it does not matter much how close our equations are to the ones chosen by nature, as long as the model is in the same universality class ... as the real system. This means that we can get the right physics out of very crude models."[33] In other words, insights about the behaviour of a system do not require ever more refined modelling, as is the case with linear models. It is simply a matter of determining the class of model characterising that particular system. The findings from one network are valid for any other network displaying the same *structure*, whether the components are alligators and fish in an ecosystem, electrons in an electrical circuit, or money in an economy.

For instance, electrical power grids have been optimised for decades for greater technical and economic efficiency. It may come as a surprise to many engineers that it is precisely because these power grids have approached maximum efficiency that large-scale electrical blackouts are occurring in the technologically most advanced countries (e.g. Germany or the USA). Over-efficient streamlining has caused them to lose their resilience.

---

32 Goerner (1999) p.153.

33 Predrag Cvitanovic, *Introduction to Universality in Chaos* (1984), p.11.

Similarly, one can intuitively grasp that a balance between efficiency and resilience is key to economic sustainability. For example, vibrant businesses must maintain resilience by creating and maintaining well-knit systems of production, marketing, delivering, accounting and training that have numerous interconnections. Once these are in place, organisations must stay competitive by honing their processes following efficiency principles, typically through streamlining. Yet to survive changing times, organisations must also be able to adjust their business strategies to respond to changes in markets and in the economic climate. Overemphasis on efficiency through streamlining can become problematic when it reduces the diversity needed for adaptability and for the multiplicity of paths. In a business model, this diversity can be seen as agility and choice among different strategic options for dealing with unexpected problems, failures or opportunities.

Since the 1990s, stock options for top management in public corporations have become a widespread practice. This approach was successful in getting CEOs focused on short-term and immediately measurable financial results. Using our sustainability framework, we can observe that such myopic profit-maximising pressures are dangerous because they force managers to over-emphasise streamlining, rigid control and short-term efficiencies at the expense of long-term adaptability and resilience. Over-emphasising efficiency produces rigidity and brittleness, so that one little break in the chain can lead to an sudden breakdown. We can thus predict that overly streamlined corporations are more likely to experience major crises when encountering unexpected challenges.

Recent events illustrate the implications of sudden disruptions in systems overly optimised for the sake of efficiency. For instance: "The 2010 Icelandic volcanic ash disrupted air transport across Europe, and gave the world's manufacturing supply chain one of its biggest tests since the advent of the low-inventory, just-in-time era. Japan's quadruple disaster – earthquake, tsunami, nuclear alert and power shortages – has put the supply chain under far greater stress. ...Over the past decade or so the just-in-time concept of having supplies delivered at the last minute, so as to keep inventories down, has spread down the global manufacturing chain. Now, say economists at HSBC, this chain may [need to] be fortified with 'just-in-case' systems to limit the damage from disruptions."[34]

Conversely, *too much* diversity and connectivity could lead to excessive overhead and insufficient efficiency.

In short, poorly connected networks are fragile, brittle and may collapse when they meet an unexpected challenge; while overly connected networks tend to become stagnant. The key to a successful sustainability strategy is therefore *the appropriate balance*, in all complex flow systems, be they corporations, ecosystems, or economies.

---

34 *The Economist*, 2 April, 2011, p.59.

5. Application to Monetary Systems

Our global monetary system is a network of monopolistic national currencies, one for each country. The technical justification for enforcing a monopoly of national currencies is to optimise the efficiency of price formation and exchanges in national markets. In a seminal paper written in 1953, Milton Friedman similarly justified the introduction of floating exchange rates to improve global efficiency by letting free markets determine the prices of each national currency.[35] This idea was actually implemented by President Nixon in 1971 when he took the dollar off the gold standard. Since that time, an extraordinarily sophisticated and efficient global communications infrastructure has been built to link and trade these national currencies. As explained in Chapter III, the trading volume in the foreign exchange markets reached an impressive $4 trillion per day in 2010, to which another several trillion of currency derivatives should be added. No-one questions the throughput efficiency of these markets or their capacity to process huge volumes of money.

However, the system's lack of resilience shows up, not in the information technologies where back-up systems are universally in place, but in the financial realm where no back-up systems exist. The hundreds of systemic crashes that have occurred over the past forty years demonstrate this. Such a crisis, particularly a combined monetary and banking crash, is, other than a war, the worst thing that can befall a country. All evidence points to monopolistic national monies having evolved into an overly efficient and brittle system. This situation is illustrated in Figure 4.6.

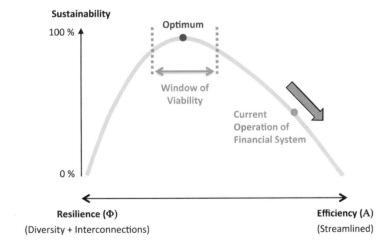

Figure 4.6: Today's global monetary ecosystem significantly overshoots the optimal balance between efficiency and resilience. This is due to an overemphasis on efficiency which leaves the overall system insufficiently adaptive. The general belief that all improvements must go further in that same direction (red arrow) will drive us yet further away from sustainability.

35 Milton Friedman, 'The Case for Flexible Exchange Rates', *Essays in Positive Economics* (1953), pp.157-203.

The path to monetary sustainability will come as a surprise for Traditional Economic thinking, where *de facto* monopolies of national monies are considered a given. Monetary sustainability requires a diversity of currency systems, so that multiple and more diverse channels of monetary linkage and exchange can emerge, as illustrated in Figure 4.7.

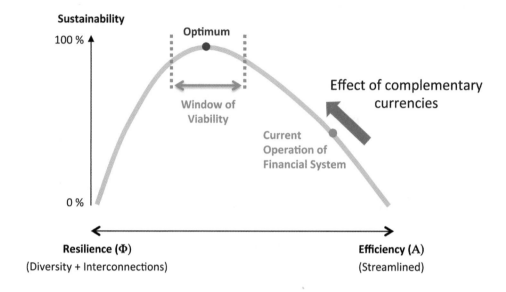

Figure 4.7: The effect of diverse types of exchange media. The operation of diverse and multiple currencies pushes the economy back towards optimal sustainability (green arrow), facilitating transactions via connections that would otherwise not exist and increasing economic resilience. The cost of this improvement is necessarily a reduction in efficiency.

Proponents of the Traditional Economics paradigm will raise a predictable argument against this idea: using multiple media of exchange within a national economy reduces the efficiency of the price formation process and of the exchanges between economic agents. The lesson from the physics of complex flow networks is that pushing for greater efficiency when a system is already beyond the optimal balance increases the likelihood of the next crash. The analogy would be to tell a driver that the more congested and accident-strewn the road looks, the more he or she should accelerate rather than brake.

Dealing with crashes, naturally?

Natural ecosystems can also experience a crash: a major forest fire, a flood, a clear-cut harvest and or some other disaster exerting significant stress on the overall environment. What happens to a natural ecosystem in such cases? The system responds by first operating at the extreme resilience level, where diversity is highest but where efficiency is extremely low. Then, as species best adapted to the new context start thriving, the system gradually returns to the window of viability (see Figure 4.8)

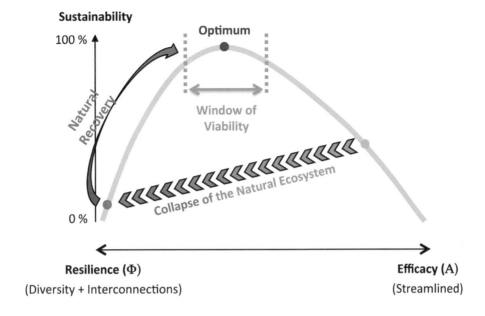

Figure 4.8: The recovery path after the collapse of a natural ecosystem.

What do we do when the financial system collapses completely, as was the case in Germany in the 1920s, or Argentina in the late 1990s, or possibly a euro breakup or a dollar collapse? The beginning is similar to the case of a natural ecosystem: individuals and businesses resort to barter, where in principle all sorts of things can become 'survival' currencies. This is obviously very inefficient. Until now, the same old recipe has been applied: the banking system and the monopoly of bank-debt money are forcibly re-established as quickly as possible. Typically, the largest banks that are 'too big to fail' are bailed out and helped to absorb the smaller ones, fuelling further concentration in a few financial institutions.

Should we not learn from nature that growing to the point of becoming 'too big to fail' should never be allowed to happen? Instead, in the USA, the ten largest banks now control 42% of the market, compared to 28% before the 2008 crisis. This pattern is the perfect demonstration of what are known as 'autocatalytic forces' in natural ecosystems – forces that automatically lead to systemic crashes. The very institutions that were already 'too big to fail' are made to grow bigger still. This promotes higher volume, and possibly higher throughput efficiency, but also a further increase in brittleness.

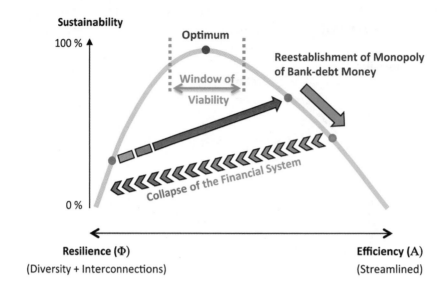

Figure 4.9: As soon as possible after a financial crash, the monopoly of bank-debt money is re-established, creating a loop where systemic crashes or crises are predictably repeated over and over again.

The autocatalytic forces in the business realm today take the political form of lobbying, which in the case of the financial system has proven remarkably effective. Wealth begets power and power begets laws that favour the interests of those who pay. This begets more wealth and the cycle continues until exorbitant excesses cause its breakdown. For example, in Washington in 2010 there were three high level registered lobbyists working for the banks for every elected person in town! Furthermore, practically all governments are now heavily indebted, further tilting the bargaining power against them. As US Secretary of State Hillary Clinton has said according to WikiLeaks, "it is difficult to be tough with your banker..."[36] So, at least in the financial sector, a return to business as usual has been taking place remarkably quickly.

The Wall Street Journal even reports that banking business is better than ever: the bonuses paid out for 2010 by the twenty-five largest Wall Street institutions amounted to $135.5 billion, surpassing even the all-time record of 2007. For instance, the top executive of Goldman Sachs increased his bonus to $12.6 million while 738 executives of Citigroup each received more than $1 million.[37] More disturbing still is information revealed by the Federal Reserve, after it had been forced to partially open its books from the bailout era by the Wall Street Act in 2009. Bernie Sanders, the independent US senator from Vermont, who initiated the amendment that forced

---

36 Hillary Clinton was referring to China as "banker for the US", but her choice of metaphor also reflects the validity of the image at the first degree, namely when it comes to actual banks.

37 Jerôme Fourel, 'Wall Street et ses bonus: $135.500.000.000 pour 2010', *Le Monde*, 7 February 2011.

this unprecedented disclosure of the relevant data by the Federal Reserve said: "Our jaws are literally dropping as we're reading this". Some of the Federal Reserve rescue programmes, such as the Term Asset-backed Loan Fund (TALF), have revealed a blatant degree of cronyism. This programme was introduced after President Obama's election in November 2008 to spur consumer lending which had dried up during the financial crisis. "But instead of lending directly to consumers, credit card holders or students, the Fed handed out a trillion dollars to banks and hedge funds..."[38]

We have been caught in the loop shown in Figure 4.9 for several centuries – actually since the time when a monopoly of bank-debt money was established. We now can predict with 100% certainty that more crashes will occur in the near future, as long as this currency monoculture is maintained.

Independent confirmation

The application of network theory to financial and banking systems is not uniquely ours. Indeed, a growing literature is emerging that uses complex network theory in economics and finance.[39] For instance, several years after our published work on the application of complex flow networks to the financial system, a paper entitled 'Systemic Risk in Banking Ecosystems'[40] was published in *Nature,* the world's most cited interdisciplinary scientific journal.[41] The two authors are prestigious: Andrew Haldane, the Bank of England's Executive Director for Financial Stability, and Professor Robert May, former President of the Royal Society in England. They, too, have been using complexity theory to model today's financial system as an ecosystem. Although they use a different complexity methodology from ours[42], they come to remarkably similar conclusions:

- Models from ecosystem research offer important and valid insights for understanding the resilience of the financial sector. "This quest to understand the dynamics of what might be called 'financial ecosystems' has interesting parallels with ecology."[43] The substantial knowledge accumulated from work

---

38 'The Real Housewives of Wall Street', *Rolling Stone*, 4 November, 2011.

39 See, for instance, M. Kosfeld (2004); Y. Leitner (2005); Frank Schweitzer *et al.* (2009a); Frank Schweitzer *et al.* (2009b); and C. Jones (2010).

40 Andrew Haldane and Robert May, 'Systemic Risk in Banking Ecosystems', *Nature*, Vol. 469 (20 January, 2011), pp.351-355.

41 This ranking was computed in 2010 in the *Journal of Citation Reports* Science Edition (Thomson Reuters, 2011) See also: *www.nature.com/nature/about/*

42 Specifically, the Haldane-May team used agent modelling as their key tool to explore the complex flow network of the financial system. Agent modelling is the favoured methodology of the Santa Fe school of complexity. In contrast, our methodology is grounded on thermodynamics and information theory applied to natural ecosystems.

43 Haldane & May (2011) p.351.

on natural network systems can and should be used in the evaluation of systemic risks in the banking sector.

- Taking into account system-wide properties of the financial system rather than individual institutions is important. "The cornerstone of the current international regulatory agenda is the setting of higher requirements for banks' capital and liquid assets. ...In regulating the financial system, [too] little effort has as yet been put into assessing the system-wide characteristics of the network."[44]

- Greater diversity across the financial system is needed. "In rebuilding and maintaining the financial system, this systemic diversity objective should be given much greater prominence by the regulatory community", because "homogeneity breeds fragility".[45]

- Increased concentration in the financial sector is one key factor contributing to the brittleness of the entire network. "Tentative evidence comes from the fact that the world's five largest banks have shown increasing concentration of assets over the last ten years."[46] Because governments are cornered into bailing out institutions that are 'too big to fail', the authors conclude, "In financial ecosystems, evolutionary forces have often been survival of the fattest rather than the fittest".[47] We have described this same phenomenon as the 'autocatalytic forces' growing in size and power at the expense of the stability of the whole.

For two different and independent teams using different complexity methodology to reach similar conclusions increases the robustness and credibility of these findings. Further research efforts in this direction should obviously be worthwhile.

Differences in the two approaches also exist. The most important difference is in the recommended solutions. Because Haldane and May remain within the paradigm of a single currency, they must live with the contradiction of needing to encourage diversity on the one hand and needing to advocate stricter regulation on the other.

6. Towards a Structural Solution?

Our own position is best summarised in William McDonough's quote at the beginning of this chapter: "The need for regulation is *always* a sign of a faulty design". This is why our solution considers the structural design of the monetary system itself. We recommend a monetary *eco*system, in which exchange media other than a monoculture of bank-debt money are allowed to play a role. This would provide greater structural

44 *Ibid.*, p.355.
45 *Ibid.*, p.355.
46 *Ibid.*, p.354.
47 *Ibid.*, p.351.

diversity in both the media of exchange and in the institutions creating them. If and when such complementary systems are in place, more spontaneous adjustments to economic instability and/or sudden scarcity of bank-debt money become possible. Such complementary arrangements would also reduce the extraordinary stranglehold the banking system exerts now on governments and the entire economy.

Coming from a completely different perspective, Friedrich Hayek, one of the leaders of the Austrian school of economics, wrote a short book in 1976 that has remained mostly ignored, entitled *Denationalization of Money*.[48] His premise was that a monopoly can no more competently manage the equilibrium between the supply of, and demand for, money than it can for shoes, automobiles, food or health care. As a solution he recommended competition between financial institutions: each bank should be allowed to print its own paper money. Such competition between banks would keep the value of money stable, since money losing in value hurts creditors, while money gaining in value hurts debtors. Hence the market would select the 'best monies', the ones that strike the best balance between depreciation and appreciation. Although we do not agree with Hayek or the Austrian school in other domains, we certainly can agree with Hayek's assessment of the current monetary system:

"It has the defects of all monopolies: one must use their product even if it is unsatisfactory, and, above all, it prevents the discovery of better methods of satisfying a need for which a monopolist has no incentive. If the public understood what price in periodic inflation and instability it pays for the convenience of having to deal with only one kind of money in ordinary transactions, and not occasionally to have to contemplate the advantage of using other money than the familiar kind, it would probably find it very excessive. For this convenience is much less important than the opportunity to use a reliable money that will not periodically upset the smooth flow of the economy - an opportunity of which the public has been deprived by the government [enforced] monopoly. But the people have never been given the opportunity to discover this advantage."[49]

We similarly wholeheartedly concur with Hayek's conclusion:

"What we now need is a Free Money Movement comparable to the Free Trade Movement of the 19th century. ...There is thus an immense educational task ahead before we can hope to free ourselves from the gravest threat to social peace and continued prosperity inherent in existing monetary institutions. It will be necessary that the problem and the urgent need of reform come to be widely understood. The issue is not one which, as may at first appear to the layman, concerns a minor technicality of the financial system which he has never quite understood.

---

48 This book was written two years *after* Hayek received the Nobel Memorial Prize in Economics.
49 Hayek (1976) p.28.

...I wish I could advise that we proceed slowly. But the time may be short. What is now urgently required is not the construction of a new system but the prompt removal of all the legal obstacles which have for two thousand years blocked the way for an evolution which is bound to throw up beneficial results which we cannot now foresee."[50]

However, like all economists of his time and like many still today, Hayek remained a prisoner of the paradigm we call Traditional Economics (shown in Figure 2.1 on page 28). His concern was predominantly to find an appropriate balance between inflation and deflation, two important but purely financial issues. This is why his solution is about re-shaping the money creation process as a competition between financial institutions each emitting the same type of bank-debt money.

From our perspective, based on the Ecological Economics Paradigm illustrated in Figure 2.3 (page 31), the issue of keeping both inflation and deflation at bay is also relevant, but represents only one of several relevant issues with regards to sustainability.

The effects of crashes, as documented in Chapter III, are obviously detrimental to many aspects of sustainability. But what is taking place during times when the monetary system is *not* in crisis, when it is operating smoothly in a 'business as usual' mode? The next chapter describes five additional biases generated by our monetary system, directly due to the fact that money is created through bank-debt. Hayek's solution is therefore one step in the right direction, but it does not go nearly far enough.

7. Conclusion

This chapter has provided a step-by-step explanation, with backing from scientific evidence, that a structural cause is behind the repeated systemic crises described in Chapter III. The complex flow network approach to monetary and financial stability is *not* a metaphor: it is systemic bio-mimicry. Peer-reviewed theoretical and empirical evidence shows that *any* complex flow network is sustained only when diversity and interconnectivity lie within a specific range. A monoculture – a plurality reduced to only one single type of currency produced by one single type of agent – will, with 100% predictability, turn out not to be sufficiently resilient.

Our methodology allows the quantitative measurement of sustainability for any complex flow network. However, it also requires detailed real-life field data. This methodology has successfully been applied to a wide variety of natural ecosystems, of very different scales and complexity. No theoretical reason exists for it not being applicable to human-made complex flow networks. Please remember: two complex flow networks with the same structure will behave in the same way.

---

50 *Ibid.* pp.133-134.

There are two ideal candidates for empirically testing and proving our claims: electrical distribution networks and the banking system. In both cases, we are dealing with a complex flow network, which may run very efficiently most of the time; but both have also been victims of repeated large-scale systemic crashes, worldwide. The practical impediment to performing these tests is the same in both cases: the data exist, but are considered confidential because of competitive relevance. There is an urgent need for this methodology to be further tested with real-life financial data. We discuss possible next steps to do so in Chapter IX.

Three hundred years of cat-and-mouse games between regulatory authorities and the financial system have proven that regulation – while useful and necessary – may reduce the frequency, but never avoid the re-occurrence, of systemic crises. Paul Romer, a Senior Fellow at the Stanford Institute for Economic Policy Research, says: "Every decade or so, any finite system of financial regulation will lead to a systemic financial crisis".[51] Is infinite regulation really the only solution?

Similarly, the likelihood that we might change 'human nature' – Alan Greenspan's explanation for the next crisis – amounts to renouncing on trying to stabilise the system. As long as we remain within the confines of a bank-debt money monopoly, there is indeed little hope.

Let us conclude this chapter with a metaphor. Conventional money plays the role of the red blood cells in your blood stream: they carry vital oxygen to all parts of the body. While red blood cells are necessary, they are not sufficient to keep your body healthy. Such a focus on only one type of cell would ignore the roles of white cells, platelets and dozens of other specialised hormones playing complementary functions to sustain your health. The existence of these complementary elements does not reduce the critical role or negate the existence of red blood cells. Likewise for the monetary domain, the key lesson from natural systems is to allow and even encourage the development of specialised media of exchange – other than a monoculture of conventional money created by bank debt – to circulate in parallel with the conventional national currency. While this approach may seem unorthodox, please remember that it is orthodoxy that has led us into our current troubles. Complex flow systems theory demonstrates that continued orthodoxy will compound the trouble. A plurality of media of exchange would provide new incentives and opportunities for all protagonists in the global economy, as will be illustrated in Chapters VII and VIII.

The remainder of this Report will explain why a strategy of multiple media of exchange makes not only theoretical, but also pragmatic sense. Randomly implementing exchange media other than conventional money may not be the best way forward. Rather, correctly designing and implementing exchange media to complement the current system and compensate for biases inherently generated by the conventional

---

51 *Institutional Investor*, May 2011, p.16.

monetary system would be critically useful. The starting point for such a corrective, complementary strategy is to identify any existing biases and incentives that lead to unsustainable behaviour patterns. Only after understanding this built-in drift can we meaningfully choose from an infinity of potential new currency designs those that will best compensate for these propensities. Identifying these generally unacknowledged biases is the topic of the next chapter.

Chapter V

The Effects of Today's Money System on Sustainability

"The Earth is not dying – it is being killed.
And the people who are killing it have names and addresses."
– U. Utah Phillips[1]

We have seen how diversification of the types of exchange media, forming together a monetary ecosystem, would structurally be beneficial to an economy. From this perspective, the most pressing thing to do is not to get rid of the existing bank-debt money system, as many monetary reformers claim should be done. Instead, the focus should be on identifying the kinds of systems that best *complement* the existing bank-debt system. This chapter will therefore explore the relationship between money and sustainability by identifying biases built into the existing system and their impact on human behaviour patterns.

Money is generally assumed to be a passive accounting instrument that facilitates exchanges more efficiently than barter. Money is seen as an oil lubricating the exchange process, but not otherwise changing its nature. It is therefore automatically assumed that the type of exchange medium one uses does not affect the nature of exchanges, the time horizon of our investments, or the relationships between us as users. We will demonstrate why all these assumptions are wrong.

The modern money system should be credited with giving birth to the industrial age, with both its positive and negative effects. It has spawned a quantum leap in scientific knowledge, and the most materially productive civilisation in the history

---

1   Quoted in Naomi Klein, *No Logo: Taking Aim at the Brand Bullies* (2000), p.325.

of mankind. It has also been an extraordinary wealth-producing mechanism, and we hope that it can continue to play that role in an evolving monetary ecosystem.

However, there are unfortunately also several mechanisms that turn out to be incompatible with sustainability. Specifically, we identify five effects that are detrimental to sustainability, and we can trace them back to characteristics of bank-debt money itself.

These five detrimental processes are:

1. the pro-cyclical character of the money creation process which amplifies both the upturns and downturns of the business cycle
2. the systematic encouragement of short-termism because the interest feature of the money system programs 'rational' investors to discount the future
3. compulsory growth due to the mechanism of compound interest
4. concentration of wealth
5. a devaluation of social capital.

From a systemic perspective, none of these effects is a simple linear cause-effect relationship. They also interact and even reinforce one another. The outcome is a set of built-in mechanisms that cause a bank-debt monopoly to be incompatible with sustainability in the long-term. We discuss each of these effects separately and attempt to describe their interactions at the end of the chapter.

1. The Pro-Cyclical Tendency of Money Creation and Flow: 'It Never Rains, but it Pours'

Because conventional modern money is created by bank debt, this money creation process amplifies the fluctuations of the business cycle.[2] Banks often display a herd instinct when making credit available or restricting it for particular countries, industries or individuals. When business is good, banks more generously provide credit and tend to fuel a shift from a merely good economic period to an inflationary boom period. Conversely, when the business horizon darkens, banks simultaneously reduce credit availability and thus can transform a small business dip into a full-blown recession. This is what is meant by a 'pro-cyclical' money creation process. The US real-estate boom of the 1990s is a perfect example of this process. The boom years led to a bust in 2007-2008 and, since then, desperate attempts to make banks lend money to businesses have followed, without much success. In the past, central banks were still able to have some influence by giving countercyclical interest rate signals. However we are currently at a point where central banks have tried everything without much success. *The Economist* concludes: "For central bankers in the rich world, unconventional is

---

2   See Appendix A for a layperson's introduction to how bank debt creates money.

the new conventional"[3] Interest rates hover around zero in the USA, Europe, and Japan, but without much impact. Euro zone banks prefer to deposit their funds with the European Central Bank rather than lend them out to businesses.[4]

Let us emphasise that the actions of the banking system are not consciously intended to produce such results. Banks do not like recessions any more than other businesses do. However, they do not want to be the last ones to bail out if they see a sinking ship. Their decisions are thus similar to the actions of a portfolio manager not wanting to be the last to hold on to a stock with plummeting value. The net effect of these 'rational' micro-decisions is that the financial sector, *as a whole,* tends to exacerbate the business cycle in both the up- and the downside directions. This finding has strong theoretical grounds[5] and is also amply supported by empirical evidence.[6]

The effects of pro-cyclical money creation

The typical boom-and-bust of the business cycle tends to waste investment capital and many other resources. In an amplified business cycle, corporations are often under-equipped in plant, equipment and qualified staff during the boom period, then suddenly over-equipped and over-staffed during the downturn.

This results in joblessness and the host of social problems it causes. Most social indicators (such as mental health, crime or suicide) deteriorate significantly during recessions. Political instabilities including violent revolutions are usually triggered by economic downturns.

The financial sector itself is not insulated against the amplified business cycle it helps to create. One typical cause of banking crises is a situation where borrowers cannot repay their loans, while the collateral upon which those loans are based

---

3 Heading of an article in *The Economist* January 7th, 2012 p.58.

4 At the time of this writing (in January 2012) bank deposits held overnight at the ECB are reaching an unprecedented level of more than €400 billion (see *The Economist*, 31 December 2011, p.56).

5 All Austrian-school theorists consider the unsustainable expansion of bank credit through fractional reserve banking as the driving force of most business cycles. See, e.g. Detlev S. Schlichter (2011). From a different perspective, Irving Fisher in the 1930s, Hyman Minsky in the 1970s and Barry Eichengreen nowadays have also pointed to this pro-cyclical money creation process as an amplifier of the business cycle. See also Milton Friedman, 'The Role of Monetary Policy', *American Economic Review*, vol. 68 (1968), pp.1–17. We are not claiming that this process is the only cause of the business cycle, but that it is a contributing factor directly attributable to the prevailing monetary system. See Olivier J. Blanchard & Mark W. Watson (1987). See also 'Shadow Government Statistics' at *www.shadowstats.com*

6 See Milton Friedman & Anna Jacobson Schwartz (1993); J. P. Keeler (2001); Barry Eichengreen & K. Mitchener (2003); Carmen Reinhart *et al.* (2004).

depreciates. These conditions are understandably aggravated by an amplified business cycle.[7]

Furthermore, since the financial deregulation of the 1980s, the volume of 'hot' money or money moving around the world in search of short-term returns has increased significantly. It further accentuates these pro-cyclical tendencies whenever it enters or leaves a particular market.[8]

Implications for sustainability

Asset bubbles are an automatic result of this pro-cyclical money creation process. When asset price bubbles burst, banks tend to fail in great numbers. The assets on which these bubbles occur have varied in time and place. During the 1630s in Holland, it was all about tulips. Three hundred years later, in 1929, the object was US trust stocks; in the late 1980s, real estate in Japan; in the 1990s, high-tech US dot-com stocks; and during the first years of the 21st century, real estate in the USA. They all have in common the pro-cyclical debt-creation mechanism acting as their overheating engine. Such bubbles invariably burst with destructive consequences for society in general, and for the banking system in particular.[9] These boom-and-bust cycles negatively affect the formation and maintenance of financial, human and natural capital.

2. Short-Termism: Why the Future is Discounted

The second built-in bias we will discuss is related to short-term vision. 'Short-termism' is the tendency to focus attention on *short*-term gains, at the expense of long-term success or stability. In the business and financial world this tendency has become widespread. Part of this process is independent of the monetary system: the further away events are in the future, the more difficult it is to make accurate predictions about them, and thus the greater the risk. Short-termism can therefore be correctly associated with lower risk tolerance.

However, the Discounted Cash Flow (DCF) technique used for financial decision-making should also bear part of the responsibility. The readiness to make long-term investments depends to a significant extent on current and anticipated interest rates. Interest is one of the three factors involved in discounting any future cash flow. The other two are the intrinsic risk of the investment project and the cost of equity capital. (see Box 5.1)

---

7   Adrian Blundell-Wignall and Paul Atkinson, 'Thinking Beyond Basel III: Necessary Solutions for Capital and Liquidity', *Financial Markets Trends*, vol. 2 (2010), issue 1, pp.9-33.

8   See *The Global Economic Crisis: Assessing Vulnerability With a Poverty Lens* (2009) *www.siteresources.worldbank.org ~ bit.ly/TPlink35*

9   Richard Duncan, *The Dollar Crisis: Causes, Consequences, Cures* (2003).

Box 5.1 – Time Perception and Interest *versus* Demurrage

The purpose of this box is to show how interest encourages short-term time horizons. Figure 5.1 below shows how interest rates affect the investment process. To keep the numbers simple, it is assumed that all numbers are inflation-adjusted and that the risk of investment is independent of the time frame. Furthermore, we will consider only a choice between two projects: planting a pine forest or an oak one. Here, a pine tree is assumed to be harvestable after ten years, when it will bring a yield of $100. An oak tree can only be harvested after a hundred years and it is estimated to be worth $1,000. So the two investments could be seen as equivalent as one could harvest and replant the pines every ten years, ending up with the same $1,000 in 100 years.

When we put on financial glasses, things change. For example, a deposit of $61 in a bank account with a guaranteed interest rate of 5% automatically becomes $100 after ten years.[10] That is why the $100 pine ten years from now is equivalent to only $61.39 today.

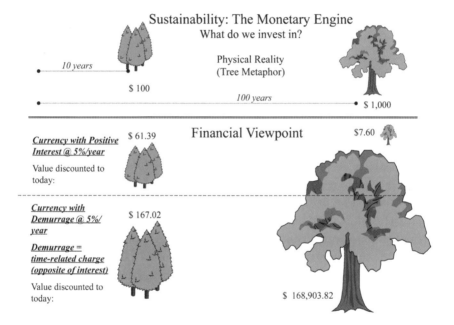

Figure 5.1: Investment behaviours differ according to the monetary system. Any currency with a positive interest rate discounts the future. A currency with a demurrage fee – equivalent to a negative interest rate – amplifies the value of the future.

Therefore, when the investor asks, "What are these two investments worth *as seen from today?*", the answer depends on the applicable interest rate. We have seen that at an interest rate of 5%, $100 in ten years is worth $61 as seen from today. This is so because at 5%, only $61 would have to be deposited in the bank in order to have $100 in ten years' time.

---

10 The multiplier in the formula is $(1+i)(n-1)$, where i is the interest rate and n the duration, in number of years, of the investment project.

At the same 5% interest rate, the value today of the future $1,000 oak tree is only $7.60. This difference in value is only due to the interest rate on the money used to finance the investments. This explains why there is currently a lot of commercial interest in harvesting old-growth forest, but very little in planting trees with long maturation periods. This difference also generally explains why our society has difficulty thinking of the proverbial seventh generation. Every 'rational investor' is programmed by the interest feature of our money to focus primarily on the short term.

In contrast, past societies have imposed a 'circulation fee' to discourage the hoarding of a currency, a bit like libraries charging a 'late fee' for books not re-circulated on time. Such a time-related charge on holding on to money is technically called a 'demurrage' fee, from the French *demeurer* – a term dating back to the railroads who charged for idle wagons not used for transport. Viewed from the perspective of an investor, demurrage – or negative-interest-bearing – currencies clearly change the relationship with the future. If the currency used in our tree-planting example carried a 5% demurrage fee, the oak tree would suddenly be worth more than $168,000 when discounted to today. Planting oaks would become the obvious choice if such a currency were used to make the investment. In short, with demurrage-charged currencies, investment with longer-term horizons would increase in value.

This 'pine versus oak' metaphor shows that the time horizons of investments depend significantly on the currency type one financially analyses and plans with. All other things being equal, if the currency one uses has positive interest rates – as do all our conventional bank-debt moneys – then short-term priorities will logically prevail. In contrast, a demurrage-charged currency would automatically provide an incentive for taking into account longer-term priorities. Figure 5.1 synthesises this metaphorical scenario and illustrates the link between short-term decision-making and the given monetary system.

The hypothesis that investment decisions depend only on risk profiles is therefore not valid. The type of money used also significantly influences what a society as a whole chooses to invest in. This is not just a theoretical statement: societies that used demurrage currencies – as in ancient Egypt for more than a millennium or in Western Europe from the 10th to the 13th century – made investments in infrastructure and buildings that were designed to last forever, as evidenced by the fact that pyramids, Egyptian temples and European cathedrals are still standing today.[11]

Implications for sustainability

Conventional bank-debt money reinforces a particular perception of time: it mandates short-term priorities. If a different type of currency – one with a negative interest rate – were used, society and businesses would be encouraged to value more long-term opportunities and costs. This change would affect the entire spectrum of economic and environmental activity and directly promote long-term sustainability. Greater concern for sustainable policies in relation to non-renewable resources and for humanity's relationship with the rest of the biosphere would result. These lessons will be used in the design of the TRC (see Chapter VII), a currency that would make it profitable to corporations to think long-term.

---

11   These historical case studies are detailed in Lietaer (2000) and Lietaer & Belgin (2011).

3. Compulsory Growth Pressures: On Debt and Compound Interest

"I find to my personal horror that I have not been immune to naïveté about exponential functions… While I have been aware that the interlinked problems of loss of biological diversity, tropical deforestation, forest dieback and the climate change are growing exponentially, it is only this very year that I think I truly internalized how rapid their accelerating threat really is."

– Thomas E. Lovejoy[12]
Chief biodiversity adviser to the president of the World Bank

The third structural bias we will discuss is compulsory growth pressures due to compound interest. Too often, growth is confused with progress. Growth is the quantitative increase in size or throughput of an entity. In contrast, progress is the idea that the world can increasingly become better. The former is purely quantitative, while the latter is primarily qualitative. One should not automatically assume that all growth leads to progress. That is why American essayist Edward Abbey could claim that "growth for the sake of growth is the ideology of the cancer cell".[13]

Furthermore, while growth is a natural process, some types of growth are intrinsically sustainable and others are not. Figure 5.2 illustrates three classical types of growth.[14]

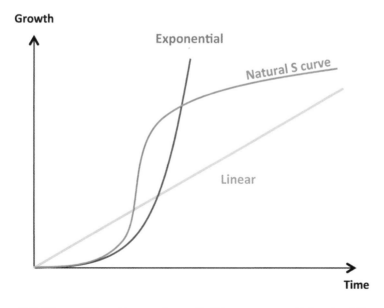

Figure 5.2: Three different types of growth: Linear, exponential, natural S curve.

---

12 Quoted in Meadows *et al.* (2004) p.17.

13 Edward Abbey, *The Second Rape of the West* (975) p.183

14 Margrit Kennedy, *Interest- and Inflation-Free Money* (1995).

The first type is linear growth, which is the easiest to grasp. A second type is exponential growth, which, when it occurs in a finite world, becomes unsustainable at some point in time. According to systems theory, this is what occurs when a positive feedback loop is allowed to operate in an unmitigated manner. Nature embodies the third type of growth and almost always exhibits an S curve: all biological systems including cells, trees, animals and populations start out by growing rapidly and eventually asymptotically taper-off to a point of stability. From a systems perspective, this tapering off reflects increasing pressures from a negative feedback loop acting to stabilise the initial positive feedback loop. This is a sustainable, natural growth process. A well-known example from nature is the relationship between predators and prey. If predators – 'foxes' – multiply too quickly, they eliminate the population they prey on – 'rabbits'. All things being equal, insufficient prey will limit the growth of the predator population until the prey population has sufficiently recovered. At some point a state of relative balance is reached.

Since bank-debt money in our current system is created with interest, it is subject to compounded interest or 'interest on interest' which automatically implies exponential growth. In a finite world, exponential growth is mathematically incompatible with sustainability.[15] Indeed, what exponential growth processes all have in common is that the amounts involved increase *at an increasing rate* over time. For a complex dynamic system to be sustainable, feedback mechanisms must be in place to avoid exponential, runaway growth. The examples described in Box 5.2 demonstrate the mathematical impossibilities of exponential growth.

BOX 5.2 – Two examples of exponential growth

Water lilies spreading in a pond

Let us assume water lilies double the surface they cover in a pond every day. Initially, their growth may seem quite reasonable. If a quarter of the pond is covered in 50 days, how many days will it take for the lilies to cover the entire pond? If the growth were linear, it would take another 150 days. If the growth were exponential, it would take one day to cover a second quarter of the pond and by day 52 it would be completely covered!

Caesar's one-cent debt

If Julius Caesar had borrowed one cent at 4% compound interest from a bank as he left Rome to conquer Gaul (52BC), by today, the interest on that one cent would have compounded to approximately 2,000 gold balls each weighing as much as the Earth, using the current price of gold! Had the interest been compounded at 5% instead of 4%, several trillion gold balls would be needed to pay his debt two millennia later. In the real world, Caesar would have had to default many times on the way. If the accumulated debt were big enough at the moment of his default, he would bring down the bank and possibly the entire banking system.

---

15 Hazel Henderson, *The Politics of the Solar Age: Alternatives to Economics* (1981) p.228. and P. F. Henshaw, 'Linking Economics and Natural Systems Physics', 20 March, 2009. Online at *www.synapse9.com ~ bit.ly/TPlink36*

> In short, without countervailing forces to stabilise them, exponential growth rates are mathematically impossible in the long run. In the language of general systems theory, compound interest is a perfect example of a positive feedback loop unmitigated by a correspondingly powerful negative feedback loop to stabilise it. Because of the interest feature of bank-debt money, and specifically because of compound interest, the monetary system is driving our economies into a reckless compulsory growth pattern.

The core question is therefore: what kind of growth does the financial system require from the real economy? The short answer is that compound interest requires exponential growth. Compounded interest is a mathematical impossibility on a finite planet.[16]

The idea of a built-in exponential curve in the financial and monetary domain is not merely theoretical, but has striking ramifications in the real world. Figures 5.3 and 5.4 illustrate the growth in the money supply of the USA and India.

Figure 5.3: US money supply, in trillions of US dollars, (1959-2010)[17].
Notice how closely the growth curve follows exponential growth.

---

16 In fact, our system's permanent growth pressure is made up of at least three aspects: first, marketing strategies that inducing constantly shifting desires; second, planned obsolescence (where objects, services or practices are no longer wanted or usable even though they could still be); third, the credit system whose effects we are emphasising in this book. See Serge Latouche (2004) and (2005).

17 Source: *www.chrismartenson.com ~ bit.ly/TPlink37*

We are fast approaching Ann Pettifor's prediction in her 2006 book *The Coming First-World Debt Crisis* whose cover was an ominous-looking time bomb.[18] This 'exponential-growth' effect is not only relevant for developed economies.

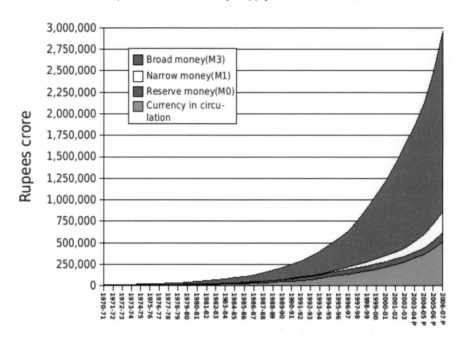

Components of the money supply of India 1970-2007

Figure 5.4: India's money supply (1970-2007) and its different components, the most relevant of which is the broad money supply (M3). The fact that exponential growth in the money supply prevails not only in the USA but also in developing countries like India illustrates the systemic nature of the process.[19]

The same process also tends to apply to a developing country's external debt. After the G8 summit in Okinawa in 2000, President Obasanjo of Nigeria commented on Nigeria's debt: "All that we had borrowed up to 1985 or 1986 was around $5 billion and so far we have paid back about $16 billion. Yet we are being told that we still owe about $28 billion. That $28 billion came about because of the foreign creditors' interest rates. If you ask me what is the worst thing in the world, I would say it is compound interest." At the time Obasanjo spoke out, the developing world was spending $13 on debt repayment for every one dollar it had received in foreign aid and grants. For the sixty poorest countries in the world, $550 billion have been paid in both principal and interest over the last three decades on a total of $540 billion of loans, and yet there are still $523 billion outstanding in debt burden.

---

18 Ann Pettifor, *The Coming First-World Debt Crisis* (2006).

19 Source: *http://en.wikipedia.org ~ bit.ly/TPlink38*

Implications for sustainability

The debt treadmill is most dangerous when the debt is incurred in a foreign currency. This is invariably the case for developing countries. It feeds a compulsion to earn foreign exchange. The consequences can be drastic: as the debt burden increases, many developing countries recklessly exploit their natural resources and/or their people. Governments are forced to neglect their domestic economies since there is no alternative but to export an ever-larger proportion of their resources to service their debts. Sometimes, they are even driven into adopting policies that predictably reduce their future opportunities for servicing debt. For example, 'structural readjustment policies' imposed by creditors have often obliged countries to cut education, public services or maintenance of the transport infrastructure funding as a precondition for obtaining loans. In summary, our current monetary mechanisms do not promote long-term financial sustainability, even narrowly defined.

From a broader perspective, the monetary sector forces indebted entities and individuals into compulsory growth, regardless of the environmental and social costs inflicted in the process.[20] Highly indebted protagonists therefore get trapped into hurried, short-term growth paths. Such pressures are partly responsible for the erosion of non-renewable natural resources, pollution of the air and water, and mounting pressure with negative social and environmental consequences.

Ecological economist Herman Daly has referred to this as 'uneconomic' growth or, growth whose short-term benefits are dwarfed by inadequately actualised future costs.[21] Uneconomic growth can only continue to be called 'economic growth', according to Daly, if some of the associated costs are not accounted for or kept invisible. This is what our current monetary system does by requiring compound interest on money. Short-termism is thus ubiquitously embedded in our current monetary system.

4. An Unrelenting Concentration of Wealth: the Poor vs. the Super-Rich

"The most profound danger to world peace in the coming years
will not stem from the irrational acts of states or individuals,
but from the legitimate demands of the world's dispossessed."
— Statement of 100 Nobel laureates, January 2002[22]

---

20 H. C. Binswanger goes considerably further in citing reasons for forced growth. See H. C. Binswanger, *Geld und Natur: Das wirtschaftliche Wachstum zwischen Ökonomie und Ökologie* (1991)

21 See, e.g., Daly (1996).

22 *www.lovearth.net ~ bit.ly/TPlink39*

The fourth built-in mechanism causing our current monetary system to be unsustainable is the tendency over time for wealth to become concentrated. The renowned historian Arnold Toynbee concluded that the collapse of twenty-one different civilisations could be attributed to just two causes:

- the excessive concentration of wealth in the hands of the few
- the inability to introduce significant changes in the face of shifting circumstances. [23]

A market economy must offer incentives to encourage people to take entrepreneurial initiatives. The remarkable innovations of the Industrial Age were triggered by the desire to achieve and create beyond the simple requirements of survival. This logic has also justified the existence of disparities of income and wealth over the past 150 years.

Nobel laureate economist Joseph E. Stiglitz writes:

"Economists long ago tried to justify the vast inequalities that seemed so troubling in the mid-19th century – inequalities that are but a pale shadow of what we are seeing in America today. The justification they came up with was called 'marginal-productivity theory'. In a nutshell, this theory associated higher incomes with higher productivity and a greater contribution to society. It is a theory that has always been cherished by the rich. Evidence for its validity, however, remains thin. The corporate executives who helped bring on the recession of the past three years – whose contribution to our society, and to their own companies, has been massively negative – went on to receive large bonuses. In some cases, companies were so embarrassed about calling such rewards 'performance bonuses' that they felt compelled to change the name to 'retention bonuses' (even if the only thing being retained was bad performance). Those who have contributed great positive innovations to our society, from the pioneers of genetic understanding to the pioneers of the Information Age, have received a pittance compared with those responsible for the financial innovations that brought our global economy to the brink of ruin." [24]

Developments in compensation habits over the last two decades have led to a distribution of assets bearing less and less relation to individual achievement or willingness to take personal financial risks.

---

23 Toynbee (1960). For more recent work along the same lines, see for instance Jared Diamond (2005).

24 Joseph E. Stiglitz, 'Of the 1%, by the 1%, for the 1%', *Vanity Fair,* May 2011.

What is the relevance of excessive concentration of wealth for overall sustainability? Hard-nosed geopolitical thinkers such as Zbigniew Brzezinsky, President Carter's National Security Advisor, have always focused on raw power relationships:

"Global turmoil manifests itself in a variety of ways. It is intensified, though not entirely caused, by persistent mass poverty and social injustice. ...It does not lend itself to sloganeering or rouse the American people as viscerally as terrorism. It is more difficult to personalise without a demonic figure like Osama bin Laden. Nor is it congenial to self-gratifying proclamations of an epic confrontation between good and evil on the model of the titanic struggles with Nazism and Communism. Yet not to focus on global turmoil is to ignore a central reality of our times: the massive worldwide political awakening of mankind and its intensifying awareness of intolerable disparities in the human condition."[25]

We have witnessed a remarkable concentration of wealth over the past decades with resulting increases in wealth disparities. Depending on the definitions of poverty used, different pictures of wealth disparities can be identified. However, social tensions arise from the relative rather than from the absolute minimum level of poverty in relation to *excessive concentration of wealth*. This aspect is further discussed along with the different definitions of poverty in Appendix F.

Economic effects of wealth concentration

Economic equity is not just about justice. Economic development itself depends on a minimum of equity. Recent evidence shows that successful economic development does not occur in the presence of too much or too little economic equality. Communism, with its attempt to impose too much equality proved to be an economic failure. However, too little equality in a capitalist society is not economically advantageous either. For instance, a key reason for the difference in development between Latin America and 'Asian Tiger' countries in East Asian and the Pacific is that wealth inequality in Latin America is too high.[26] Appendix F provides some of the evidence for these economic effects of excessive inequality.

---

25 Zbigniew Brzezinski, *The Choice: Global Domination or Global Leadership* (2004), p.217.

26 For instance, the Equity Index developed by Franz Joseph Radermacher that empirically measures the full-range degree of income distribution in a country puts Brazil and Mexico at 0.27 and 0.28, respectively. (Theoretical communism, which would impose exactly the same income for everybody, would be at 1.00). In contrast, this index reaches 0.65 for China, 0.55 for Korea and 0.62 for Japan. (Note that the US is at 0.47 on that scale, and the European Union at 0.54.) It seems that economic growth is hurt when the index remains roughly below 0.45 or above 0.65. For full details, see Franz J. Radermacher (2004) pp.85-120.

Equity effects of wealth concentration

In his *Theory of Justice*, philosopher John Rawls formulates two central conditions for social justice (see box 5.3) under which an uneven distribution of income and wealth is, in the long run, acceptably just.[27]

Box 5.3 – What is just? What is unjust? John Rawls on inequality

From his exploration of liberal-egalitarian political philosophy, Rawls extracts two practical imperatives: Social and economic inequalities must be controlled in such a way that they (a) offer those who are the least favoured the best possible prospects and (b) render offices and positions accessible to all, thus providing the same opportunities for everyone.

While Rawls justifies differences in wealth and income, even relatively substantial ones, he places specific conditions on them. Based on condition (a), it is morally unacceptable for the poorest to have no share in economic growth. Condition (b) points out that sufficient social mobility must exist so that the fortunate do not occupy their positions permanently. This implies being critical of socio-economic systems with entrenched *structurally unequal* income distribution mechanisms that generate *compound imbalances* over time.

In summary, Rawls claims that freedom cannot exist if there is not enough equality. Communism went in the direction of too much equality and proved unsuccessful. Our recent history with capitalism is now giving a warning that market fundamentalism may push us too far in the opposite direction.

Wealth concentration: connection with the monetary and financial system

The current economic system is thus not a 'rising tide that lifts all boats'. With a track record such as the one just presented, 'trickle-down economics' – the belief that the poor will somehow get their fair share as the rich get richer – has lost its credibility. The following paragraphs describe three systemic mechanisms built into the current monetary system that lead to wealth concentration. These mechanisms are interest, the money creation process and the role of lobbies. We will treat each of them separately.

Interest

The first built-in mechanism or bias leading to wealth disparity is interest. The definition of interest is a charge or payment for the use of money. Interest is thus a transfer of money from those who do not have enough money, to those who have surplus money. In ancient Greece, Aristotle forcefully condemned the 'chrematistic' way of life, which consisted of making money from money. Judaism, Christianity and Islam each had strict rules against 'usury', defined as any interest on money. Today, only Islam still reminds people that interest was considered a problem of justice or, as it were, injustice.

---

27   John Rawls, *A Theory of Justice* (1971).

We have found only one study of the transfer of wealth via interest. It was performed in Germany in 1982 when interest rates were at 5.5%.[28] The German population was grouped into ten income categories of 2.5 million households each. Over a one-year period, transfers between these ten groups totalled Deutsche Mark (DM) 270 billion in interest paid and received. Graphing the net interest transfers (interest gained minus interest paid) for each of these ten household categories allows us to see the net effect (see Figure 5.5).

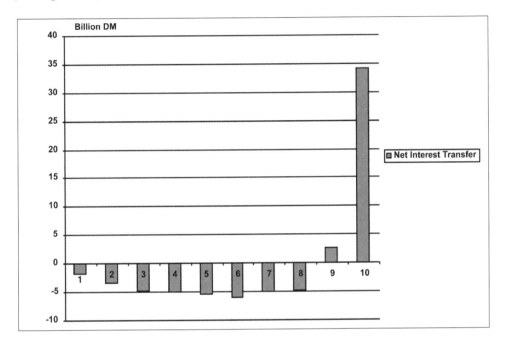

Figure 5.5: Net Interest Transferred (billion DM) for 10 groups of households of 2.5 million each (Germany - 1982).

In this graph, we see that the highest interest transfers occurred from the middle class. Categories 3 to 8 each transferred approximately DM 5 billion to the top 10% of households in category 10. Category 1, the lowest-income households transferred DM 1.8 billion in interest per year to the highest group. The net effect is that the top 10% of households received a net transfer of DM 34.2 billion in interest from the rest of society during that one year.

Figure 5.5 clearly displays the systematic transfer of wealth from the bottom 80% of the population to the top 10%. This transfer was due exclusively to the monetary system in use. It is independent of the degree of cleverness or industriousness of the participants, the standard arguments given to justify large income differences.

---

28 Kennedy (1995) p.26

The money creation process

The second built-in mechanism or bias leading to wealth disparity is the money creation process itself. The common belief is that capital is financed through savings. In reality, capital is generated through *credit*. However, the catch is that credit is only given to people who *already have savings.*[29] Good banking practice dictates that loans be backed by good collateral. The quip by comedian Bob Hope: "A bank is a place that will lend you money at the condition you can prove you don't need it" has more than a grain of truth. In a society imposing a monopoly currency created through bank debt, an automatic bias towards concentration of wealth will predictably occur.

'Lobbycracy'

The third built-in mechanism leading to wealth disparity is related to special interest groups, and lobbying. Lobbies can play a positive role in a democracy. They provide a feedback loop between the branch of government that creates laws and the citizens and organisations affected by those laws. Good lobbyists are expensive. Individuals and corporations who can thus pay for them have an advantage over those who cannot afford them. Grass-roots organisations, some non-governmental organisations and ordinary people affected by the same laws are often unable to pay for those expensive lobbyists.

Thus, money begets power and power begets political influence, which in turn begets laws making it possible for the powerful to make more money. This positive feedback loop is well known in politics. It explains why so many of our laws favour powerful interests rather than the ordinary people that democracy should protect. At a certain point, the line between lobbying and crony capitalism can get blurred. When money speaks more powerfully than people, democracy gets replaced by plutocracy, which takes the form of a 'lobbycracy' today.[30] The manner in which money is currently created encourages this problematic bias by generating structural wealth concentration.

Wealth disparities and implications for sustainability

Strongly unequal wealth tends to concentrate purchasing power in the hands of the people who adopt the most consumption-intensive, and hence resource-intensive, lifestyles. But what is at stake is more than food or the necessities of life for the average wage-earners, or even justice and economic performance. As US Supreme Court Justice Louis Brandeis claimed, "We can have a democratic society or we can have great concentrated wealth in the hands of a few. We cannot have both."[31] The

29 Louis and Patricio Kelso, *Two Factor Economy: How to turn a million workers into capitalists on borrowed money* (1967) quoted in Hazel Henderson (2006) p.164.

30 See, e.g., Belén Balanya *et al.* (2003) and Greg Palast (2003).

31 *http://en.wikiquote.org ~ bit.ly/TPlink40*

Dalai Lama has said: "A society in which the rich are too rich and the poor too poor generates violence, crime and civil disorder. Agitators can easily excite the masses to make them believe that they are fighting for them."[32] Violence and war are the exact opposite of sustainability since they mean a lose-lose proposition for all segments of society – including the wealthy. As US President John F. Kennedy remarked, "Those who make peaceful revolution impossible will make violent revolution inevitable".

5. The Devaluation of Social Capital: Why Competitive Behaviour CAN Overpower Cooperation

Regions, countries and groups feeling left behind will face deepening economic stagnation, political instability and cultural alienation. They will foster political, ethnic, ideological and religious extremism, along with the violence that often accompanies it.
Central Intelligence Agency (CIA), April 2007[33]

The fifth and last mechanism leading to unsustainability in our current monetary system pertains to how it devalues and erodes social capital.

Defining social capital

Sociologist Robert Putnam defines social capital as "Features of social organisation, such as trust, norms and networks, that can improve the efficiency of society by facilitating coordinated actions".[34] The content of this concept has not evolved for almost a century, as illustrated by the 1916 definition by Lyda Judson Hanifan: "The whole community will profit from the co-operation of its parts, and the individual, as a result of the links forged, will experience benefits such as help, compassion and community spirit from its neighbours … When people in a community trust each other, and when it has become customary to come together for entertainment purposes, to exchange views or for personal pleasure, skilful leaders can easily employ this social capital for the general improvement of welfare in the community as a whole."[35] Hazel Henderson uses a very short but effective label for it all, referring to the "love economy".[36]

---

32 *www.commondreams.org ~ bit.ly/TPlink41*

33 *Global Trends 2015* (Central Intelligence Agency, April 2007).

34 Robert Putnam *et al.*, *Making Democracy Work: Civic Traditions in Modern Italy* (1994), p.167. One of Putnam's more recent definitions also remains very much in line with this: "Social capital refers to connections among individuals – social networks and norms of reciprocity that arise from them". Putnam (2000) p.19.

35 Lyda Judson Hanifan, 'The Rural School Community Center', *Annals of the American Academy of Political and Social Science,* no. 67 (1916), p.130. See also Alexander Grimme (2009).

36 Hazel Henderson: *Building a Win-Win World: Life beyond Economic Warfare* (1996) p.212.

Cohesion within a society arises not as a result of spatial proximity, common language, religious beliefs or relationships, but through that society's ability to create mechanisms, rituals and behaviour patterns that generate a spirit of cooperation, trust and shared responsibility.[37] These behaviours are learned and continually reinforced through socialisation. Studies have demonstrated that the acts of giving and receiving activate the same regions in the brain; and giving usually leads to greater happiness than spending on oneself.[38] Social capital can be private or public, can vary in formality and organisation, but always has an aspect of social commitment. It also defines the types of institutions and rules that give a society its identity. "A peculiar feature of social capital is that it is not accumulated through a standard mechanism of individual investment, since most of its benefits are not privately appropriable. Rather, or at least to a much greater extent, it is accumulated through social participation in group activities."[39] Social capital is therefore not a mere by-product of society. It is the 'glue' that makes a collection of individuals into a human society. It is a precondition for a functional democracy[40] and for securing economic prosperity.[41] Indeed, political action and efficient markets are both unthinkable without a modicum of social capital.

Democracy and economic prosperity become possible only when a society has a sufficient sense of responsibility, mutual trust, solidarity and cooperation. Increasing crime rates,[42] poverty and the exclusion of ever-larger groups from society[43] are the first indications of social capital erosion. Several studies have shown that social capital is not only dwindling in most parts of the world, but also undergoing a change in its very nature.[44] One of its dimensions is the balance between competition and cooperation.

Encouraging Competition

The following story (Box 5.4) illustrates the way interest is woven into our money fabric, and how it stimulates competition among the users of this currency.

---

37 Marcel Mauss (1920); Claude Lévi-Strauss (1949); Lewis Hyde (1983); Charles Eisenstein (2011).

38 Elizabeth W. Dunn *et al.* 'Spending Money on Others Promotes Happiness', *Science* 319 (21 March 2008), pp.1687-8.

39 Paolo Vanin *et al.* 'On the Possible Conflict Between Economic Growth and Social Development', in Benedetto Gui & Robert Sugden (2005).

40 Putnam *et al.* (1994).

41 Francis Fukuyama, *Trust: Social Virtues and the Creation of Prosperity* (1995).

42 Manuel Castells, *Das Informationszeitalter* (Bd. II, 2002, pp.275sq) and (Bd. III, 2003, chapter 3).

43 Gerry Rodgers, Charles G. Gore and Jose B. Figueiredo (eds), *Social Exclusion: Rhetoric, Reality, Responses* (1995) and Enzo Minigione, *Urban Poverty and the Underclass – A Reader* (1996).

44 James Coleman (1990), especially Chapter 12, and Putnam (2000).

Box 5.4 – The Eleventh Round

Once upon a time, in a small village in the Outback, people used barter for all their transactions. On every market day, people walked around with chickens, eggs, hams, and breads, and engaged in prolonged negotiations among themselves to exchange what they needed. At key periods of the year, such as during harvests or when someone's barn required big repairs after a storm, people recalled the tradition of helping each other out, brought from the old country. They knew that if they had a problem someday, others would help them in return.

One market day, a stranger with shiny black shoes and an elegant white hat came by and observed the whole process with a sardonic smile. When he saw one farmer running around to corral the six chickens he wanted to exchange for a big ham, he could not refrain from laughing. "Poor people", he said, "so primitive". The farmer's wife overheard him and challenged the stranger, "Do you think you can do a better job handling chickens?" "Chickens, no", responded the stranger, "But there is a much better way to eliminate all that hassle. "Oh yes, how so?" asked the woman. "See that tree there?" the stranger replied. "Well, I will go wait there for one of you to bring me one large cowhide. Then have every family visit me. I'll explain the better way."

And so it happened. He took the cowhide, and cut perfect leather rounds in it, and put an elaborate and graceful little stamp on each round. Then he gave to each family 10 rounds, and explained that each represented the value of one chicken. "Now you can trade and bargain with the rounds instead of the unwieldy chickens", he explained.

It made sense. Everybody was impressed with the man with the shiny shoes and inspiring hat.

"Oh, by the way", he added after every family had received their 10 rounds, "in a year's time, I will come back and sit under that same tree. I want you to each bring me back 11 rounds. That 11th round is a token of appreciation for the technological improvement I just made possible in your lives." "But where will the 11th round come from?" asked the farmer with the six chickens. "You'll see", said the man with a reassuring smile.

***

Assuming that the population and its annual production remain exactly the same during that next year, what do you think had to happen? Remember, *that 11th round was never created*. In the end, one of the 11 families will *lose* its 10 rounds to provide the 11th round to the 10 others. This will occur even if everyone manages his or her affairs well.

So when a storm threatened the crop of one of the families, people became less generous with their time in helping to bring it in before disaster struck. While it was much more convenient to exchange the rounds instead of the chickens on market days, the new game also had the unintended side effect of actively discouraging the spontaneous cooperation that traditionally existed in the village. Instead, the new money game *generated a systemic undertow of competition among all the participants*.

This is how today's monetary system pits participants in the economy against each other. This story isolates the role of interest – the 11th round – as part of the money creation process, and its impact on the participants.[45] The point of the '11th Round'

---

45 The story of the Eleventh Round is extracted from *The Future of Money* (Bernard Lietaer, 2001). It is a simplified illustration for non-economists, isolating the impact of interest on money on the system. To isolate that one variable, the hypothesis of a zero growth society is assumed: no population increase, no production increases, or quantity of money increases. In practice, of course, all three of these variables can grow over time, further obscuring the impact of interest.

is simple: competition to obtain the money necessary to pay the interest, which is not initially created along with the principal, is structurally embedded in our current system. How does such a permanent undertow affect social capital? Can we measure such an effect? Can social capital even be measured in the first place?

Measuring social capital

Despite the relative stability in the definition of social capital, the capacity to measure it has not improved a lot over time. One reason is that "the idea of social capital sits awkwardly in contemporary economic thinking. Even though it has a powerful, intuitive appeal, it has proven hard to track as an economic good. Its difficulty to measure isn't because of a recognised paucity of data, but because it's not quite known what should be measured. Comprising different types of relationships and engagements, the components of social capital are many and varied and, in many instances, intangible."[46] The essentials of social capital are forms of goodwill mediated through generalised social exchanges,[47] which includes social networking, feeling a sense of belonging to one's neighbourhood or community, and civil participation.

Perhaps the reason why social capital is so hard to quantify is that the term itself is an economic projection on a foreign realm. It represents a reductionist view, objectifying the human spirit and the most elevated of human capacities as just another input into material production. It implicitly assumes that material production is the only relevant criterion for the good and wellbeing of a society.

Many indirect indices have been used to measure social capital. They have ranged from education and income, to the percentage of women at work; from forms of business organisation and social safety nets, to the degree to which we can participate in the running of our society; from the freedom of the press, to the legal constitution of states. The availability of jobs and the quality of working conditions has a key influence on the formation of social capital. Regardless of the definition or data set used, the tendency over decades is a decrease in social capital in most developed societies.

One key question that remains unanswered is: What role does the monetary system have in these processes? The evidence comes from three different sources: from game theory, from neuro-imagining and from empirical behaviour testing.

---

46 Partha Dasgupta, 'Social Capital and Economic Performance: Analytics' in Ostrom & Ahn (2003)..

47 Putnam (2000); Paul S. Adler & Seok-Woo Kwon (2002); Yaojun Li *et al.* (2003).

1. The Input from Game Theory

The first input comes from Game Theory. The 'tit-for-tat' strategy in non-cooperative games can be described as, *"I will give you something in the first place and you will give me something if I need it in the future; but should you decide not to give anything back, I will end our collaboration"*. The work of Robert Axelrod and Elinor Ostrom demonstrates that tit-for-tat (an essentially cooperative strategy) as a cultural norm is better than an attitude of competitive egoism. With competitive egoism behaviour, participants tacitly transmit to one another the message *"I will, in each and every interaction, pursue my self-interest regardless of whether it benefits you or not. Each of us should look out exclusively for him- or herself."* After fifteen repetitions of such games however, cooperative and altruistic behaviours start to dominate the competitive ones. They are more successful and attract more participants.[48]

We saw in the above story of the Eleventh Round that our money system has a built-in bias towards generating competition between its users. In contrast, evolutionary game theory lends broad support to the superiority of cooperation over competition. By extension, sustainability is possible only in the presence of sufficient social cooperation and low levels of socially disruptive competition and rivalry. In conclusion, because our money system generates competition rather than cooperation, it pushes us in a direction that game theory has demonstrated is the opposite of what would be desirable.

2. Evidence from Neuro-imaging

The second source of evidence of the role money plays in eroding social capital comes from clinical psychology. Neuro-imaging studies have demonstrated that the mere presence of conventional money can alter social behaviour. Greed, as well as other negative emotions such as fear, anger, intolerance, scapegoating, and panic are increased whenever money is present. It even measurably decreases the performance of the brain in making rational decisions! [49]

According to neuro-scientific findings, these processes involve two conflicting brain regions. One is the impulsive circuit[50] responding to stimuli and seeks immediate reward; the other is the prefrontal cortex, which tries to rationalise, control and anticipate behaviours. In all addictive disorders the impulsive

---

48 See e.g. Martin A. Novak *et al.* (2004). Among the seminal contributions to this vast area of evolutionary game theory, see Robert Axelrod (1984) and Elinor Ostrom (1990).

49 George Loewenstein, Scott Rick and Jonathan D. Cohen, 'Neuroeconomics', *Annual Review of Psychology*, vol. 59 (2008), pp.647-672; Dan Ariely, *Predictably Irrational: The Hidden Forces That Shape Our Decisions* (2009).

50 Including the *Nucleus Accumbens*, the *amygdala* and the *ventral pallidum.*

circuit is overactive and the same has been shown to be true for financial incentives involving conventional money. The activations that occur with conventional money are even stronger than activations from sex or crime![51]

3. Evidence from Clinical Psychology

In 2006, Kathleen Vohs and her colleagues published in the journal *Science,* empirical evidence on how the monetary system influences behavioural patterns.[52] They conducted a randomised controlled trial to demonstrate the effect of money on social behaviours. In this study, participants were randomly assigned to two groups and asked to answer identical questionnaires. During the study, one group was primed with visual symbols of money, such as an artistic dollar bill on the wall, while the other group was primed with a neutral symbol, such as a shell.

In comparison to the neutrally primed participant group, participants in the money-primed group demonstrated significantly higher rates of playing alone, working alone, and put more physical distance between themselves and their neighbours. The money-primed group also hesitated to ask others for help, and tended to respond to requests for help as if they were insensitive to others. They also preferred the pursuit of individualistic goals and individual freedom to that of collaboration. The results of this and other similar studies strongly support our hypothesis that money is non-neutral with regards to human interactions and behavioural patterns. Indeed, it increases social isolation and thereby a decline in human social capital.

This might be the first 'hard science' evidence that conventional money acts as an unconscious programming device negatively affecting human values and behaviours. As discussed in Chapter IV, 'human nature' has often been blamed as the engine that drives financial follies and crises. We can now subscribe to that idea with one caveat. These problems are triggered by *"human nature as programmed by a monopoly of bank-debt money"*. This monopoly of bank-debt money generates a specific human *culture* with associated problematic *patterns of behaviour*. The use of exchange media not created through bank-debt money leads to other types of behaviour patterns. Several examples of such systems will be presented in Chapters VII and VIII.[53]

51 Alain Dagher, 'Shopping Centers in the Brain', *Neuron*, vol. 53 (2007), pp.7-8; Brooks King-Casa *et al.* 'Getting to Know You: Reputation and Trusting in a Two-Person Economic Exchange', *Science,* 308 (1 April 2005), pp.78-83.

52 Kathleen D. Vohs *et al.*, 'The Psychological Consequences of Money', *Science* 314 (17 November 2006), pp.1154-6; Carole B. Burgoyne and Stephen E. G. Lea, 'Money Is Material', *Science* 314 (17 November 2006), pp.1091-2.

53 S.G. Lea, R.M. Tarpy and P. Webley, *The Individual in the Economy: A Textbook for Economic Psychology* (1987); and G. Seyfang and K. Smith, *The Time of our Lives: Using time banking for neighbourhood renewal and community capacity building* (2002).

Social capital and implications for sustainability

If a monetary system fostering competition, fear, mistrust and anxiety is imposed as the only legally acceptable exchange medium, how can participants be expected to generate cooperation, trust, responsibility and confidence?

Social capital is a mediator between different social variables. One measure of this is the prevalence of stress-related psychosomatic syndromes, which is inversely correlated to perceived social capital.[54] Eroding social capital is also accompanied by large income inequality and higher mortality rates.[55] Such findings point to a link between social capital, money, wealth distribution and health parameters. A motivation system relying primarily on monetary incentives to promote unconscious competition among its users may currently not be the best way forward. As explained above, we know that cooperative approaches yield superior results for all participants in the long run. In view of the sustainability challenges we face in the 21st century (see Chapter I), massive behaviour changes will be required. Is it time to reconsider the use of motivation tools relying primarily on conventional money based – and therefore competitive – incentives?

6. Money as an Attractor

We have covered a wide range of theoretical and empirical results that all confirm that bank-debt-generated currency is not behaviourally neutral. We have described five systemic effects of the conventional money system which generate pressures that are not sustainable. They are pro-cyclical money creation, short-term thinking, compulsory growth, increased income disparity, and decline in social capital. All substantially affect the type of day-to-day economic activities we engage in. While these factors are differently generated and interconnected, they all play a crucial role in how the human brain is conditioned in relation to money. Our monetary system acts as an attractor towards which all other variables mentioned in this chapter are pulled. Figure 5.6 illustrates this in a schematic way.

---

54 Cecilia Åslund, Bengt Starrin and Kent W. Nilsson, 'Social Capital in Relation to Depression, Musculoskeletal Pain, and Psychosomatic Symptoms: A Cross-Sectional Study of a Large Population-Based Cohort of Swedish Adolescents', *BMC Public Health*, vol. 10 (2010), issue 715 (10 pages).

55 See I. Kawachi, B. P. Kennedy, K. Lochner and D. Prothrow-Stith, 'Social Capital, Income Inequality and Mortality', *American Journal of Public Health*, vol. 87 (1997), no. 9, pp.1491-1498.

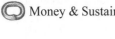
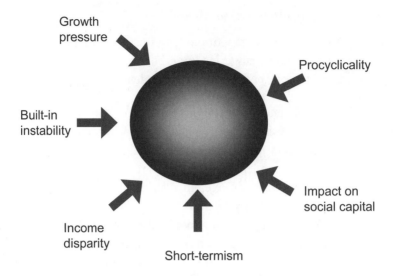

Figure 5.6: The official monetary system as an attractor.

An attractor can be described as a dynamic process in which a wide range of variables converge over time. James Buchan in his book *Frozen Desire* captured the reason for this universal power of attraction of money.[56] Money is seen as the necessary means to fulfil any mortal purpose, our very personal dream. That dream may be different for each of us, but money has become its common denominator. This makes money elusive and, as a result, seductive. That seduction power is captured in Figure 5.7.

Figure 5.7: Money: everybody's different frozen desire.[57]

56 James Buchan, *Frozen Desire: the Meaning of Money* (1997).

57 Extracted from Margrit Kennedy and Bernard Lietaer, *Regionalwaehrungen: Neue Wege zu nachhaltigem Wohlstand* (2004) p.30.

As shown in Chapters III and IV, the official monetary system is systemically unstable. This chapter has demonstrated that it is also not behaviourally neutral. Furthermore, the *homo sapiens* brain is sensitive to different incentive types, which leads to unconscious programming. Every time people interact using conventional money, the five negative mechanisms explored in this chapter are perpetuated and mutually reinforced. These mechanisms counteract the painstaking efforts undertaken to secure a common sustainable future, and may be the most significant unacknowledged obstacle to attaining it.

7. Conclusion

Far from being the behaviourally neutral and purely facilitative exchange tool that the Traditional Economics paradigm assumes, the conventional monetary system acts as a large-scale, unconscious programming tool. It generates five processes that directly conflict with various dimensions of sustainability. Today's monetary system combines a pro-cyclical money supply with deregulated capital flows, and uncontrolled speculative incentives. Furthermore, this money is created with built-in compound interest that makes growth obligatory and renders the concentration of wealth automatic. None of these features is a law of nature. They are all conventions that can be systemically counter-balanced by other systems to neutralise these effects.

Before we can consider what form such adaptations could take, we still must elucidate perhaps the most sensitive topic of all: the role of *power* with regards to money. This is the topic of the next chapter.

Chapter VI

The Institutional Framework of Power

"The study of money, above all fields in economics,
is the one in which complexity is used to disguise truth,
or evade truth, not to reveal it."
– John Kenneth Galbraith[1]

The final aspect we must consider is how power relates to money, and *vice versa*. We do this by examining the respective roles of governments and the financial system in the monetary domain. Historically, governments and banks have had a complex and sometimes conflicting relationship. This chapter examines some aspects of this relationship.

1. Semantic Traps

The domain of money and the relationship between governments and the banking system is fraught with semantic traps. For instance, the usual label used to describe conventional money is 'national currency', implying that the national government plays a key role in the creation and circulation of money. In reality, the money supply consists primarily of privately issued bank-debt money. This private proportion hovers now somewhere between 95% and 97% in most countries.

There is also a great deal of emphasis on central banks being 'independent', meaning 'independent from any political influence'. What is *not* meant is 'independent from the influence of the banking system'; however this remains unstated. For instance, the majority of board members of the US Federal Reserve are bankers.

---

1   John Kenneth Galbraith, *Money: Whence It Came, Where It Went* (1975), p.5.

Most economics textbooks define money as: a unit of account, a medium of exchange and a store of value. Because these are three *functions* of money, they characterise what money *does*. This is different from a definition of what money *is*. With such a widely accepted functional definition, there is actually little real inquiry into the *nature* of money. Our own working definition of money is as follows: 'money is an *agreement* within a *community* to use something standardised as a *medium of exchange'*. In contrast with the traditional functional definition, if an agreement does not work, one can at least imagine changing it. One might also envisage that different instruments could perform some – but not necessarily all three – functions.[2]

There are other examples of language traps.[3] When an individual or a business gets a loan, the word used is 'credit'. With governments however, the word used is always 'debt'. The two processes are identical. But 'credit' has positive connotations – someone trusted you and considered you 'creditworthy'; while 'debt' has negative connotations (you are indebted to someone). Similarly, individuals pay 'interest to the bank' while governments 'service their debt'. Here again two different terms refer to the same process. However, servicing a debt is an anonymous process without an identifiable receiver. Many countries, including France, do not even have statistics separately tracking the interest they pay on their national debt. Only the total debt (principal plus accumulated interest) is actually published, so that neither the amounts nor the recipients of this 'debt service' are visible.

Notice that all these semantic signals are consistent: they always support what we will describe below as the 'Official Paradigm' of money and finance. These semantic signals are not accidental, even if some of them can be traced back several centuries. We can therefore assume that these semantic signals reveal a coherent power strategy related to the issue of control and power. Governments have the right to exert power over their citizens and over the businesses active on their territory. Therefore, whoever can control governments can project power all over the world.

The Nexus of Power and Money

Power as conceived in this context is 'power over': the capacity to mobilise resources and control the behaviours of populations. A more powerful country or person is therefore one that can mobilise more resources, and motivate or control a greater number of humans, than another country or person. Many tools exist to obtain and exert power. They include the creation of specialised institutions (e.g. central banks, armies,

2   For instance, the Natural Savings instrument presented in Chapter VII would mainly be a savings tool, not a medium of exchange or unit of account. In many civilisations, the unit of account was also different from the medium of exchange. A case in point is Homeric Greece, where the unit of account was the ox but where, for the sake of convenience, actual exchanges were often performed with ingots of bronze or other commodities.

3   For the arguments offered in this paragraph, see Philippe Derudder and André-Jacques Holbecq (2008) p.17.

etc.); the bestowing of hierarchical or honorific titles; the capacity to offer rewards or inflict punishments in conjunction with an effective enforcement mechanism (e.g. police, prisons). The most extreme forms of power are a country's capacity to use coercion internally (e.g. requiring the payment of taxes or drafting someone into the army), or externally (through war or the threat of war).

Friedrich Nietzsche defined money as "the crowbar of power".[4] Napoleon similarly claimed that three things were needed to effectively wage war: "Money, money and money". Napoleon's realisation of an ironclad connection between money and war was hardly new. Twenty centuries earlier, the Roman statesman and orator Cicero concluded that, "the sinews of war are unlimited money".[5]

Political and financial historian Niall Ferguson provides an insightful analysis of the connection between money and power in modern times in his book *The Cash Nexus*. He shows how most significant financial and fiscal innovations of the past three hundred years have evolved from the need to finance wars. "The costs of war have fluctuated quite widely throughout history. These fluctuations have been the driving force of financial innovation."[6] Today's monetary framework is therefore an institutionalisation of arrangements between government and the financial system, historically negotiated in a context of war.

Ferguson's 'square of power' singles out two key institutions as particularly relevant on the governmental side: the parliament (i.e. representative democracy) and a professional tax bureaucracy. Within the financial system, he similarly bestows specific roles on the central bank and on national debt (see Figure 6.1).

According to Ferguson, the dynamic between these four institutions explains the evolution of the nexus between power and modern money. A particularly effective synergy among these four institutions emerged for the first time in Britain during the 18th century. It is this synergy that made it possible for Britain to industrialise, defeat Napoleon, and build its empire. Let us briefly summarise the specific role played by each institution.

---

4   Friedrich Nietzsche, *Thus Spoke Zarathustra,* translated by Adrian del Caro and edited by Robert Pippin (2006).

5   The original is elegantly succinct: *"Nervos belli, pecuniam infinitam"* from Cicero's *Fifth Philippic.* See Jon Hall, *The Philippics*, in *Brill's Companion to Cicero: Oratory and Rhetoric*, translated by James M. May (2002), pp.273-304.

6   Niall Ferguson, *The Cash Nexus: Money and Power in the Modern World, 1700-2000* (2001), p.25.

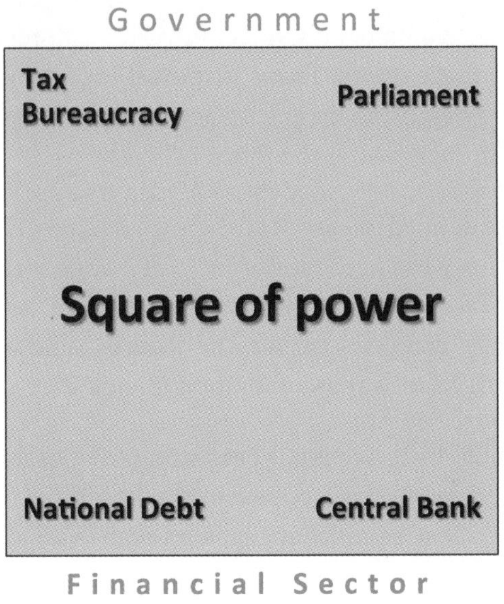

Government

Tax
Bureaucracy   Parliament

Square of power

National Debt   Central Bank

Financial Sector

Figure 6.1: Niall Ferguson's 'Square of Power'.[7]

A *professional tax bureaucracy* was an innovation introduced in England in the early 18th century. It proved significantly more effective at raising government income than the private 'tax farmers' or individuals mandated by the king to collect taxes, as was still the practice in France at the time.

Today we could call the French approach a privatised tax collecting system. It is estimated that half the revenues that the French tax farmers generated never reached the government, simply because they kept it for themselves.[8] In contrast, between 1650 and 1715, the new fiscal bureaucracy in England managed to multiply government revenues by a factor of 8, and a century later by a factor of thirty-six.[9] The relevance and importance of a professional tax bureaucracy prevails even today: when this institution appears too weak, as was the case during the Greek sovereign-debt crisis of 2011, the financial markets will tend to require higher interest rates, which can make the burden of servicing national debt unbearable.

The second player in the square of power is *parliamentary institutions,* which were created to represent taxpayers politically. Parliaments legitimised the budgetary process, thus enhancing a government's capacity to raise revenue. "For most of history, direct taxation could be collected only with the cooperation of the richer group of society. For that reason, the widening of the direct tax 'base' has very often been

7   *Ibid.*, p.23.

8   Donald Winch, 'Political Economy of Public Finance in the 'Long' Eighteenth Century', in Maloney (1998), pp.8-26.

9   Patrick O'Brien and Philip Hunt, 'The Rise of the Fiscal State in England, 1485-1815', *Historical Research*, vol. 66 (1993), pp.129-176.

associated with extensions of political representation, as taxpayers have traded shares of their income for participation in the political process, a fundamental part of which is the enactment of tax legislation. ...The slogan 'no taxation without representation' neatly encapsulates the trade-off."[10] The expansion of access to the electoral process from a wealthy landowner elite to universal suffrage was the keystone marking the political evolution of the 19th century. The final step in achieving universal suffrage was attained during the early 20th century, when women were allowed to vote in most countries.

On the side of the financial sector, the development of a *market for government debt* made it possible to deal with sudden increases in expenditures, typically triggered by wars. For a government, the benefit of borrowing was to spread the costs of a war over time, and smoothing out the subsequent need for increased taxation over many years. While private debt has more than 5,000 years of recorded history, the emergence of public debt is much more recent. The earliest government debt goes back to 12th century Venice. At that time, public debt was secured through a state tax monopoly on salt, of which the revenues were earmarked for debt service and redemption. The modern market for governmental debt took off only after the English Consolidating Act of 1751, in what became known as the British 'consols' (the predecessors of today's 'gilts', and all other government bonds). The confidence that interest will be paid on such debt critically depends on the government's capacity to tax its citizens.

Finally, a *central bank* was created to become the 'guardian' of the monetary paradigm with the task of maintaining the monopoly of a single currency, created through bank-debt. Central banks were also given responsibility for stabilising the entire system – saving it even from its own follies if needed – during a currency or banking crisis. In this way, central banks were also entrusted with the role of lender of last resort, a systemic fireman role. Whether central banks are willing or allowed to play that role can matter a lot to both governments and banks.[11]

Each of these four institutions has its own specific historical roots and characteristic path of evolution in different countries. The two strategic questions raised by the evolution of the square of power are:

- Why should we expect that a synergy that was effective when money took the form of precious metals – during the early industrial age, a period of intense nationalism and empire-building in which environmental concerns could be ignored – still remain appropriate for a post-industrial society? Since the 1970s and the official abandonment of any trace of the gold standard, money has officially taken the form of pure 'fiat money', meaning pure information.

---

10 Ferguson (2001), p.77.

11 Greece, Ireland, Portugal and other eurozone governments are discovering the consequences of the fact that the European Central Bank (ECB) is allowed to play this 'lender of last resort' role only for the banking system, and specifically not for governments.

The 21st century is also a time when the notion of empire building has become obsolete, and when our society faces some unprecedented challenges.

- Why do three out of the four corners of Ferguson's square of power – parliament, a tax bureaucracy and national debt – all have as their common denominator the core issue of taxes? We will explore the critical role of taxes in defining the relationships between government and the financial system later in this chapter.

How did we get here?

Aristotle is acknowledged as the originator of the 'science of money'. He asserted that money exists "not by nature, but by law".[12] Thus, money is not something that comes out of a farm, a mine, a mint, even a printing press or a computer. Laws are created by those who exert sovereignty. How did the creation of money become predominantly privatised if it only exists by law? While the answer to this question and the timing are different in each country, they all share a similar sequence which Heinrich Rittershausen has well documented:[13]

1. In exchange for financing a war, a private bank receives the exclusive licence to issue paper notes, thereby becoming a central bank.

2. Government tax offices accept these paper notes for tax payments in addition to metallic money.

3. The central bank becomes a source of credit.

4. An emergency occurs – usually another war or major political crisis – and a shift of power takes place between the government and the bank.

5. More paper money is issued than there are metallic reserves. To avoid a run on the bank, the convertibility to metallic money is legally abolished and the acceptance of the notes becomes compulsory.

6. The paper currency becomes the only measure of value.

The oldest agreement prototyping this sequence can be traced back to 1668 in Sweden, when the power of emitting paper money was granted to the Bank of the Estates of the Realm (now the *Riksbank* or Swedish central bank). This took place when the Swedish crown urgently needed to fund a war against Denmark. Similarly, the Bank of England, founded in 1688, was granted the monopoly of paper money emission by King William of Orange in 1694 to fund a £1.2 million war against the French. From England, this approach to money creation spread throughout the world.

---

12 Aristotle, *Nichomachean Ethics*, v.5, 1133.

13 Heinrich Rittershausen, *Die Zentralnotenbank* (1962), pp.18-19, quoted in Greco (2009) p.40.

The Old Lady of Threadneedle Street, as the British central bank in the City of London is still referred to, "is in all respects to money as St. Peter's is to the Faith. And the reputation is deserved, for most of the art as well as much of the mystery associated with the management of money originated there."[14] For the USA, this same sequence was completed with the Federal Reserve Act of 1913.[15]

While it is often assumed that the relationship between the banking system and governments has remained unchanged over the centuries, this has not necessarily been the case. The case study of the Banque de France and the French 'Law of 3 January 1973' illustrates how a more conflicted relationship between governments and the financial system can be generated. These tensions are currently being manifested in the ongoing sovereign debt crises of 2011-12.[16]

Box 6.1 – Chronicle of a Predictable Debt Crisis

THE CASE STUDY OF FRANCE[16]

The creation of the French central bank, the 'Banque de France', dates back to 18 January, 1800. It follows the sequence described by Rittershausen. It was initially set up as a privately owned joint stock company with a share capital of 30 million francs. Napoleon Bonaparte, still only 'Consul' at the time, owned parts of the shares, as did several members of his entourage. Annual general meetings were open to the two hundred largest shareholders, who became known as France's richest 'deux-cents familles'. Fifteen Regents were appointed to sit on the General Council administering the Bank, as well as the three Censors who supervised the Bank's management.

The Banque de France experienced several difficulties during its first years, including a crisis in the government's finances and a fall in its gold reserves. This led to a restriction in the redemption of bank notes. As a result, Napoleon implemented reforms giving him greater say in the management of the Bank. On 22 April, 1806, a new law replaced the Central Committee with a Governor and two Deputy Governors, all three of whom were appointed by Emperor Bonaparte. Two years later, the Imperial Decree of 16 January, 1808 set out the 'Basic Statutes' which governed the Bank's operations until 1936.

The political upheaval of 1848 led to the imposition of 'forced currency' acceptance, freeing the Bank from the obligation to redeem its own notes for metal (i.e. step 5 in Rittershausen's sequence). The Bank's notes became legal tender and individuals were obliged to accept them for all payments. Forced currency and legal tender were eliminated by the law of 6 August 1850 but reinstated during the Franco-Prussian war of 1870. Thereafter, there were no further challenges to the status of the Bank's paper money as legal tender.

---

14 Galbraith (1975).

15 The genuine conspiracy saga of how this law was passed in the USA on Christmas Eve, 1913, just before World War I, is the topic of Edward Griffin, *The Creature From Jekyll Island: A Second Look at the Federal Reserve* (1994).

16 Much of the description below is taken from the Banque de France website: *www.banque-france.fr ~ bit.ly/TPlink42*

Following the victory of the *Popular Front* in the 1936 general election, the French government decided that it was no longer in the public interest for the Bank to be governed by private company law. The Act of 24 July 1936 gave the government the means to intervene more directly in the management of the Bank. Most of the Councillors were appointed by the Government to represent economic and social interests as well as the general interest of the nation. This was only a prelude to the nationalisation of the Bank, decided by the Act of 2 December, 1945, just after France's liberation from German occupation. This Act stipulated that the capital of the Bank would be transferred to the State on 1 January, 1946. The shareholders were to receive four 20-year bonds for each share. The last 3% Banque de France bonds were redeemed on 1 January, 1965.

Throughout its entire history, the Banque de France handled the Treasury's cash transactions free of charge and granted the government interest-free advances to meet its financial needs. This changed with the Law of 3 January, 1973.[17] Article 25 of this law states tersely: "The national Treasury cannot present its own instruments for discounting at the Banque de France."[18] In other words, for the first time since 1800, the French government had to borrow exclusively from the private sector, and thereby pay interest on any new debt it contracted. Figure 6.2 shows what this has meant in practice.

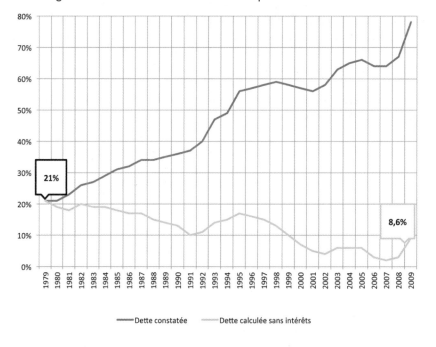

Legend: ━━ Dette constatée   ┄┄ Dette calculée sans intérêts

Figure 6.2: French government debt as % of GDP: Official debt vs. debt computed without interest, 1979-2009[19]. The lower line presents what would have happened to France's national debt under the pre-1973 rules: a drop from 21% to 8.6% today. In contrast, under the new rules, national debt surged from 21% to 78%. No 'spendthrift government' can be blamed in this case... Compound interest explains it all!

---

17 *http://fr.wikipedia.org ~ http://bit.ly/TPlink43*

18 The laconic original in French is worth quoting: "Article 25. – Le Trésor public ne peut être présentateur de ses propres effets à l'escompte de la Banque de France".

19 Taken from Derudder & Holbecq (2008) p.68.

At the end of 1979,[20] France's government debt was the equivalent of €239 billion or 21% of its GDP at the time. Thirty years later, by the end of 2009, this almost quadrupled to €1,088 billion or 78% of GDP. Had Article 25 of the Law of 3 January, 1973 not been in force, the French government would have saved €1,306 billion in interest by 2009, and the country's total public debt would currently only be 8.6% of GDP. These figures should challenge the often made claim that increases in sovereign debt are due exclusively to 'spendthrift' governments. For France, the cost of this additional interest amounts to "€45 billion per year, which represents the cost of building three 'Charles de Gaulle' aircraft carriers *every year*; or buying 600 Airbus A320 planes; insulating (at the rate of €10,000 per household) some 4,500,000 homes; or the salary (at a French median salary of €18,000) for 2,500,000 people!"[21] Should commitments of this scale not be democratically debated before they are implemented? Does financing *even one* additional aircraft carrier not require some form of parliamentary debate and approval?

A version of the French Article 25 has been embedded in the EU's Maastricht Treaty as Article 104, and in the Lisbon Treaty as Article 128. These decisions seem to have been reached without much open debate or explanation about their implications for future European governmental finances. As French economist Jacques Sapir stated:

> *"The single [European] currency is a vector of [the] rise in debt, because it imposes on countries the obligation to finance themselves on the financial markets. The institutions of the single currency, from the Maastricht Treaty to the Lisbon Treaty, indeed forbid states either to go directly to the central bank's discount window, or to impose on banks the purchase of government debt in proportion to their assets. ...In France this was forbidden by a 1973 Law. But what a law has done, another law can also undo. ...The financial markets become the only possible source of public financing. As a result, they sanction heavily both the level of [government] debt and the weak growth prospects."[22]*

What changes are available to Europe that would reverse or soften the impact of today's monetary arrangements? The most radical policy option proposed used to be known as the 'Chicago Plan' and dates back to the 1930s. While it would indeed be a far-reaching policy shift, it is not an option we actually recommend for reasons explained at the end of this chapter.

---

20 This series should be started in 1973, but given that France does not have a statistical series that tracks the interest paid on government debt separately, the interest data had to be reconstructed. But data were not available to reconstruct the interest payments before 1979. The difference by 2009 should therefore be still larger than this graph shows..

21 *Ibid.* p.65

22 Jacques Sapir, *Faut il sortir de l'Euro?* (2011); p.16 and footnote 1. *italics added.*

7. The 'Chicago Plan'

"If the American people ever allow private banks to control the issue of their currency, first by inflation, then by deflation, the banks and corporations that will grow up around [the banks]will deprive the people of all property until their children wake-up homeless on the continent their fathers conquered. The issuing power should be taken from the banks and restored to the people, to whom it properly belongs."

US Congressional Subcommittee Record, 1937
Usually attributed to Thomas Jefferson[23]

After the 1929 crash, two banking reforms were proposed in the USA to make sure that 'it would never happen again'. One of them was the Banking Act of 1933, also known as the Glass-Steagall Act. It strictly separated banking activities between Wall Street investment banks and high-street banks. However, the best-known academics of the time favoured another proposal known as the 'Chicago Plan'. Its promoters included most leading American economists of the 1930s: Henry Simons and Paul Douglas from Chicago University, Irving Fisher from Yale (who published a book about it [24]), Frank Graham and Charles Whittlesley from Princeton and Earl Hamilton from Duke University. Among its supporters was also a young economist called Milton Friedman, later to be known for very different monetary views.

The quickest way to explain the Chicago Plan is that bank-debt money would be made illegal. The government would itself issue a currency to be used in payment of all debts, public and private.[25] Banks would thereby become simple intermediaries, service providers taking in deposits, holding a fraction as reserves and lending out the remainder. They would be forbidden to lend out *more* than the deposits they collected. In other words, banks would have to apply a 100% compulsory reserves rule and, since no bank-debt money could be created at all, banks would *de facto* be limited to the role of money brokers. Ironically, that is exactly what those who believe the Official Paradigm have believed all along!

---

23 Although many letters of Thomas Jefferson, 3rd President of the United States (1743-1826), confirm that he was highly suspicious about banks, the attribution of this particular quote to him should be considered spurious. The first printed reference to this quote has been traced back to 1937 in the US Congressional Subcommittee Record.

24 Irving Fisher, *100% Money* (1935), re-edited in 2011 by ThaiSunset Publications.

25 Notice that while the Chicago Plan or its most recent versions (such as the one presented in Huber & Robertson [2001]) propose to nationalise the *money creation* process, they have no intention of nationalising the banking system itself. Banks would continue to compete with each other and to allocate financial resources as they do today. The only – but significant – difference is that their functioning would be based on 100% reserves and they would therefore not be able to create debt money *ex nihilo*.

Under powerful and effective pressure from the banking lobby, the Chicago Plan was abandoned and the Glass-Steagall Act was enacted. Banks presumably preferred this solution since it would lessen the impact on their core business model. They may also have thought it would be easier to eventually repeal Glass-Steagall than to re-privatise money creation once governments had realised the advantages of the Chicago Plan. And right they were: Glass-Steagall was repealed with the Gramm-Leach-Bliley Act in 1999, signed by President Clinton. Since then, this repeal has been blamed for having triggered the subprime crisis and the collapse of Lehman Brothers in September 2008, which precipitated the global banking scramble leaving so many governments over-indebted.

Reinstating some form of the Glass-Steagall Act, or implementing some version of the Chicago Plan, are once again being debated. Predictably, it is the former that meets with more approval from both bankers and regulators. In the UK, the equivalent of the Glass-Steagall Act was enacted in 2011. In the USA, Paul Volcker, ex-Chairman of the Federal Reserve, is similarly pushing for some version of Glass-Steagall. In contrast, Congressman Dennis Kucinich is proposing the American Monetary Act,[26] an equivalent of the Chicago Plan. On 26 July 2011, Kucinich invited Professor Kaoru Yamaguchi from the University of California at Berkeley and Doshisha University in Japan, to give a congressional monetary briefing on this idea. Yamaguchi's paper[27] uses a systems approach to show that the liquidation of debts under the current monetary regime will trigger multiple recessions and massive unemployment in the USA with contagion to other economies. In contrast, under the American Monetary Act, debt reduction and even debt liquidation can be put into effect without causing recessions, unemployment and inflation, either in the USA or abroad.

Realistic debt reduction is not the only argument in favour of nationalising the money creation process. James Robertson[28] shows that this change would provide the government with significant additional revenue to spend on what it considers relevant. In the case of the UK, this would represent both:

- an annual total bonus to all taxpayers of about £75 billion
- a one-off benefit to the public purse totalling some £1,500 billion over a three-year period of transition from the existing commercial-bank-created money supply to the new debt-free money supply

---

26 See *www.monetary.org* ~ *bit.ly/TPlink44*

27 The paper, 'Workings of a Public Monetary system of Open Macroeconomics', was presented at the 29th International Conference of the System Dynamics Society, Washington D.C., 25 July, 2011. See *www.monetaryorg* ~ *bit.ly/TPlink45*

28 James Robertson, *Future Money: Breakdown or Breakthrough* (Totnes: Green Books, forthcoming). Chapter 3 of this text is available on *www.jamesrobertson.com* ~ *bit.ly/TPlink46*. See also James Robertson and John Bunzl, *Monetary Reform: Making It Happen* (2003) and Huber & Robertson (2001).

Professor L. Randall Wray from the University of Missouri-Kansas City offers another strong argument: the availability of government-issued currency would make it possible to ensure zero unemployment[29] without inflation.[30] In conventional economic theory or practice, such an outcome is considered impossible – the equivalent to squaring the circle. Notwithstanding all these positive arguments in favour of the Chicago Plan and its contemporary variants, it is not the solution we recommend in this Report. Let us explain why.

Reasons for Not Recommending the Chicago Plan

While we appreciate the strengths of the idea of nationalising the monetary creation process, there are five reasons why we do not recommend this solution.

1. Replacing a monoculture with another monoculture is not the way to generate diversity in exchange media. As was shown in Chapter IV, any monoculture leads to a structural instability. Replacing a private monopoly with a public one wouldn't resolve the problem of structural fragility.

2. While it is true that a 'Chicago Plan' reform would eliminate the risk of widespread banking crashes and of sovereign debt crises, there would still be monetary crises. In other words, as was shown in Chapter III, the 145 banking crises and 76 sovereign-debt crises that have hit the world since 1970 would have been avoided if such a reform had been in place. The 208 monetary crashes would not necessarily have been avoided.

3. If governments were the only ones in charge of creating money, there might be a risk of inflation rising to a greater extent than it has in the past. Such a risk is real and most recently demonstrated in 2009 by the hyperinflation crippling the Zimbabwean dollar after President Mugabe instructed the central bank to print its currency by the trillions.

4. The fourth reason can be summarised as 'political realism'. Any version of the Chicago Plan will be fought to the death by the banking system because it threatens both its power base and its business model. Even after the excesses triggering the 2007-2008 collapse, or in the middle of the Great Depression of the 1930s, the banking lobby managed to deflect the implementation of any significant changes. Recall that in 2010, for every elected official in Washington, there were three high-level lobbyists

---

29 Zero unemployment would correspond to a much higher rate of employment than what is known as the rate of unemployment associated with a constant inflation rate, technically defined as the NAIRU ("non-accelerating inflation rate of unemployment"). However, zero unemployment would not necessarily mean that all those who would like to work are indeed working. There could still be "frictional" unemployment (i.e., people in the process of changing jobs) or voluntary unemployment.

30 See L. Randall Wray, *Understanding Modern Money: The Key to Full Employment and Price Stability* (1998).

working full-time for the banking system. Thomas Friedman writes in the *New York Times*: "Our Congress today is a forum for legalised bribery. One consumer group using information from *Opensecrets.org* calculates that the financial services industry, including real estate, spent $2.3 billion on federal campaign contributions from 1990 to 2010, which was more than the health care, energy, defence, agriculture and transportation industries combined. Why are there 61 members on the House Committee on Financial Services? So many congressmen want to be in a position to sell votes to Wall Street."[31] In Europe, there is no awareness of this problem because no legislation is in place requiring lobbyists to register at the European level. What are the chances of something as radical as the Chicago Plan being implemented when legislators themselves are part of an army of bank lobbyists?

5. The final argument is about risk. Nationalising the money creation process cannot be done on a small pilot scale. It must be implemented on a massive, national scale or, in the case of the euro, a multinational scale. Any change always involves the risk of unintended consequences. Logically, large-scale change involves greater risk. It is certainly a higher risk than any of the options presented in the next chapters.

If not the Chicago Plan, then what can governments do at this point? Two stories are relevant. The one most people are familiar with is referred to as the 'Official Paradigm' because it is embedded in the majority of financial media and mainstream economic textbooks.[32] It does not offer governments many options except that of submitting to the dictates of the 'financial markets'. The second story is the 'Fiat Currency Paradigm' which opens up a very different set of possibilities.[33]

3. The Official Paradigm

Governments must, like any household, raise the money needed to pay for what they do, either through income (levying tax revenues) or debt (issuing governmental bonds). Banks are intermediary service providers that collect deposits, hold a small fraction as reserves, and lend out the remainder to creditworthy private or governmental entities that require it.

---

31 Thomas Friedman, 'Did you hear the one about the bankers?', *The New York Times*, 21 Oct 2011.

32 For a conventional description of today's system, see for instance Gregory Mankiw (2003); McConnel & Bruce (2008); or Mishkin (2007). These textbooks provide no critical analysis of the limitations of the prevailing system and, in particular, offer no comparison with alternative systems.

33 For a critical analysis of the limitations of today's monetary system, see for instance: Wray (1990) and (1998) and Moore (1988). One of the most readable pieces for the general public is the almost humorous text by Warren Mosler, *Seven Deadly Innocent Frauds of Economic Policy* and *Soft Currency Economics*, available on *www.warrenmosler.com*. A more complete list of relevant heterodox economists and their publications is given later in this chapter.

If this story sounds familiar, it is because it provides the implicit and/or explicit background for most financial commentaries in the media, as well as for many banking and finance economic courses. It is the narrative used by rating agencies, which is not surprising since they are mostly bank-owned. This official story is what some politicians refer to as 'sound government finances', particularly when austerity measures are introduced. According to this story, governments are at the mercy of opaque 'financial markets'. It justifies the joke by James Carville, the director of President Clinton's 1992 electoral campaign: "I used to think that if there was reincarnation, I wanted to come back as the President, or the Pope. But now I want to be the financial market: You can terrify anybody!"[34]

A long time ago, this official story did indeed reflect reality. This was the case, for instance, when the Byzantine Empire issued the bezant, a gold coin issued with the same weight (4.55 grams) and same purity (98%) for a record 700 years.[35] Producing these coins on such a consistent basis required a continuous supply of the precious metal. This gold was obtained through mining, conquest, trade and taxation.

By the late 19th century, the official story became less and less true. During the latter days of the gold standard, the actual gold reserves of the Bank of England were treated as a state secret, because the amount of gold backing for the pound Sterling was much lower than publicly claimed.[36] President Nixon removed the last vestiges of the gold standard in August 1971 when he suspended convertibility between the US dollar and gold, thereby severing the last remaining link between the money system and any physical reality or commodity.

The key point is that whatever governments choose to accept in payment of taxes automatically gives enormous power to those who produce or control that particular item. When sovereigns chose to be paid in wheat, as in Mesopotamia, everyone dealt directly or indirectly with wheat producers, and farmers played a pivotal role in such a society. When governments chose to be paid in gold, gold producers and gold hoarders held the power. If governments choose a fiat currency created through bank debt, it will be banks. If the issuer of the currency is the government itself, then it will be the government that is empowered.

---

34 *Financial Times*, 4 February 1998.

35 Its official name was the *solidus*. It was first issued by Emperor Constantine (306-337 AD), and circulated widely until well into the Middle Ages, even beyond the Byzantine empire in both Europe and Asia.

36 A governor of the Bank of England (a private company at that time) was being questioned by the British Parliament:
– Can you please inform us about how much gold there is at the Bank of England?
– In ample sufficiency, Sir.
– Can you be more precise?
– No, Sir.

4. The Fiat Currency Paradigm

Officially since 1971, all national currencies operate as pure 'fiat' currencies, i.e. where money is created out of nothing ('*ex nihilo*') through simple bookkeeping entries. This fiat currency paradigm is succinctly summarised by James Galbraith: "When government spends or lends, it does so by adding numbers to private bank accounts. When it taxes, it marks those same accounts down. When it borrows, it shifts funds from a demand deposit (called a reserve account) to savings (called a securities account). And that for practical purposes is all there is."[37] In other words, sovereign governments are *not* like any household, as claimed in the Official Paradigm.

"The government taxes us and takes away our money for one reason – so we have that much less to spend, which makes the currency that much more scarce and valuable. Taking away our money can also be thought of as leaving room for the government to spend without causing inflation."[38] This does not mean that there are no consequences when a sovereign government overspends by over-using these accounting entries. Such consequences take the form of inflation and/or reduction in value of the currency on the international markets.

What is the role of the banking system in all this? Simply put, they administer the giant accounting system that keeps track of money flow. They are also in the business of creating bank-debt money with the expectation of making a profit. By 'making loans', banks buy IOUs from borrowers in exchange for providing them with a credit in fiat money.

In principle, banks can make loans only to the extent they have sufficient reserves.[39] In practice, however, "banks do not wait for excess reserves before making loans and creating deposits. Rather, if faced with a credit-worthy customer and a request for a loan, a bank makes the loan. It then operates to obtain reserves as necessary to meet legal requirements. If banks in the aggregate are short of required reserves, the central bank automatically *must* supply them.[40] In spite of rhetoric about Fed policy to discourage such borrowing it is simply impossible for the Fed to refuse to supply the reserves needed by the system."[41] It is even harder for a central bank to get banks to make more loans if they are not inclined to do so. When central banks try to push banks to lend, as was the case after the crash of 2007-2008, it is like trying to "push on

---

37 James Galbraith in the Preface to Mosler (2010) p.2.

38 Mosler (2010) p.27.

39 This is the usual way of explaining the process by which bank-debt money gets created, which is the one we used initially in Appendix A to explain the process. In practice, the reserve limit is basically not binding.

40 If a bank is short on reserves, this 'short' is in fact an overdraft on its reserve account with the central bank. This overdraft is effectively a loan from the central bank. So there is no way that a central bank could deny credit to a bank.

41 Wray (1998) p.118.

a string".[42] All four major central banks of the rich world – those of the USA, Britain and Japan and the European Central Bank – have their lending rate near zero. Japan's has basically been stuck there since the 1990s, without succeeding in a relaunch of its economy.[43]

So, contrary to what is often claimed, the degree of control central banks exert over the creation of bank-debt money is more theoretical than practical. Central banks are reduced to the role of pricing the marginal cost of reserve funds for the banking system. They determine only the cost of getting additional reserves from the central bank, a cost that banks pass on to their clients with an additional mark up. They do not determine the amount or timing of bank-debt money being created by the banks. The development of the massive interbank market has further reduced the need for banks to go to the central bank's discount window. This has further marginalised the influence of the central banks. Central banks thus have more limited control over the banking system's money creation process than is generally believed.

They also seem to have difficulty grasping the notion that in a floating-exchange world, when a country such as the USA pumps trillions of additional dollars into its economy, the inflation that is being created may manifest on the other side of the world. For instance, these additional dollars could end up being spent by wealthy Russians on real estate on the French Riviera, regardless of what the French or European Central Bank may want to do about it.

In contrast, governments are not as powerless as they seem, at least in theory. *Governments are needed continuously for giving value to any fiat-created currency.* However, based on their actions, governments are not making use of the power they have over the private banking system.

When governments require payment of taxes in a specific medium of exchange, they automatically increase its scarcity. As a result, that medium acquires more value. A sovereign government can therefore *choose the instruments of payment it wants to give value to. In so doing, it can determine the kind of effort its citizens must make or the types of behaviour they must engage in to obtain these instruments.* This conclusion will be critically important for the design of government-initiated monetary solutions, as discussed in Chapter VIII.

---

42 This is one of the reasons why central banks are even more worried about deflation than about inflation. To reduce inflationary pressures, they can make loans more expensive by increasing interest rates. But when central banks are facing deflation, interest rates can only go as low as zero to convince people to borrow (although the Bank of Japan has even gone as far as charging a negative interest rate to the banks to stop deflation, without much success).

43 Central banks' policies in January 2012 were compared to "crazy aunts on the loose" in their desperate attempts to use Quantitative Easing, a tool that "is best kept in a locker marked 'for Emergency Use Only' is how Charlie Bean, the Bank of England's deputy governor, put it in 2010". *The Economist*, 7 January 2012 p.58.

There is still one last veil to be lifted in the monetary domain. The financial system exerts power over governments by influencing beliefs. As George Soros pointed out with his reflexivity theory,[44] *belief creates reality*. It is a world of self-fulfilling prophecies. In finance, if enough people believe gold will defy gravity and double in price, the price of gold will actually double! Although the belief may not be solid enough to keep the gold price at that level when real-life supply and demand manifest, a big price movement will have occurred in the interim. Similarly, if enough people believe a particular government will default on its debt, investors will divest themselves of enough bonds to create substantial real pressures on that government. These pressures can even directly provoke the default.

Box 6.1 – Academic backing for the Fiat Currency Paradigm

The ideas resulting from the Fiat Currency Paradigm are not new, and certainly not our creation. They can even be traced back to Adam Smith in the heyday of the Gold Standard.

Smith was aware of the role of taxation in creating value for a currency, including gold. He gives an example in which a non-redeemable paper money issued by a bank could even carry a premium over its face value in gold specie.

"A prince, who should enact that a certain proportion of his taxes should be paid in paper money of a certain kind, might thereby give a certain value to this paper money; even though the term of its final discharge and redemption should depend altogether upon the will of the prince. If the bank which issued this paper was careful to keep the quantity of it always somewhat below what could easily be employed in this manner, the demand for it might be such as to make it even bear a premium, or sell for somewhat more in the market than the quantity of gold or silver currency for which it was issued."[45]

Smith thus already knew that the key to a paper currency's value is neither its conversion to gold, nor any 'legal tender laws'. Rather, the acceptance of this paper in payment of taxes was the key to give it value.

Many other economists have put forward this same idea. Here are some of the more significant contributors and a selection of their relevant ideas and sources appears in the corresponding footnotes.

---

44 George Soros, *The Alchemy of Finance* (1987).

45 Adam Smith: *The Wealth of Nations,* Cannan Edition (1937) p.312.

The main proponents of the Fiat Currency Paradigm in rough chronological order include Mitchell Innes,[46] Georg Friedrich Knapp,[47] Irving Fisher,[48] Abba Lerner[49] and John Maynard Keynes.[50] Fiat-currency economists sharing similar views have even been regrouped as an economic school variously labeled Chartalists, neo-Chartalists,[51] the Endogenous Money School or the State Money School. They include contemporary economists like Paul Davidson,[52] Nicholas Kaldor,[53] Hyman Minsky,[54] Stephen Rousseas,[55] Warren Mosler,[56] Charles Goodhart,[57] Wynn Godley[58] and Randall Wray[59].

While these scholars don't all necessarily agree on many topics, they all concur that *the systemic role of taxes is to give value to a currency, which, in the case of a fiat currency, would otherwise have no intrinsic value whatsoever.* If these ideas appear new or strange, it is because they have been systematically ignored in practice, rather than because they have been proven invalid or wrong.

---

46 Mitchell Innes, 'What is Money?', *Banking Law Journal*, vol. 30 (1913), no. 5, pp.377-408.

47 Georg Friedrich Knapp claims that "All means by which a payment can be made to the State form part of the monetary system. On this basis, it is not the issue, but the acceptation, as we call it, which is decisive." (Georg Friedrich Knapp, *The State Theory of Money* [Original publication 1924; republished, New York: Augustus Kelley, 1973, p.95])

48 Fisher (1935).

49 Lerner created a framework called the "functional theory of finance", which builds on the premise that "money is a creature of the state. Its general acceptability, which is its all-important attribute, stands or falls by its acceptability by the state." (Abba Lerner, 'Money as a Creature of the State', *American Economic Review*, vol. 37 (1947), no. 2, p.313). See also Abba Lerner, 'Functional Finance and the Federal Debt', *Social Research*, vol. 10 (1943), pp.38-51.

50 Keynes was aware that the value of money is not generated by its intrinsic properties. "Money is the measure of value, but to regard it as having value itself is a relic of the view that the value of money is regulated by the value of the substance of which it is made, and is like confusing a theatre ticket with the performance." (John Maynard Keynes, *The Collected Writings, Vol XI: Economic Articles and Academic Correspondence*, ed. Donald Moggridge [1983], p.402).

51 For the first time, to our knowledge, *The Economist* has provided a four-page briefing about "Heterodox Economics", mentioning Warren Mosler as part of a "neo-chartalist" school. (*The Economist*, 31 December 2011, pp.49-52).

52 Paul Davidson, *Money and the Real World* (1978).

53 Nicholas Kaldor, *The Scourge of Monetarism* (1985).

54 Hyman Minsky, *Stabilizing an Unstable Economy* (1986).

55 Stephen Rousseas, *Post-Keynesian Monetary Economics* (1986).

56 Warren Mosler, (1995), (1997/8) and (2010).

57 Charles E. Goodhart, *Money, Information and Uncertainty* (1996).

58 Wynne Godley and Marc Lavoie, *Monetary Economics: An Integrated Approach to Credit, Money, Income, Production and Wealth* (2007); Wynne Godley and T. Francis Cripps, *Macroeconomics* (1983).

59 Wray (1990) and (1998).

5. Comparing the Two Paradigms

The same components identified in Ferguson's 'Square of Power' (see Figure 6.1 above) are present in both paradigms: governments and the financial sector, governmental debt, taxes and central banks. They fit together in different ways depending on which of the two stories one selects.

The advantage of the Official Paradigm's storyline is that it is shorter, easier to understand and ties in with ordinary people's daily experience. Most of us have first-hand experience with the constraints of living within budgets. Anyone who has opened a savings account or obtained a loan is privy to the idea that banks take deposits and lend money for interest. However, when this official story is applied to our current system, it presents governments as having no options except to do whatever the financial system desires. Moreover, it depicts the banking system as a passive intermediary and service provider, and not as a central protagonist creating fiat money through bank-debt.

The Fiat Currency Paradigm story is more abstract and does not neatly fit with ordinary people's experience. This paradigm describes a significantly different power relationship between a sovereign government and the banking system. In this version, the banking system is totally and permanently dependent on governments to give value to bank-debt money. The government, on its side, also always has the power to require payments of tax liabilities in a currency other than, or in addition to, bank-debt money.

6. Conclusion

A public debate about monetary reform that could include the Chicago Plan and/or other regulatory initiatives is overdue. If an initiative akin to the Chicago Plan were implemented, it would still be necessary to introduce greater diversity in the exchange media as such diversity is an essential condition for the structural stabilisation of our economic system. Putting the public sector in charge of the system and making it the main beneficiary of a fiat money mechanism – instead of the private sector – would not solve this structural issue. It would, in structural terms, simply replace a private monopoly with a public one.

As we showed in Chapter IV, a structural solution requires creating a monetary ecosystem with diversity in terms of means of exchange and types of issuing institutions, including the government. If the objective is to create diversity, the most logical step is not to get rid of the one large-scale system already in place. The logical focus should be on innovative, non-financial incentive systems that can function in parallel and *complement* current financial incentives based on bank-debt money. The next two chapters provide examples of such complementary incentive systems, some combinations of which, taken together, would provide the diversity needed to structurally stabilise our 21st-century economies.

One important source of hope is the explosive growth of NGOs that now number over a million organisations worldwide. According to Paul Hawken's research: "By any conventional definition, this vast collection of committed individuals does not constitute a movement. Movements have leaders and ideologies. People *join* movements, study their tracts, and identify themselves with a group. ...Movements, in short, have followers. This movement, however, doesn't fit the standard model. It is dispersed, inchoate, and fiercely independent. It has no manifesto or doctrine, no overriding authority to check with. ...Rather than a movement in the conventional sense, could it be an instinctive, collective response to a threat? ...Can it successfully address the issues that governments are failing to do: energy, jobs, conservation, poverty, and global warming?".[60] More significant than their sheer numbers is the qualitative shift from being simple observers and critics to being actors implementing innovative policies. We concur with Hawken that 'this movement that isn't a movement' could become a key actor in finding a solution to the impending challenges coming our way. That is why five out of the nine solutions that we propose in the next two chapters are examples of initiatives that can be implemented by NGOs, if they so choose.

---

60 Hawken (2007) p.3.

Chapter VII

Examples of Private Initiative Solutions

"The future belongs to people who see possibilities
before they become obvious".
Anonymous

The most common complementary currency systems today are commercial loyalty systems, popularised initially by the airline industry over thirty years ago under the generic name of 'frequent-flyer programmes'. There are now more than 15 trillion 'miles' in circulation managed by five airline alliances, each with their specific names. These systems have proven that it is possible to operate efficiently very large-scale complementary currency systems. However, commercial loyalty systems are also the least interesting complementary currency applications from a societal viewpoint: they simply motivate customers to use the same airline alliance, or return to the same supermarket chain or shop. Using one airline instead of another doesn't make much difference for society, although it does, of course, for the specific airline or shop.

We will therefore focus here only on complementary currency innovations that have a really beneficial impact on society. There is a great variety of such systems and they already exist in their thousands around the world; they have been described – and their valuable effects abundantly documented – elsewhere.[1] In truth, the people participating in these systems have been the real pioneers and trail blazers of a broad monetary awareness movement on which we are simply commenting here.

However, many of these existing social purpose systems are intentionally small-scale (e.g. building social capital in a particular neighbourhood), and some of their

---

1   Lietaer (2001); Lietaer & Kennedy (2008); Greco (2009); Lietaer & Belgin (2011); Hallsmith & Lietaer (2011).

design features limit their capacity to scale-up to meet the challenges that we can expect to face in the near future. Their function can be compared with that of capillary vessels: they play the important role of keeping us warm and give us a pleasant colour. However, it would be naïve to expect capillary vessels to be able to replace the role of an aorta in the event of a heart attack. To use a different metaphor, in a natural ecosystem, life forms are needed at very different scales: from microbes, earth worms, frogs and rabbits all the way to buffaloes and elephants. Each is vitally important at its own scale. The health of a natural ecosystem depends critically on thriving subsystems at such different scales.

Similarly, in the monetary ecosystem that this Report recommends, systems of different scales are needed. That is why we focus here only on systems that meet two criteria: they should be capable of delivering a significant beneficial societal effect, and of scaling-up as necessary.

Dozens of designs exist for innovative exchange media that meet these two criteria, some already operational, many still at the design stage. In combination with the conventional money system, mixes of these could create a great variety of monetary ecosystems. In the next two chapters we discuss nine examples. Each of the examples describes a system that:

- is useful in today's unstable socio-economic environment, while government budgets are under pressure

- addresses a different theme or socio-economic issue such as health care, education or the environment

- can be implemented as a stand-alone system; and when combined in various ways, could play a useful role in unleashing the synergies that characterise a successful monetary ecosystem

We start with the least controversial and finish with the most controversial, moving from systems against which we expect little resistance to those which will elicit the most. For instance, we proceed from purely voluntary systems not requiring anyone's permission to be started, to compulsory systems that would require new legislation. We are not claiming, however, that the most demanding systems are also the most desirable.

Obviously, not *all* these systems need to be implemented for significant improvements to materialise. The German 'Iron Chancellor' Bismarck is reported to have claimed that politics is the art of the possible. Each community, city or country can therefore decide how far it wants to go and how far it is possible, in practice, to stretch policies in new directions. We deliberately present a very broad range of pragmatic solutions simply to illustrate what is possible.

Five innovations can be implemented without government initiative or new legislation: they are the ones presented in this chapter. The other four examples, more appropriate for governmental initiative, are presented in Chapter VIII.

For all their diversity, the nine systems we describe share two common denominators. First, they are all designed to act as *complementary systems*, i.e. they are designed to operate in parallel with the existing national bank-debt money system. Second, they should ideally all be as transparent for their users as possible. For example, before making an exchange, each party could have the right to see the other party's account. Transparency allows these systems to be self-policing and reduce potential fraud. These systems would be most cost-effective if they used mobile electronic devices such as mobile phones.

Again, each of these initiatives could be made viable on its own. However, if several of them were to be implemented in parallel, their cumulative effect could demonstrate the synergistic power and resilience of what we refer to as a 'monetary ecosystem' in Chapter IV. They could also combine with systems that are already operational, many of which have been documented elsewhere.[2]

We propose the nine examples as if they were on a menu in a restaurant. Choose the one(s) that are most intriguing or relevant to your own specific domain and interest. The page refers to the place where the detailed 'kitchen recipe' for that particular system is to be found. We do not recommend the average reader to study all nine, it could be like ordering the entire menu at one sitting and might lead to indigestion...

Box 7.1 – Menu of Motivation Systems

PRIVATE SECTOR

NGO Initiatives:
Doraland p.142
Wellness Tokens p.144
Natural Savings p.151

Business Initiatives:
C3 on a regional or national scale p.155
TRC on a global scale p.158

PUBLIC SECTOR

Government Initiatives:
Torekes at city level p.168
Biwa Kippu environmental project p.171
Civics at the city or regional level p.173
ECOs at the national or European level p. 179

---

2   For applications at a city level, see in particular Gwendolyn Hallsmith and Bernard Lietaer, *Creating Wealth: Growing Local Economies with Local Currencies* (2011).

Below is a brief description of the first five models, none of which requires governmental permission to be implemented.

1. *Doraland* is a system that has been proposed to help Lithuania to become 'A Learning Country' by stimulating grass-roots educational initiatives. It would be best implemented by NGOs, organised around a new Learning Foundation.

2. *Wellness Tokens* is a NGO initiative in cooperation with health care providers to deal with health care issues in a preventive fashion, thereby reducing society-wide medical expenses.

3. *Natural Savings* is a financial savings product fully backed by living trees. It would be a savings currency superior to any national currency in terms of inflation protection. It would provide an incentive to reforest areas and promote the creation and maintenance of long-term carbon sinks.

4. *C3* is a Business-to-Business (B2B) system that reduces unemployment by providing working capital to small and medium-sized enterprises outside the constraints of the mainstream currency. It is currently operational in Brazil and Uruguay.

5. *TRC* is a global B2B currency proposal that would make longer-term thinking profitable for multinational companies by resolving the conflict between short-term financial corporate priorities and long-term societal and environmental needs.

1. Doraland: Creating a 'Learning Country'

Lithuania was the first of the three Baltic States to become independent from the Soviet Union in 1990. More than twice the size of Belgium, it has a population of only 3.2 million. During the 14th century, it was the largest country in Europe, stretching from the Baltic Sea to the Black Sea. Given its small current size and lack of stereotypical tourist attractions, Dalia Grybauskaitė, the first woman to become Lithuanian president, would like foreigners to visit Lithuania in order to learn something. There are two areas in which Lithuania leads the world today: it is currently the most optically wired country in the world, and it has mobile phone penetration reaching 120% of the population (many people have more than one SIM card).

In October 2011, a group of public sector representatives, business and NGO leaders as well as some students, were convened by Ms. Rasa Balciune, leader of an international consultancy headquartered in Vilnius. They were asked the question: *How could Lithuania become a 'Learning Country'?*

Doraland was one of the proposals to emerge from that process.

The starting point was the formation of a Lithuanian Learning Foundation with the working title 'Doraland'. This foundation is designed to enable individuals or groups to make one of their dreams come true, in exchange for a contractually agreed amount of 'Dora' currency. This currency is earned through teaching and/or learning activities, such as offering courses in English, in computer skills, in Italian cuisine or in any other skill that can be contributed.

For example, one 17-year-old at the Vilnius event had the dream of learning Buddhism in the mountains of Burma. The Doraland Foundation would contractually promise to make this experience possible in exchange for 3,000 Doras. Doraland would not only raise the funds — through sponsorships and donations — to purchase the airline ticket payable in national currency, but also arrange for the necessary contacts in Burma. The teenager could earn 3,000 Doras by teaching 300 hours of conversational English to others, for example, or perhaps by training adults wanting to acquire computer skills. Another young person wanted to spend a weekend with her hero, a Nobel laureate in physics. In exchange for 2,000 Doras or the equivalent of 200 hours of teaching an art skill, the Foundation would facilitate the meeting with the physicist. Another group might want to learn to sail around the world or to create a neighbourhood greenhouse for year-round food production. The media attention attracted by these endeavours will help to raise sponsorships and donations and can also help generate more creative and socially useful dreams, as well as more offers to teach/train a range of skills.

Under this scheme, Doras will be obtained directly from the Foundation and can be easily tracked using mobile phone technology. Non-profits are to be involved in organising the learning activities. In addition, another new non-profit would be created to independently audit the earning and exchanges of the Doras.

This Dora learning-economy is intended to operate in parallel with the conventional monetary system. We are, therefore, witnessing the beginnings of an exchange media ecosystem. At the end of the first planning session, one of the participants asked the 17-year-old whether he would be willing to teach English and get paid in *Lita* (the Lithuanian national currency), in dollars or in euros. His answer was, "No, I'd prefer to get paid in Dora, because that would get me closer to my dream. These other currencies only would get me the airline ticket!" For this teenager, the Dora had already become a 'superior currency', a currency that he preferred over all others. Doraland is an example of a complementary system that encourages non-spontaneous but desirable behaviour patterns. Figure 7.1 summarises the Doraland model in a flow diagram.

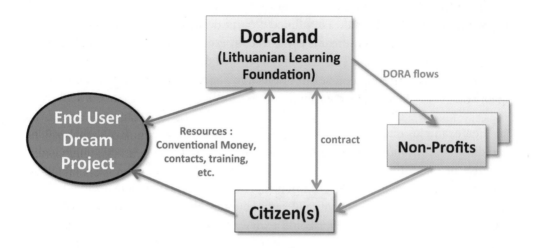

Figure 7.1 Doraland Flow Diagram. The process starts with a citizen's dream project. Doraland makes a contract with one or more citizens to help realise their dream in return for a certain amount of Doras. People who provide teaching/training are compensated in Doras. Non-profit organisations would play the same role in the Dora economy as corporations do in the conventional currency world: organise, motivate and audit the relevant activities.

2. Wellness Tokens: Overcoming Market Failures in the Health Care System

The cost of health care has been growing faster than GDP in most developed countries. One medical reason is that patterns of disease burden have shifted from infectious diseases to chronic diseases. In contrast to infectious diseases, which have shorter periods of illness and faster mortality, chronic diseases allow people to live with their illness for longer periods of time. While technology to treat both infectious and non-infectious conditions has continued to improve significantly over the past decades, preventing the development of chronic diseases has not. Furthermore, medical costs are expected to continue to rise steeply in the near future due to the demographic bulge of baby boomers reaching retirement age. The challenge for current and future generations is how to achieve and optimise the health of a population without having its costs absorb an ever increasing proportion of the economy.

Identifying a Market Failure: The 'sick and alive' bias

Market failures in health care have been well documented. Causes of these failures include asymmetric information, adverse patient selection, entry barriers, absence of risk pooling and moral hazard.[3] We hypothesise the existence of an additional market

---

3   Arrow (1963) and Reinhardt (2001).

failure. In fact, no developed country really has a 'health care' system; rather, they are all funding 'medical care' systems. The economic incentives in a medical care system are therefore skewed towards keeping sick people alive, rather than preventively keeping the general population healthy. This is because medical care stakeholders, including the pharmaceutical industry, medical technology suppliers and health care professionals — all acting rationally — end up earning most of their money by treating sick or unwell individuals, as opposed to providing preventive health care to a healthy population.[4]

Because the vast majority of the global medical care budget is spent on acute and chronic diseases, preventive health care accounts for only a very small fraction of the overall health care services provided in industrialised countries.[5] For instance, recent studies in the USA estimate that 50% of all mortality is linked to social and behavioural factors such as smoking, diet, alcohol use, sedentary lifestyle and preventable accidents.[6] Yet, less than 5% of the approximately US$1 trillion spent annually on health care is devoted to addressing the root causes of these preventable conditions.[7]

Even if the medical care market were a theoretically 'perfect' one – with fully informed actors, no moral hazard, less asymmetry, more efficiency, fair access and so on – the economic preference for 'sick and alive' clients would remain a problematic bias. The current system thus makes it tempting to treat an obese patient who develops diabetes by using medication, rather than by using an early detection/prevention approach with exercise and weight-loss programmes, to mitigate or even avoid the disease. In addition, improved technology has allowed an increase in the life expectancy of chronically ill individuals, with a corresponding increase in the consumption of health care resources. Prevention is thus side-lined in the face of this additional disease burden. The 'sick and alive' bias then becomes an additional cause for a market failure that contributes to the ineffective systemic organisation of health care services.

A Wellness Token system is proposed next to counteract this specific market failure. Interestingly, people who study the 'long wave' of technological changes, called the

---

4   M. Rothschild and J. E. Stiglitz, "Equilibrium in Competitive Insurance Markets" (1976); D. Cutler and R. Zechhauser, *Insurance Markets and Adverse Selection: A Handbook for Health Economists* (1998).

5   Committee on Capitalizing on Social Science and Behavioral Research to Improve the Public's Health (2000) *Institute of Medicine.*

6   *U.S. Health* (2005) National Center for Health Statistics, Department of Health and Human Services, No: 2005-1232.

7   "Behavioral and social interventions therefore offer great promise to reduce disease morbidity and mortality, but as yet their potential to improve the public's health has been relatively poorly tapped." Committee on Capitalizing on Social Science and Behavioral Research to Improve the Public's Health (2000) *Institute of Medicine.*

Kondratieff wave, expect that Wellness technologies will be the breakthrough in the next technological wave.[8]

Wellness Tokens

Wellness Tokens are specifically designed to use a preventive approach to promote and maintain the good health of participants. Just as 'Frequent Flyer Miles' are issued by airline alliances to induce a habit of taking the same airline for all one's trips, Wellness Tokens would be issued by a Wellness Alliance to induce healthy habits. The members of the Wellness Alliance would be those organisations that have a financial interest in keeping the population healthy (e.g. insurance companies, local government and local employers). One of the purposes of the Wellness Token would be to generate changes in habits towards health promotion and disease prevention by encouraging healthy behaviours and emphasising preventive health care. Such an approach would also be a means of financing supportive care so that the elderly, the chronically ill and the disabled can remain in their own homes, and delay for as long as possible their entry into a long-term medical facility, where the costs escalate.

Earning Wellness Tokens

The Wellness Token Alliance, which could be run by an NGO or by a group of insurance companies[9], would issue Wellness Tokens for two types of activities:

1. *Promoting preventive health care programmes* including primary, secondary and tertiary disease prevention measures, focusing on lifestyle modification for people with or without chronic conditions – including nutrition, physical activity and stress management interventions. Such health-educational programmes have an impact on health care costs and health outcomes.[10] The return on investment (ROI) of such preventive programmes is estimated to range from 300% to 1000% depending on the programme.[11] That such rates of return are available in preventive

---

8   L.A. Nefiodow, *Der Sechste Kondratieff* (2001). See also Appendix G for more information on Nicolai Kondratieff and 'long waves'.

9   In the Netherlands an alliance involving the largest insurance company is planning to introduce several city-scaled experiments for motivation systems to deal with the ageing wave of the next decades.

10 Indeed not all preventive programmes are cheaper than the treatment . Studies show that it is more cost effective to treat tuberculosis rather than prevent it. See Borgdorff *et al*. (2002). Influenza vaccination is not cost effective for healthy working adults. See Bridges *et al*. (2000). However, all of these studies only compare the costs for treatment and the costs for prevention. They do not take into consideration the decrease in productivity and the absenteeism due to illness.

11 The most significant benefits occur after the second or third year of the programme. One hundred dollars or euros spent on preventive care programmes per year and per employee will have an ROI after the third year of 300 dollars or euros. See Goetzel (1999); Erfurt (1992); Powell (1999) and Chapman (2003).

programmes provides hard evidence that the 'sick and alive' market failure is quite real.

Wellness Tokens would encourage the adoption and maintenance of healthy habitual behaviours. The payment of individuals for maintaining specified healthy behaviours has already been documented through the use of conditional cash transfers, for example to remain HIV negative.[12] For example, a family with two obese children could participate in a weight reduction programme, monitored either through weight or, even more precisely, through the Body Mass Index (BMI). For every kilogram or BMI improvement, the family would receive 10 Wellness Tokens.

2. *Helping the elderly or disabled people requiring chronic care.* In industrialised countries, the proportion of people over 60 years of age is growing faster than any other age group due to longer life expectancy and declining birth rates. By 2050, the number of people over 60 will almost double. Technological advances tend to be less relevant for home care than for other health care fields and home care is structurally linked to personal face-to-face interactions, which makes it less costly and more humane in many cases. Therefore, having recourse to home care instead of anonymous, hi-tech hospital treatment, even in the case of chronic conditions, will make a significant positive difference to health care costs and, in many cases, to treatment outcomes.[13]

We should insist that while the Wellness Token system is indeed aimed at improving behaviour with respect to health, it does not fall into the category of 'neo-Victorian' sanction mechanisms where people are denied financial support when they fall ill due (arguably) to specific behavioural patterns (i.e. get lung cancer while having been heavy smokers or get heart disease while having a history of detrimental eating habits). Our objective here, as we explained, is educational and has more to do with awareness building and the quest for personal autonomy. That is why the system clearly emphasises preventive rather than curative measures. The idea is not to use 'financial incentives' in order to scare people into changing their ways, as is the case with a sanction mechanism that kicks in when the disease is already present. There is indeed a *personal-responsibility-building* dimension to the Wellness Tokens, in the direction of what has been called 'genuine autonomy' of the patient in recent literature

---

12 Lia *et al.* (2008); Bastagli (2009).

13 See *www.cdc.gov ~ 1.usa.gov/TPlink47*

inspired by Ivan Illich.[14] The system offers positive rather than negative incentives to motivate and reward people for their behaviours rather than punish them for 'mis-behaviours'. The perception should be that the system increases the opportunities available to people rather than imposing restrictions on them.

This approach would also be useful in setting up support groups. Creating pods of people who are tackling a weight problem can be a very effective way to get longer-term commitment. One could then create group objectives, which — when met — earn extra Wellness Tokens for the entire group. Group support is well known as a key for longer-term maintenance of changes and improvements.

Spending Wellness Tokens

People earning Wellness Tokens could use them in a number of ways, including paying part of their insurance premiums with them[15] or purchasing goods and services related to prevention or health promotion from providers pre-qualified by the Wellness Alliance. After a formal audit, local and regional businesses providing goods and services supporting preventive health care would become certified if their services and goods met specific health promotion criteria. This could include partial payment in Wellness Tokens for preventive care, biological or organic food or restaurants, health promotion/disease prevention courses, and sports equipment such as bicycles, to name just a few examples. In this way, a family earning Wellness Tokens because their children are maintaining their BMI could go shopping within the local community to buy organic food or a bicycle from participating vendors.

What could the businesses accepting Wellness Tokens do with them? The owners of participating businesses could use them in the same way as their customers, to start their own wellness programme. However, the more typical option would be to cash the Wellness Tokens in for conventional currency through the Wellness Alliance.

---

14 See Christian Léonard, *Croissance contre santé: Quelle responsabilisation du malade?* (2008). While Léonard, a leading Belgian health care expert, is strongly critical of the current ideology of punitive 'responsibilisation' of patients, he does argue in favour of a "genuine" autonomisation, which he links to Ivan Illich's ideas of autonomy and conviviality: genuine personal responsibility can only flow from a reappropriation, by the patient him/herself, of his/her health. This requires preventive measures, which are under-financed in the current "alive and sick" logic. The Wellness Token system, therefore, moves in the direction called for by Léonard.

15 The Elderplan insurance company in the New York area has implemented successfully part of this idea with a Time Dollar currency. They have discovered that people participating in a Time Dollar system remain on average healthier because of a better social capital environment.

The business case for Wellness Tokens

The logic for the insurance companies and other members of the Wellness Alliance to pay for cashing-in practices works only if the savings in the cost of an unhealthy population are higher than the costs of the programme. For instance, if the cost of a non-lethal heart attack is €100,000, and if we know that losing 5 kg in weight will reduce the probability of a heart attack by 20%, this would generate an expected cost saving of €20,000 for each at-risk individual achieving that target. The rate at which Wellness Tokens are redeemed would be calculated in such a way that half the savings would be used for Wellness Token redemptions, while the other half would reduce costs for the members of the Wellness Alliance. In the above example of an expected saving of €20,000, €10,000 could be used to redeem the tokens used. The other €10,000 would be used to reduce the costs incurred by Wellness Alliance members.

For the preventive care providers, the Wellness Token could function as a loyalty currency by attracting customers who might otherwise not patronise them. From a purely financial viewpoint, the role of a loyalty currency is to ensure that the value to the business generated by an exchange is always larger than the marginal cost in conventional money of serving an additional customer. The most logical participants are therefore businesses with comparatively low marginal costs. This is the case for many preventive health care providers. Some businesses have virtually no marginal monetary costs – think, for example, of a massage therapist who is not fully booked. But even a restaurant, for example, typically has marginal costs of about one third of its customers' bills. This means that only one third of what customers spend pays for the food itself. There is usually another third that goes to fixed costs: renting the location, heating the room, paying the staff, etc. The final third is profit. Therefore, as long as a restaurant would not otherwise be full, it makes economic sense to bring in additional customers who pay partly in conventional money and partly in complementary currency.

The Wellness Token is a win-win approach. Going back to our example, the children become healthier and less prone to illness; the family has additional resources to spend on health-related and health-promoting goods and services; the insurance alliance incurs fewer health care costs as a result of healthier clients; and healthcare providers increase their turnover. On a macroeconomic level, society benefits through lower rates of sick leave, increased productivity, less unemployment and greater social capital.

Wellness token = steering towards a healthy society

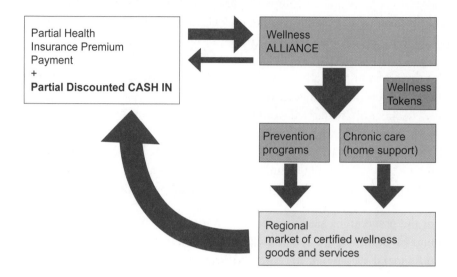

Figure 7.3 Wellness Token system running in parallel with the conventional medical care system.

Although research on these aspects is incomplete, the existing literature on conditional transfer systems has proved that they can have a positive health impact on the population.[16] While simple cash transfers in conventional currency may have similar effects, they do not ensure that the cash flow remains within health-promoting goods and services. We believe this is crucial when it comes to introducing diversity: the Wellness Token system allows a durable preventive health sector to develop in a parallel economy. Would this create entrenched privilege and generate monopolistic behaviour on the part of care providers? We do not believe so, for two reasons: first, the mentality in prevention is probably quite different from the 'big bucks' approach that prevails in the curative care industry, since preventive care is intrinsically less lucrative, less technology-intensive and less open-ended; second, the conditions for participating, if appropriately designed, would allow dubious firms or practitioners to be expelled from the system if necessary. The ideal is that the advantages of participating should be so desirable that exclusion is the only punishment needed.[17]

Wellness Tokens introduce an alternative way to encourage and finance preventive health care and home care programmes. This approach would also allow long-term cost reduction for insurance companies, and for governments subsidising them.[18] The Wellness Token program provides positive encouragement – rather than punitive

---

16 Lia *et al.* (2008); Paxson & Schady (2007).

17 The Swiss business-to-business currency system WIR has been successfully operating on this principle for 75 years.

18 C. J. Ruhm, *Macroeconomic Conditions, Health and Government Policy* (2006).

threats – for individuals to acquire healthy habits. Finally, by making people more explicitly responsible for their own health, Wellness Tokens counteract moral hazard and risk pooling, which are two other major market failures at play in health care.

3. Natural Savings

This idea was initially developed as a micro-savings instrument for India, but can easily be adapted to many other environments.[19] It consists of a savings instrument fully backed by a natural growth process and useable as a local medium of exchange. The backing could be any commercially valuable product that grows organically over time, whose ownership can be secured and which can be maintained and harvested without unduly high costs. Examples of such products include trees or any other commercial plant that grows organically in value over years, or breeding fish in a protected lake, or wild game in an enclosed forest. Here we will focus on the example of a tree plantation, because the benefits are wide ranging. Forests act as carbon sinks and deforestation is a growing global ecological concern that makes a significant contribution to climate change.

Objectives of Natural Savings

The proposed savings tool has four objectives:

1. to provide an inflation-proof and robust savings instrument.
2. to reduce the wealth gap between rich and poor without having to rely exclusively on tax redistribution mechanisms.
3. to encourage sustainable resource management, including reforestation and sustainable forestry, with the positive environmental benefits it entails.
4. to make available a local medium of exchange that increases liquidity and thus fosters on-the-spot economic activity.

   Investing in a natural resource as a secure long-term savings tool is not a new idea and has been done on an individual level for millennia. Even from an institutional standpoint, major insurance companies today own large forest plantations in Europe and the US for exactly that purpose. The novelty of this proposal is that such investments would be made available as an inflation-proof savings tool for everyone, including the poorer segments of the population.

---

19 The text of this section is extracted and summarised from Marek Hudon and Bernard Lietaer, 'Natural Savings: A New Microsavings Product for Inflationary Environments – How to Save Forests with Savings For and By the Poor?', *Savings and Development*, vol. 4 (2006), pp.357-381

Natural Savings step by step

Let us assume the initiative comes from a local government and/or NGO owning a piece of land suitable for a commercial forestry project. The process would start with the creation of a legal entity, which we will call a 'Natural Savings Company'. This entity becomes the owner of the timber but not of the land, which remains the property of the government or NGO.[20]

The Natural Savings Company issues 100,000 shares backed by the trees planted on the land. The labour costs for planting and maintaining the forest are payable in those shares. To avoid dilution of the value of the shares, the company is not allowed to issue more shares without creating additional plantations to back further issues. This underlines the need for a robust governance structure to ensure the transparency of the system and all managerial decisions, further strengthened by periodic external audits and other safeguards against fraud.

A value curve would be established using the value of the timber over time based on a conservative growth estimate of the species of trees in the particular climate, and on their market value at maturity. If there were 100,000 'tree shares' in the Savings Company, then one share would represent 1/100,000 of the total timber value in the plantation. If the trees were ready for harvest after twenty years, the value curve between planting and harvest would resemble figure 7.4 below. The curve provides an easy reference for the number of shares paid for a day's work. As long as the members of a community clearly understood the value of a 'tree share' in their own terms, the exchange of the shares for goods and services among themselves would be facilitated. Hereafter, we will express the value in terms of workdays.

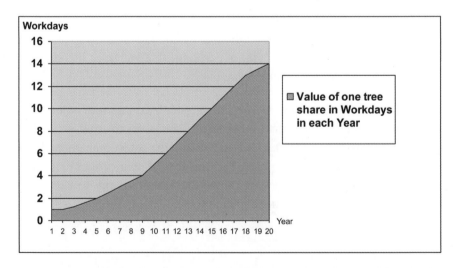

Figure 7.4: Example for the value over time of one tree share, expressed in workdays.

---

20 If the property is owned by a third party, one could also arrange for a long-term lease of the necessary land and pay the owner in part or whole with shares in the Natural Savings Company.

Let us assume that the value of a 'tree share' at maturity after twenty years is fourteen workdays, and that its growth is reflected in the value curve above, expressed in workdays. For the first two years of the project, one day's work earns one share. But by the ninth year the shares have grown in value to be worth four days of work, so a day's work is payable with a quarter of a share. (Note: it is always possible to pay labour partially in tree shares, and the rest in conventional money.)

At maturity, the forest would be harvested and the timber sold for conventional money. All the shares earned by workers up to that point would be redeemed with the proceeds of the sale of the timber. Because the value curve was based on a conservative estimate of the timber value, this would have the potential of windfall profit. The entire process could begin again with a new plantation on the same land and a new issue of shares for the next generation of workers.[21]

Risk management

Any investment carries some form of risk. These risks could be reduced with well-known approaches, such as fire insurance in the case of a forest. The Natural Savings Company should purchase insurance against this and other hazards.

It would also be possible to diversify the risk *ex ante* by launching a variety of natural savings products such as different tree species, different maturities, or even totally different natural savings bases such as a fish-breeding project in a local lake. Diversification can occur *ex post* by facilitating exchanges of shares of one project for another in the same region or country, or beyond.

Using the Natural Savings shares

What can a community member who has earned some tree shares in the Natural Savings Company do with them? The shares could be kept to full maturity and then cashed in for the proceeds of the harvest, thus using the tree share purely as a savings instrument. This would be a valid option for anyone saving for retirement or any other long-term goal such as higher education for one's children.

A second option would be to trade shares for goods or services within the community. The tree shares would thus function as a local medium of exchange and provide some additional liquidity in that community. In principle, the value of the exchange should reflect the value of the tree currency at the time of the exchange, but the owner of the shares and the person accepting them could decide for themselves the most appropriate arrangement.

---

21 Depending on the size of the land and the community, one could make this a continuous process, with new plantations and harvest on parts of the total forest on a periodic, rotating basis. Well-known forestry management techniques should be applied as appropriate.

A third option, requiring prudent management, would be for the Savings Company to allow the shares to be 'cashed in' for payment in conventional money before reaching maturity. This would be useful to build trust in the system. In situations where immediate cash was required, such as after an accident or disease, or for a wedding, this option would allow an individual or family to address the situation without having to dump the shares at a price below their real value.

The value of an early redemption could be based on a value curve such as that shown in Figure 7.4, less a transaction fee. This fee would encourage share owners to use them primarily as a store of value continuing exchanges within the community rather than cashing shares in for conventional money. If this third option were made available, the Natural Savings Company would need to have access to sufficient cash (e.g. by securing a line of credit with a bank), to avoid a 'run on the savings company' – the equivalent to a 'run on the bank' in a conventional system.

Some theoretical considerations

Notice that this 'tree currency' is intentionally designed not to perform all three classical functions of money. Its main function is as a store of value, and it would play that role better and more reliably than any national currency. Even the Deutsche Mark (the world's least inflationary currency between 1945 and 2000) lost more than half its value during that time period. In contrast, trees have biological growth between 3% and 7% per year and this growth has been historically more reliable than any government bond. The 'tree currency' could occasionally function as a medium of exchange, but not as a unit of account, nor as legal tender. With regards to these later functions, the national currency would continue to play its usual role.

Natural Savings could potentially reduce the gap between rich and poor. The conventional way of reducing this gap is to increase taxes on the rich and redistribute the proceeds in programmes benefiting the poor. In the Natural Savings system, those willing to work could create real wealth by themselves with long-term protection against inflation, banking or monetary crashes. The best way to earn tree shares would be by participating early in the tree plantation project or other community project approved by the local government and the Natural Savings Company. Those in the poorest levels of society could thus be able to reliably accumulate wealth. An investment in living trees would not only be inflation-proof and secure against monetary crashes, but would organically grow in value until maturity.

4. C3: 'Commercial Credit Circuits' for Small and Medium-Sized Enterprises

In most countries, the vast majority of private jobs (75% to 95%) are created in small and medium-sized enterprises (SMEs). Addressing unemployment as a genuine and serious social sustainability challenge is one way of improving the rates of development and survival of SMEs.

The problem

SMEs frequently have difficulty obtaining working capital. These smaller firms are pressured by their suppliers to pay in cash or within 30 days, while the customers of SMEs (which are often larger enterprises) may operate on a 90-day payment basis. This cash-flow quandary becomes deadly for SMEs when banks refuse to provide them with bridge financing, or charge prohibitive interest rates, or impose disproportionate collateral requirements. This problem has become critical in many industrialised countries where, as a result of the financial crisis, banks have stopped offering reasonable credit conditions to other businesses. However, it has long been endemic in developing countries.

The solution

The 'Social Trade Organisation' (STRO), a Dutch Research and Development NGO, has developed a financial innovation to address this challenge structurally. Their model has been successful in several Latin American countries. The process uses insured invoices or other payment claims as liquid payment instruments within a Business-to-Business (B2B) clearing-network. Each recipient of such an instrument can choose between cashing it in at a cost for conventional money or directly paying his or her own suppliers with the clearing-network proceeds backed by an insured invoice.

C3 step by step

The C3 mechanism involves the following seven steps:

1. An SME we call business *A* makes a sale and issues an invoice to a larger business we call business *B*. Business *B* agrees it will pay the invoice in 90 days.
2. Business *A* secures insurance on that invoice with an insurance company. In practice, the cost of this insurance can be as low as 1% because the likelihood of payment default by Business *B* – the larger, well-established firm – is small.

155

3. Business *A* then opens a 'current account' with the clearing network and exchanges the insured invoice for the same amount of 'clearing funds'. It can then pay its supplier, which we can call business *C*, with these funds via the clearing network.

4. To receive its payment, business *C* simply needs to open its own 'current account' with the network. *C* then has two options: it can either cash-in the clearing funds for conventional money at the cost of paying the interest for the outstanding period of 90 days plus the banking fees, or spend the clearing funds in turn within the network at no cost.

5. No matter when the invoice of business *A* is paid, business *C* can use the positive balance on its clearing-network account, for instance to pay its supplier, business *D*.

6. Business *D*, in turn, now simply needs to open its own account with the network. It then has the same two options as business *C*: cash its clearing funds in for conventional money at a cost or spend them at no cost within the network. And so on…

7. At maturity of the invoice, the network gets paid the amount of the invoice in national currency, either from business *B* or from the insurance company in the case of a payment default on the part of *B*. Whoever owns the proceeds of the insured invoice at that point can cash them in for conventional money without incurring any interest costs.

Benefits

The benefits for businesses are as follows:

- Because participating businesses have access to short-term funds as needed, they increase their productive capacity at a substantially lower cost than they otherwise could through bank loans. The level of credit can be built up to a stable level ranging between a quarter (an average of 90 days of invoices) and half of annual sales.

- Because suppliers are paid immediately regardless of the original buyer's payment schedule, substantial liquidity is injected into the entire SME network at very low cost. This extra liquidity attracts participation in the C3 network.

- The technology to do this already exists and the necessary Open Source software is available. It does not require new legislation or government approval. C3 encourages more efficient use of information technology infrastructure among SMEs, including the opening of new markets and marketing channels through e-commerce.

What are the benefits for governments? The greatest one is additional revenue from transactions that would otherwise not occur. Because this additional income ultimately becomes available in conventional national currency, the clearing-network does not upset existing procurement policies. The most effective way for governments at any level to encourage the implementation of the C3 strategy is for them to accept payment of taxes and fees in the C3 currency. As we argued in Chapter VI, this will encourage people to accept the C3 currency in payment. Uruguay is the first country to have applied this concept: it accepts C3 units for payments of all taxes and fees. The other advantages to governmental entities are listed below.

- The C3 approach is a dependable way of reducing unemployment without costly subsidies and without needing to nationalise money creation as in the 'Chicago Plan'.

- Any profits on transactions performed via the C3 system are taxed exactly as if they were in conventional money. Furthermore, C3 helps shift economic activities from the black or grey economy to the official economy, because SMEs must formally be incorporated to participate, and all exchanges are 100% electronic and traceable.

- In order to remain at a manageable scale, C3 systems are best organised at a regional level. Businesses within the network have an incentive to spend their balances with each other, thus stimulating the regional economy.

- All C3 networks should use the same insurance standards so they can connect across networks and facilitate exchanges, even internationally.

Sizeable benefits for banks and the financial system also exist:

- The win-win situation also extends to the financial system. Because the network is computerised, lending and management for the insurance and loan providers are streamlined. SMEs become a more profitable sector for banks because credit lines can be negotiated with the entire clearing-network rather than individual businesses. This also automatically provides for risk diversification.

- Banks and other financial institutions already provide factoring services similar to the C3 process; however, these are cost effective only for large amounts and thus available only to large firms. The computerised streamlining of the C3 system makes it possible for all parties to obtain the same results at lower costs.

- Most banks now also provide insurance services. C3 opens a new market for insurance and credit, all the way down to micro-finance enterprises. With C3 computerisation, even such small-scale entities can be serviced at low cost.

5. The TRC: an Initiative for Multinational Businesses

The Trade Reference Currency (TRC) is a global currency proposal first published in 2001.[22] Its relevance has increased significantly because of the financial crisis of 2007-2008. A leadership group for the TRC has recently been formed and is currently undertaking a feasibility study, with a view to implementation of this system.

The problem

Monetary instability has become the leading concern for international business — often greater than political or market risks. In a *Fortune 500* survey in the USA, all corporate participants reported foreign exchange instability as the largest risk of doing business internationally.[23]

The TRC system provides an effective solution for this while making it profitable for corporations to think long-term. It does this by resolving the ongoing conflict between shareholders' short-term priorities and the long-term requirement of society at large. It also stabilises the world economy through its counter-cyclical impact.

The TRC mechanism

The TRC is a privately issued currency carrying a demurrage charge. It is fully backed by an inflation-resistant, standardised basket of a dozen of the most important commodities and services in the global market.

The TRC's characteristics

- **Complementary currency.** The TRC is designed as a complementary currency circulating in parallel with national currencies. All existing monetary and financial products or practices could therefore continue to exist. The TRC mechanism would be an additional option for those international economic players voluntarily choosing to use it.
- **Trade reference currency.** The TRC is backed by a standardised basket of the most important commodities and standardised services traded on the global market. Though conceptually similar to a fully backed gold standard, the TRC backing would consist of a dozen of the main international commodities, including gold. Since it is fully backed by a physical inventory of commodities, it would be a secure, robust and stable mechanism for international contractual and payment purposes.

---

22 Lietaer (2001).
23 Dolde (1993).

- **Private issuance.** The TRC would be issued as an inventory receipt by the TRC Alliance, a non-governmental initiative with an organisational structure open to all those meeting certain pre-established criteria. In this sense, the TRC Alliance would play for the non-financial sector a role similar to the one that the Visa credit card alliance plays for participating financial institutions.

  The inventory receipts, called TRCs, are issued by the TRC Alliance in payment to the producers selling commodities in the TRC basket to the Alliance. These sales are based on the market values of the commodity involved and on the value of the TRC basket at the time of the transaction. As a private initiative, it does not require governmental negotiations or international agreements. From a legal and taxation viewpoint, the TRC is simply a standardisation of international barter technically called 'countertrade'. Legislation and reporting requirements for countertrade already exist in over 200 nations around the world.

- **Demurrage-charged.** The TRC is a demurrage-charged currency. As described in Chapter V, a demurrage charge acts like a linear parking fee applied to a currency, imposing a cost on its holder over time. The cost for holding on to the TRC currency is estimated at 3.5% to 4% per annum and corresponds to the costs incurred for storing the physical commodities included in the TRC basket. This demurrage charge ensures that the currency is used as a planning, contractual and trading device: it would not be hoarded but would remain in circulation. Thus it would strongly activate commercial exchanges and investments wherever it circulates. In sum, the TRC deliberately fulfils only two of the three traditional monetary functions: it acts as a unit of account and medium of exchange, but not as a store of value.

- **Inflation-resistant.** The TRC is designed as an inflation-resistant currency by its very composition. Inflation is always defined as an ongoing, durable process by which a standardised basket of goods and services changes its value. By selecting the appropriate ingredients to be placed in the basket, the TRC would be protected against inflation. For example, the composition of 100 TRCs could include 1 barrel of oil, 5 bushels of wheat, 10 pounds of copper, 3 pounds of tin, plus 1/10th of an ounce of gold, 10 Carbon Emission Rights, container cargo rates and so on.

How the TRC works in practice

The key steps involved in the TRC mechanism, from the creation of TRCs to their final cash-in are illustrated in Figure 7.5. The numbers in parentheses correspond to the steps labelled in Figure 7.5.

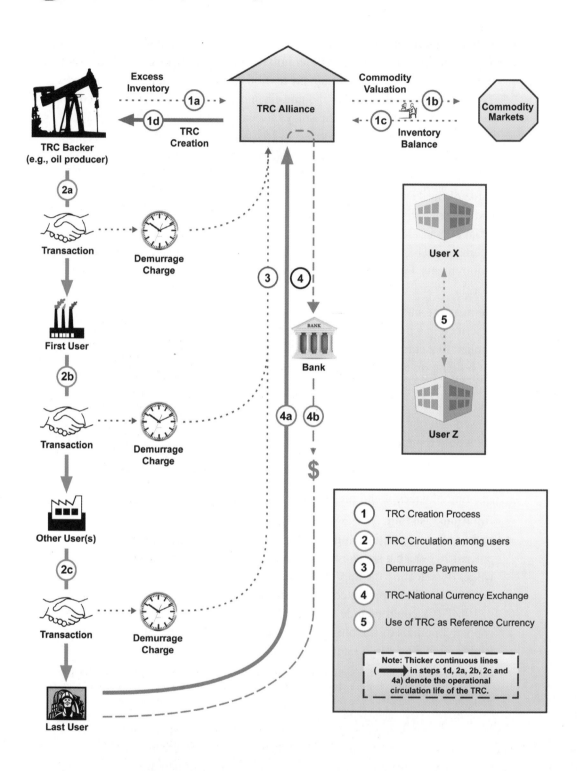

Figure 7.5: The Trade Reference Currency mechanism.

(1) The TRC creation process

(1a) Excess inventory sale. The creation of the Trade Reference Currency begins with the sale of excess commodity inventory to the TRC Alliance by one of its backer members. For example, this could be one million barrels of crude oil sold to the Alliance by an oil producer.

(1b) Commodity valuation in TRCs. The value of this sale of oil to the TRC Alliance and the amount of TRCs the one million barrels of oil are worth is calculated at market prices. Using an agreed-upon procedure, this is accomplished by determining the commodity prices at the time of the sale for both the inventory in question, in this case oil, and the sum of each of the commodities in the TRC basket. The formula used to calculate the commodity valuation is:

[Commodity value per unit x *number of units]/TRC Unit Value = Y TRCs*

Let us assume that the commodity price for a barrel of oil at the time of the sale is $100 and the price for each item in the TRC basket at the time of the sale (i.e., copper, grains, lead, one unit of carbon emissions rights, including oil) totals $200. Let us further assume that one million barrels of oil are sold. Therefore, 500,000 TRCs are issued:

[$100 per barrel of crude oil x *one million barrels]/$200 = 500,000 TRCs*

(1c) Inventory balance. The TRC Alliance rebalances its portfolio to account for the inclusion of the one million barrels of oil. This may be accomplished through future market transactions (i.e. a purchase or sale today at a given price for delivery at some future date) or through spot transactions (at the market price of the day). Thus, a TRC in circulation always has a backing in the appropriate physical or future commodity.

(1d) TRC creation. The TRC Alliance credits the oil producer's account with 500,000 TRCs. (TRC currency movements are denoted by the thicker continuous arrowed lines in Fig. 7.5.)

(2) TRC circulation among users

Once the TRC is created, it remains in circulation for a period determined entirely by the users. For example:

(2a) First user – The oil producer decides to pay one of his or her suppliers (e.g., a German engineering company for the construction of an off-shore rig) partly or completely in TRCs.

(2b) Next user(s) – The German engineering firm decides, in turn, to purchase speciality steel from a Korean steel mill partly or completely in TRCs. The Korean mill then uses the TRCs to pay a mining company in Australia and so on.

(2c) End user – Each TRC remains in circulation for as long as its various users continue to use it. This could be for just one transaction or an infinite number of transactions, without any particular date of expiration. The process comes to an end when a particular user decides to cash in the TRCs, thereby becoming the End User.

(3) Demurrage

Throughout the circulation life of each TRC, from its creation to its final cash-in, a demurrage fee of 3.5% to 4% a year is in effect. Demurrage is a time-related charge on money. The demurrage fee acts in a similar manner to a linear parking fee, with the charge increasing in proportion to the time the car is occupying a parking spot. Financially, it corresponds to a negative interest rate. Whoever is holding the TRC is, therefore, charged the demurrage fee in proportion to the time they hold on to it. With a demurrage charge of 3.5% to 4%, the actual cost of holding it for a few days or even a few months is still low compared to today's international currency transaction costs. Because the TRC exists only in electronic form, it is easy to know exactly how much time has elapsed between the moment a user receives TRCs and the moment they are transferred to others.

The demurrage charge serves two key functions:

- *TRC circulation incentive.* The demurrage charge is an incentive to keep the TRCs in circulation and ensure they are being used as an exchange mechanism rather than a savings instrument.

- *TRC operational cost coverage.* The demurrage charges are calculated to cover the costs of operating the entire TRC system: storage costs of the basket, administrative overhead, and transaction costs in the futures markets, to name a few.

The demurrage fees for a particular TRC transaction may be calculated by the following formula:

(TRC Operation Costs/time unit) x *(TRC holding period)* x *(TRCs on account)* = *Demurrage Charge*

Let us assume the TRC operation costs are calculated at 3.65% per year, or 0.01% per day. If the German engineering firm (2a in figure 7.5) received all 500,000 TRCs from the oil producer and kept them on account for a period of 10 days before paying the Korean steel mill (2b), the demurrage charge would be calculated as follows:

0.01% per day x *10 days* x *500,000 TRCs* = *500 TRCs*

(4) TRC cash-in

The existence of a TRC unit comes to an end when any user (designated the End User in our diagram) decides to cash it in, perhaps to pay its taxes and/or payroll and needing national currency to do so. A transaction fee is charged at the time of cash-in and proposed at 2% of the amount of TRCs cashed in. This serves two purposes:

- *TRC circulation incentive.* The transaction fee is an additional incentive to keep the TRCs in circulation rather than being cashed in. The 2% amount is based on the consideration that cashing in the TRCs is equivalent to paying demurrage for more than six months. TRCs probably will be used as payment before this time as most suppliers prefer being paid earlier rather than later.

- *Cash-in operational costs.* When the end user decides to cash in TRCs, the TRC Alliance sells the necessary volume of commodities from its basket to the commodity markets in return for conventional currency.

The End User returns the TRCs to the TRC Alliance (4a). They are converted either to national currency or a corresponding volume of TRC commodities (which is called 'taking delivery' in the commodity market) chosen by the End User, minus the transaction fee of 2%. The cash-in may take place directly with the TRC Alliance or through an intermediary bank, just like any foreign exchange transaction today (4b).

(5) Reference currency

Once the TRC mechanism is operational and the advantages of using an inflation-resistant international standard are known, there is nothing to prevent two entities (user X and user Z in the diagram) with no direct involvement in the TRC mechanism from denominating contracts in TRCs, even if the final settlement is in conventional currency. Here, the TRC functions purely as a trade reference currency, or a reliable international standard of value. This is how the gold standard functioned (contracts were denominated in gold whether or not the involved parties owned gold). The difference with the TRC is that it is backed by a dozen or more commodities and services which makes it a more stable reference than the gold standard.

Benefits of the TRC

Benefits for the global economic system

There are two main benefits for the world economy and for humanity as a whole:

- The TRC promotes long-term sustainability. As we argued in the section on 'short-termism' in Chapter V, today's financial practice is to focus on short-term profits. The demurrage function of the TRC makes long-term thinking profitable and, therefore, long-term sustainability more likely.

- The nature of the TRC basket counteracts the normal business cycle, thereby creating a more dependable economic environment.

Each of these benefits deserves further explanation. First let's look at the realignment of financial interests with long-term concerns. The demurrage feature of the TRC would provide a systematic financial motivation that realigns financial interests with long-term concerns. This is in direct contrast to the current discounted cash flow of conventional national currencies in which positive interest rates lead agents to emphasise the immediate future at the expense of the long-term. The same discounted cash flow with a demurrage-charged currency produces the exact opposite effect, reducing the conflict between stockholders' financial priorities and the long-term priorities of humanity as a whole.

Second, let's look at the TRC's role in business cycle stabilisation. The TRC counteracts fluctuations of the business cycle and thus improves the overall stability and predictability of the world's economic system. When the business cycle weakens, corporations typically have excess inventory and a need for credit. When these excess inventories take the form of raw materials included in the TRC basket, they could be sold to the TRC Alliance, which would place these inventories into storage. The corporations would be paid in TRCs, giving them immediate access to a means of payment, often necessary during such phases of a business cycle. The demurrage charge would encourage rapid payment of their suppliers, who have a similar incentive to pass on the TRCs to their own suppliers. The spread of this currency (with its built-in incentive to trade) would swiftly activate the economy at this point in the cycle.

In contrast, when the business cycle booms, both suppliers and corporations have an increased need for raw materials and demand for them goes up. The TRCs could be cashed in and used in the commodity markets. The amount of TRCs in circulation would decrease when the business cycle is at its maximum and counteract inflationary pressures. In summary, by providing monetary liquidity during phases when credit gets tight in the conventional system and contracting when business is booming, TRC-denominated exchanges would stabilise the overall business cycle.

Benefits for participating businesses

The TRC offers corporations the following advantages:

- It allows for the swift conversion of illiquid assets, such as inventories of excess raw materials into liquid working capital. This is a twofold advantage given that inventories are otherwise a cost item.
- It provides a robust international standard with a consistent value in real purchasing power for international contracts.

- It lowers the costs of doing business by reducing expensive currency hedging counter-measures, providing dependable, low-cost insurance against international currency uncertainties, and offering a more cost-effective exchange system than conventional corporate barter.

Benefits for financial services and the banking sector

The TRC would provide two main advantages to the banking system:

- It would standardise countertrade and make the countertrade mechanism bankable. Our banking system currently plays no role in the countertrade field which is growing at a rate of 15% per year – three times faster than trade facilitated by conventional currencies. Banks could provide services such as TRC account management as is currently done for any foreign exchange.
- The counter-cyclical impact of the TRC mechanism would stabilise the value of banking loan portfolios. The numerous banking-related crises often occur when borrowers cannot repay their loans and the collateral on which loans are based depreciates. These conditions are aggravated by the boom/bust cycle and currency fluctuations. Therefore, because the TRC mechanism would help stabilise economic cycles, the number and severity of crises in bank portfolios would also be reduced.

Differences from earlier proposals

The TRC is a commodity-basket currency. Well-known economists have put forward several proposals for commodity-basket currencies over the past century.[24] The main reason they have not been implemented is because they aimed to replace the conventional monetary system, thus jeopardising powerful vested interests. This is not the case with the TRC proposal. The win-win strategy of the TRC mechanism includes the financial sector. Everything in the current monetary system would remain in operation after the introduction of the TRC because it is designed to operate *in conjunction with* existing bank-debt currencies.

The political context for an international monetary treaty does not exist. The TRC avoids this difficulty by relying on private initiative. As we have already emphasised, from a legal or tax standpoint, the TRC functions within the official framework of countertrade and does not require any formal governmental agreements to be made operational.

Perhaps the most important difference between the TRC and all previous proposals is the introduction of demurrage. Demurrage provides a powerful incentive

---

24 See for example: Harmon (1959); Graham (1937) and (1944); Hart *et al.* (1964); Grondona (1975); Gondriaan (1932) and Jevons (1875).

for circulation, but also has a built-in mechanism to cover the storage costs of the basket. It thus resolves the biggest problem that previous commodity proposals faced: Who will pay for it all? We believe the TRC mechanism is a win-win approach for all participants in the global trading system, and can succeed where other proposals for monetary innovation have failed.

Conclusion

The five examples discussed in this chapter are just a small sample of the complementary systems that are possible; many others are already in existence. They include for instance: 487 operational systems providing non-medical elderly support at no cost to the government in Japan; a B2B system currently used by 65,000 Swiss businesses (that is one out of every four corporations in Switzerland) which has been in operation for the past seventy-five years and has been proven to contribute macro-economically to the legendary Swiss economic stability; and a Time Dollar system that proved successful in reducing teenage crime in Washington, D.C. and which the US Justice Department is now encouraging other American cities to adopt.

As explained at the beginning of this chapter, we are not elaborating on those useful and highly relevant systems here because they have already been described in detail elsewhere. They obviously could, and should, be part of an emergent monetary ecosystem.

The next chapter will complete our discussion of the range of systems that would be relevant in such a monetary ecosystem. Please remember (from Chapter VI) that bank-debt money acquires its value only because governments require it in payment of taxes. Therefore, the full potential of a monetary ecosystem will manifest itself only when governments and government bodies throw their weight behind the process.

Chapter VIII

Examples of Governmental Initiatives

"In a democracy dissent is an act of faith."
J. William Fulbright

This chapter focuses on the second half of the 'solutions menu', the ones where government at various levels could or should act as initiators. We will present four examples of such solutions. The appropriate level of government involvement will be specified in each case. It varies from a city, to a region, a country, and even an EU or worldwide scale. First a summary of these four last examples before we describe them in full:

6. *Torekes* is a city-based initiative to encourage volunteering while promoting green behaviour and social cohesion in a poor neighbourhood. It is currently running in the city of Ghent, Belgium.

7. *Biwa Kippu* is a proposal for the restoration and maintenance of Lake Biwa, the largest and oldest lake in Japan, without burdening the local government's budgets.

8. *Civics* is a proposal empowering a city or region to fund civic activities without burdening the local public budget. Such activities could provide the labour component for social, educational and/or ecological projects.

9. *ECOs* is a national or Europe-wide initiative that funds components of large-scale ecological project or climate change adaptation projects, that could be part of our near future.

6. Torekes: A City-Initiated System to Encourage Volunteering

Our sixth example is running in the city of Ghent in Belgium, having been started in 2010. Although a relatively wealthy town of 250,000 inhabitants, the neighbourhood called Rabot is statistically the poorest in Flanders. Half of its 8,000 inhabitants are immigrants living in low-income apartment towers called 'Torekes' (Flemish for 'Little Towers'). Its population density is among the highest in the country. More than twenty languages are spoken there, the most prevalent of which is Turkish.

The City of Ghent wanted to encourage ecological and health-promoting activities, beautify the neighbourhood and improve the overall quality of life in Rabot. They started with a survey asking local residents what was most desirable to them. The answer was access to a small plot of land to grow vegetables and flowers. The city made land available, including an unused factory lot, on which over a hundred $4m^2$ gardens were created. These little gardens have been made available for a yearly rent of 150 Torekes, payable only in Torekes.

Torekes are earned by engaging in a variety of activities in the community. The activities are organised by the local community centre, run by the city government in the neighbourhood and by several local NGOs. The activities started with the building of these small gardens themselves. They also included more modest efforts such as putting flowers on windowsills and helping to clean up a football field after a match. The list is open to local suggestions.

Figure 8.1: Photograph in the Spring of 2011 of the individual garden plots rented in Torekes.

In addition to being used to pay rent for the gardens, Torekes can also be used to buy from local shops specific goods which the city encourages, including low-energy light bulbs and seasonal vegetables. Torekes can also be used to buy tickets for public transport and for the cinema (where otherwise empty seats would have remained unused). Businesses can exchange the Torekes for euros at the community centre office. These simple arrangements with participating stores benefit the residents, the local economy and the environment.

Since its launch in November 2010, the system has been so successful that it even faced an excess of volunteers during the spring of 2011. At the request of the participants, Torekes were introduced as a paper currency (see Figure 8.2). During the first year, a total of 50,259 Torekes were earned for 526 different activities.[1] 494 users have officially registered, but the number of actual participants is larger than this because exchanges also can take place directly between the residents.

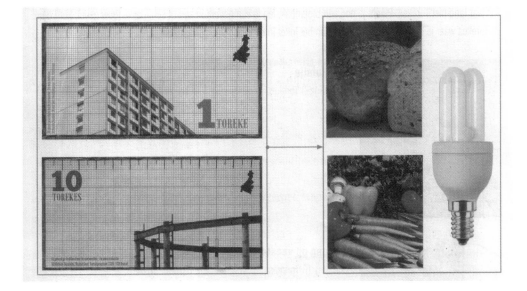

Figure 8.2: Torekes bills in denominations of 1 and 10 Torekes (left), with samples of products for which they can be exchanged at local shops (right).

First-year results:

Earning Torekes

The most popular activities were preparation of the little gardens themselves, which resulted in 21,424 Torekes being earned by 161 participants. Other activities included the creation of a little facade garden in front of some of their own residence towers

---

1   All data about the Torekes are taken from a private report about the first year of operation of the Torekes, by Wouter Van Thillo, dated November 2011. See also *www.torekes.be*.

(4,850 Torekes earned by 97 participants), the planting of flowers in common spaces (3,565 Torekes earned by 29 participants) and the installation of windowsill flower boxes facing the street (720 Torekes earned by 72 participants).

Spending Torekes

Of the 50,259 Torekes issued, 21,855 were spent on purchasing fresh vegetables and low-energy lamps at local shops. The rent of the Torekes gardens accounted for 8,400 Torekes and 2,640 were spent on movies and bus tickets. The balance is still in circulation, or saved for next year's garden rental.

Exchanging Torekes

The city reimburses businesses exchanging Torekes with Euros drawn from existing budgets allocated to the neighbourhood. The pilot experiment has had a broad social impact. Even at this early stage, the results obtained for the budget allocated in euros have been estimated at three times more than what was thought possible without the Torekes system. Because some of the operational costs are fixed, this could rise to a factor of 10 as the number of participants in the project increases.

7. 'Biwa Kippu': Funding a Regional Environmental Project

Lake Biwa in the Shiga Prefecture of Japan is one of the world's oldest lakes and is graced with a very diverse and unusual ecosystem. However, the lake has become prone to a number of environmental problems: poor maintenance of water source forests; water contamination from industry, agriculture and households; algae blooms; as well as invasion of exotic fish species that have overwhelmed the native fish population. The Shiga prefectural government has used both environmental regulations and subsidies as policy instruments to address these issues. However, the question was raised: can additional policy instruments be used to obtain greater environmental results without increasing the budgetary burden on public authorities. The Biwa Kippu has been designed to be just such an instrument.

Objectives

The primary objective of the Biwa Kippu system (literally 'Biwa Tickets') is to improve the Biwa Lake environment. Biwa Kippu, therefore, aims to promote environmental activities by residents and non-profit organisations in Shiga Prefecture without creating additional costs for the prefectural government, which is already too highly indebted. While job creation and community building are not the primary objectives, such benefits would be welcomed as positive side-effects.

Scope

The Biwa Kippu system is intended to focus on activities by residents and non-profit organisations in the Shiga Prefecture, rather than on businesses. It could be expandable so that it could deal with environmental issues relating to the whole river basin.

The Biwa Kippu System

The intention is that the prefectural government should issue a new ordinance requiring resident households to contribute a certain amount of 'Biwa Kippu' environmental activities each year, for example 10 Biwas per family. One Biwa would roughly correspond to one hour of environmental service activities.

This would be an obligation for every family, but obviously with appropriate exceptions for special circumstances such as people with handicaps or other valid excuses. Biwa Kippu would either be issued by the Prefecture itself or by an appropriate entity such as the Lake Biwa Environmental Research Institute in exchange for undertaking specific, measurable, environmental activities. The Prefecture would determine the scope of these activities each year. Residents or non-profit organisations carrying out these activities would receive Biwa Kippu. The prefectural government would not accept payments in Yen to replace the contributions in Biwa Kippu, nor would it set any exchange rate between Biwa Kippu and Yen. However, residents would be able to exchange Biwa Kippu among themselves on a free local (eBay-type) electronic market.

By balancing the quantity of contributions and the opportunities for earning Biwas, an 'ecological economy' would be activated at whatever scale is deemed appropriate for the Prefecture, and democratically accepted by the population.

Step-by-step approach

The prefectural government would launch the Biwa Kippu system using the following eleven steps:

Planning for the Biwa Kippu Intervention:

1. Implement a feasibility study to identify the major environmental problems in Shiga prefecture and prioritise these problems in terms of ecological impact, scalability, measurability and ease of implementation.
2. List the measurable environmental activities needed to solve the problems prioritised in the previous step and determine the value in Biwa for each of these activities. For instance, if it takes one hour on average to catch an exotic fish, one could estimate that one Biwa would be the value of that

type of fish's head. Determine the number of Biwa provided to the non-profit organisations performing the quality control and payment function.

3. Choose the activities and geographical areas where a pilot scheme for the first year would best be run.

4. Identify all relevant stakeholders, including existing or nascent citizen groups and non-profit organisations that could be mobilised to support such activities, as well as the relevant governmental administrative departments and research centres.

5. Make the necessary agreements with the mobile phone providers to electronically issue, exchange and collect Biwas.

6. Issue an ordinance to introduce Biwa Kippu.

Implementing Biwa Kippu:

7. Decide the amount of Biwa Kippu required as contribution by each family for the first year (e.g. 10 Biwas in the first year, corresponding to roughly one full day of activity) as well as the number of Biwas that could be obtained for each environmental activity.

8. Recruit non-profit organisations as intermediate agencies to administer Biwa for each environmental activity. These non-profit organisations would also be paid in Biwa for their verification and implementation activities.

9. Launch a communication campaign to explain how residents participating in the environmental activities decided in step 2 can obtain Biwa. Have the prefectural government and local non-profit organisations co-organise two weekends of environmental activities where participants could earn their 10 Biwas in a communal way.

10. Issue Biwas using an online system via mobile phones and collect the Biwa contributions through the existing prefectural online taxation system. Feedback to the participants about progress on each activity could be provided in real time by using the electronic Biwa payment system as an accounting and communication tool.

11. After one year of pilot testing, evaluate the results and problems; fine-tune the system, and gradually increase over time the range of environmental activities and geographical reach.

Advantages of a Biwa Kippu System

For the Shiga prefectural government the advantages of this Biwa Kippu initiative are that it would:

• allow a variety of environmental activities to take place without requiring additional Yen budgets.

- measure environmental activities more precisely than is currently the case: the number of Biwa issued is a direct measure of these activities.
- effectively mobilise all households in the Shiga Prefecture to take an interest, and participate, in environmental activities.

For environmental non-profit organisations, the advantages would be:

- the sale of Biwas earned by individuals or non-profit organisations to people who have not earned enough of them through their own environmental activities would provide an income source.
- the emergence of more non-profit organisations with a focus on environmental issues in Shiga Prefecture.

The advantages for the residents of the Shiga Prefecture would include:

- living in a better-quality environment.
- receiving real time online feedback about environmental improvements obtained through the Biwa Kippu system. This has the potential to motivate them to personally put in more work towards these improvements.
- the creation of additional and specialised non-profit organisations (encouraged by the Biwa Kippu system), which would provide a range of activities that can be tailored to their personal interests or preferences.

8. Civics: Funding Social, Cultural or Civic Activities

Suppose a city, region or a country would like to become a model of social capital or a beacon for culture and the arts.

The conventional approach

This governmental entity would start by preparing an implementation plan, which would conventionally include all labour costs at market rates. Suppose this civic entity were a city of 100,000 households politically agreeing to encourage social capital and the arts at a cost for required annual subsidies of €1,000 per household.

Figure 8.3: Conventional approach to the funding of a social project. The development of the cooperative local economy normally is supported via subsidies, which are paid by taxes, and via the non-profits whose cash is obtained through tax deductions. This graph will be most useful when compared later with Figure 8.4 below.

Conventional ways of raising funds include raising taxes or incurring debt. Although the latter involves the same amount of tax revenues over time, plus interest, both avenues directly affect city budgets. Non-profits would typically also be involved in such projects and their funding through tax-deductible donations indirectly reduce governmental income.

Another approach: Civics

Another way to fund the labour components in such a project and to strengthen a cooperative local economy in the process is through Civics. The city starts by requiring its residents to make an annual *'Civics' contribution*. A Civic is an electronic unit issued by the city that is earned by residents through activities that contribute to the city's publicly agreed upon aim. The unit of account could be one hour of time, valued at the same rate for everybody. For example, if the aim of a city is to be more green, the activities could include growing food on terraces or rooftops, or taking responsibility for plants and trees in the neighbourhood and parks, or training people in city-based horticulture, and so on. Non-profits would play a key role in the Civics economy by organising the associated activities and verifying the quality and quantity of the work performed. They would actually play in the cooperative economy exactly the same role that businesses play in the competitive economy – the role of initiating projects, organising activities, coordinating and motivating people. A specially-created new type of non-profit would be in charge of auditing all the non-profits involved in this economy to ensure transparency and trust in the system. It would play the role that auditing firms play in the competitive economy, and their reports would be published on the city's website. The benefit to non-profits would a powerful new way to reach their objectives, a big increase in their volunteer base, as well as the opportunity to pay their staff partially in Civics.

Objective of the Civics system

The first objective of the Civics system is to fund the labour component of desirable civic projects. Because manpower is often the largest component of a budget, a Civics system makes the funding of otherwise unaffordable projects possible. With Civics, a city can accomplish big goals, even in times of economic downturn. It is in bad economic times that labour is automatically more available and eager to find an alternative income stream via Civics. With conventional jobs currently in short supply, this would have a beneficial effect on individuals and the community.

A Civics system also gives opportunities to build a stronger sense of community. Modern societies suffer high levels of isolation and fractured social networks and family systems. Shared work in a local community is an effective way to counteract this loss of social capital while generating economic and environmental resilience.

The Civics system could operate at any scale: local, city, region, or even across a country as a whole. Engagement by the population in the decision-making process about which projects get implemented is essential for success. Various processes exist to accomplish this and modern civil society may still have something to learn from forms of governance in traditional communities. For instance, the Balinese banjar system has been working for over twelve centuries and has proven adaptable to modern environments.[2] New systems like sociocracy[3] and holacracy[4] also look promising.

Operation of the Civics system

The government would issue an ordinance requiring residents to contribute a certain number of Civic tokens each year. As a rule of thumb, one Civic is equivalent to one hour of service in civic activities. Every household would have this obligation, with appropriate exemptions for people with handicaps, people caring for young children or elderly parents or other reasons. Civics would be issued by the city and used to reward specific measurable civic activities. Payments could be in the form of paper tokens as in the case of Torekes, or of electronic units tracked via mobile phone as in

---

2   See Bernard Lietaer, 'A World in Balance', *Reflections (Journal of the Society for Organizational Learning – SoL)*, vol. 4, no. 4 (2003) and Bernard Lietaer and Stephen De Meulenaere, 'Sustaining Cultural Vitality in a Globalizing World: the Balinese Example', *International Journal for Social Economics*, vol. 30, issue 9 (2003), pp.967-984.

3   See *http://en.wikipedia.org/wiki/Sociocracy*.

4   See *www.holacracy.org*.

Doraland. The governmental entity would accept only Civics as a form of payment for this obligation and would not set a fixed exchange rate between the Civic and the national currency. Residents could exchange Civics for national currency on free-market principles. A local online market (like eBay could be set up to facilitate such exchanges and assure transparency and trust.

From an economic theory perspective, the Civics approach amounts to a Keynesian stimulus by creating additional demand for services at the city scale. The main difference is that the process is much more bottom-up than the usual central government Keynesian stimulus. Even more importantly: it doesn't generate any additional debt for anybody. Furthermore, the process can be targeted to specific population segments, and should be countercyclically fine-tuned to local conditions. For instance, specific programmes paid in Civics can be implemented for young people when their unemployment level is abnormally high (as is the case now in Spain, Greece, Ireland, etc.). The contributions requested in Civics should be highest during an economic downturn, and scaled back to zero when close to full employment has been restored. The timing can also be fine-tuned: Civics contributions could be requested on a quarterly basis instead of an annual one, thereby matching more closely real-life conditions. Please remember also that when more Civics contributions are demanded, their value in euros would also increase in the local eBay type market, thereby providing a higher income in euros to the most active participants.

In order to tailor the activities to different sub-populations, the process of choosing Civics-earning activities should be done democratically and in a decentralised fashion, even down to the neighbourhood level. Citizens themselves should also be able to propose Civics-earning activities to the city.

Fairness of the Civics system

In Chapter VI, we saw that governments can make a fiat currency valuable by requiring taxes to be paid in that currency. Governments have always required involvement on the part of their citizens. For example, paying taxes is universal and military service is very common. Whether or not these are fair depends mainly on the system's governance. Consultation and transparency can help create a Civics system that is welcomed by the population.

From a purely economic angle, if an annual tax of €1,000 can be replaced with 10 hours of civic activity per household, anyone earning less than €100 per hour should be interested in joining the system. Ideally, however, the Civic Economy's goals and activities would have the support of the residents, as something they would gladly volunteer for if they didn't have to earn a living. The Civics system has the added benefit of allowing people to earn an income from the activities; see Figure 8.4.

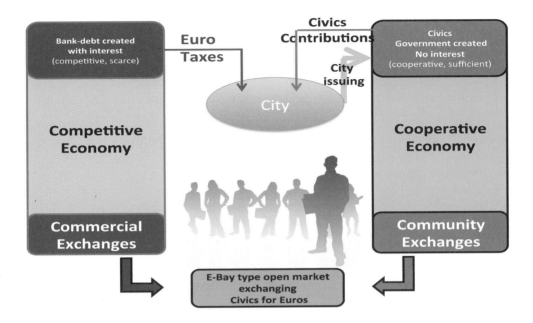

Figure 8.4: The government requires payment of taxes on the commercial activity, as well as a contribution payable only in Civics that the government itself issues. People who earn extra Civics can exchange them freely on a local online market.

Notice that there is no obligation to personally perform any of the tasks rewarded in Civics. There are two ways to avoid participating at all. The first would be opting out by paying an extra amount in euros as part of one's annual taxes. Based on our example, a logical amount would be the €1,000 per year estimated in the conventional process described at the beginning of our example. The second option for people not interested or without the time to personally perform the tasks, would be to purchase Civics via the online market openly and transparently. People having earned more Civics than they needed for their annual contribution could sell them on that market. The buyer of the Civics could make the purchase in conventional money or as an exchange for any good or service acceptable to the other party.

The government's role would be to ensure that fake Civics were not in circulation and that exchanges are transparent and fair. The government would not fix the value of the Civic in terms of national currency. If it wanted the value of the Civics to rise in terms of the national currency, the most effective way would be to require a higher contribution amount payable only in Civics. If it wanted the value to drop, the easiest way would be to reduce the quantities requested.

Advantages of the Civics System

For the governmental entity involved, the Civics system would:

- Generate an abundance of civic activities with minimal financial cost.
- Measure and track civic activities more precisely than is done currently, and thus encourage and improve this very important aspect of civil society.
- Effectively mobilise widespread participation in civic activities.

For non-profit organisations the advantages would be:

- Non-profits in this cooperative economy would play the same role as businesses do in the competitive economy: motivating and organising people in their respective domains.
- Non-profits would gain an income stream in conventional currency from the sale of excess Civics to those preferring to purchase rather than earn them.
- More people volunteer and volunteer-turnover is reduced when a complementary currency is used as reward.[5] This is the case even when there is no obligation to earn that currency.
- Non-profit organisations now tend to be in stiff competition with one another for operating funds, particularly those with similar aims that depend on the same type of donors. Such competition can become an obstacle to cooperatively attaining their goals. The Civics system would essentially give non-profits their own valuable currency. Their very activities would earn them Civics. There would still be healthy competition over how to attain the best results, but less rivalry for conventional money.

For citizens, the advantages would include:

- Residents could enjoy a flourishing community and a better quality of life.
- Residents with time and/or interest in civic activities could earn additional income from others needing Civics or preferring to purchase them.

Some legal issues

The first question usually raised is whether such a system is legal. Article 104 of the Maastricht treaty and article 128 of the Lisbon treaty specifies "The European Central Bank shall have the exclusive right to authorise the issue of euro banknotes within the Union. The European Central Bank and the national central banks may issue such notes. The banknotes issued by the European Central Bank and the national central banks shall be the only such notes to have the status of legal tender within the Union."

---

5 Robert Wood Johnson Foundation, *Service Credit Banking Project Site Summaries* (1990).

When describing the Civic system, the words 'money', 'currency' or 'legal tender' were never needed or used. The EU treaty refers to 'euro banknotes' and 'legal tender'. The Civic does not need the status of 'legal tender' in order to function. It is more cost-effective for the Civic to exist only in electronic form with a mobile phone system as the platform rather than be issued as notes. We will use the word 'contributions' when referring to Civics. and reserve the label 'taxes' for levies that can only be paid in euros.

Some countries, such as the Netherlands, have already defined a special legal status for what is called 'civil service'. Even more familiar is the concept of a 'ticket' that is required to participate in a particular event. The Civics can be seen as tickets needed to live in a particular city. If legal difficulties were to arise, a full consideration of the overall benefits of the Civics system could lead to a change in some laws. What one law created, another law can undo.

9. ECOs: Declaring War on Climate Change

Niall Ferguson's study of 'The Cash Nexus' has shown that all major innovations in the domain of government finance over the past three centuries were triggered by wars. Armed conflict seems to trigger innovations and technologies that otherwise might never come to light. The scale of destruction caused by the most-likely climate change scenarios is worse than any war ever fought on this planet and is one of our main motivations for publishing this report now. (Please refer back to Figure 1.1 and Appendix A as evidence for this statement.) Because the devastation will unfold over decades, and reducing its likelihood will require collective action by humanity as a whole, this 'war' may also be more difficult to wage than any previous one. It may not have to be so hard if governments require ECOs to win a war against climate change.

While the ECO shares many similarities with the Civic previously described, it differs from it in the following ways:

- The Civic works best on a decentralised basis (e.g. cities and neighbourhoods) whereas the ECO must be implemented on a much larger scale such as on a national or a EU-wide scale. It would best work on a global scale.
- The Civic mobilises manpower for a variety of civil activities chosen by the population itself. The ECO focuses exclusively on mobilising material resources that contribute to the reduction of climate change.
- The Civic applies to households and citizens; the ECO applies only to medium and large corporations with for example, more than $1 million sales per year.
- The Civic is on the fringe of what is currently legal; the ECO would definitely require new legislation.

- The Civic could be started on a small local scale and would thus be easy to implement; the ECO would have to start on a larger scale and might initially encounter resistance from corporate lobbies. It would therefore be a greater challenge to implement it.

In other ways, the ECO system is conceptually similar to the Civic, as illustrated in Figure 8.4. It would start with a governmental authority such as a national government, requiring an annual contribution of ECOs proportional to the total sales volume of each individual corporation. For instance, all corporations would have to contribute 1 ECO for every $1 million of global sales to the government of the country where their headquarters were located.

The ECOs would be created by governments electronically and bear no interest. Corporations would earn ECOs by providing quantitatively verifiable evidence of investment and activities reducing the risk of climate change. There would be a clear description of how many ECOs a business would earn for each type of activity. An independently verifiable audit trail would be required before any ECO payment could be obtained. Qualifying activities could include: reductions in carbon emissions (e.g., 1 ECO for each 1000 tons of verified carbon reductions), investments in natural carbon sinks (e.g. 1 ECO for each 1000 tons of carbon sequestration in new, sustainably managed forests) or in other sequestration technologies.

Corporations unable to earn ECOs would need to obtain them by buying them using conventional money from corporations earning more than their requirement. A specialised online market would be set up, as in the case of the Civic.

Wide consensus exists in both the scientific and the business world that the development of technologies to switch to a post-carbon world is possible but will require strong governmental leadership. Because many governments will experience a budget squeeze over the next decade, and because government subsidies are the usual way to fund environment conservation and protection measures, many corporations will be left passively waiting for funding to become available before deciding to tackle these issues on their own. The ECO changes this dynamic. In order to wage a war against climate change, governments could require contributions payable only in ECOs, thus giving value to the ECO. As discussed in Chapter V, any fiat currency (including bank-debt money) becomes valuable when a government requires it in payment of fees and taxes. The ECO would also spur serious innovations to reduce climate change.

Such an approach will undoubtedly be unpopular in many business circles. But let's see it in the context of what took place in President Roosevelt's office on 27 December, 1941, when he signed his executive order 9001 stating: "The Office of

Production Management will bring about the conversion of manufacturing industries to war production, including the surveying of the war potential of industries, plant by plant; the spreading of war orders; the conversion of facilities; the assurance of efficient and speedy production..."[6] The only argument given was that the United States had been at war since 7 December, and until that war was over, things would run differently. This was the only justification available and the only one needed.

If we want to reverse humanity's collective suicidal rush towards irreversible climate change, governments may have to declare war on it. From this perspective, would not corporate ECO contributions be a rather modest change, compared to what Roosevelt was ordering?

* * *

We can now pull together all the strings of the logical key elements of this Report, to check their overall coherence.

Pulling all the strings together

The central thesis of this report is that systemic financial meltdowns are pervasive because of a significant structural flaw in our monetary system (Chapters II and III). To systemically improve the resilience of our economies and the health of our societies, we must shift our monetary paradigm from a monoculture of debt-based, interest-driven money to a *monetary ecosystem* (Chapter IV). We also identified five negative effects of the prevailing monetary monoculture on sustainability (Chapter V). Our monetary monoculture needs to make room for sufficient diversity in both the types of exchange media and in the types of agents creating and managing them. Within this framework, we can map how the innovations described in Chapters VII and VIII could correct and balance out the overall economy.

We will regroup these effects in the same sequence used to identify the five problematic influences in Chapter V.

1. Pro-cyclical money creation process and flow: 'It never rains, but it pours'

Both the C3 and the TRC, if implemented on a sufficient scale, would have a counter-cyclical effect compensating for the pro-cyclical effect of the conventional system. There is quantitative proof that such built-in countercyclical behaviour works, and that the availability of a Business-to-Business (B2B) complementary currency spontaneously tends to stabilise the business cycle and the overall economy. A detailed analysis of the WIR system, a B2B system in use for seventy-five years in

---

6   See *www.presidency.ucsb.edu ~ bit.ly/TPlink48*

Switzerland, provides the evidence for this claim[7] and allows us to conjecture that the same result would occur with the C3 and the TRC. Both these systems are business initiatives, and neither requires any new legislation or permission. They are also voluntary, with substantial advantages for participating businesses, even without any interest in sustainability. Therefore, the ball is completely in the court of the business community.

It would also be possible for governments to stimulate the economy deliberately in a counter-cyclical way with Biwa, Civics and ECOs. When a country or city experiences recession in the bank-debt money economy, and unemployment is high – as is the case today in Europe or the USA – the government at the appropriate level increases the quantities of Biwa, Civics or ECOs that it requires from citizens or businesses. If and when an inflationary boom occurs, governments can correspondingly reduce the requirement for government-issued currency.

2. Short-term thinking: Why we do not take the longer-term future into account

The precise purpose for the design of the TRC is to correct corporate short-term thinking. In a different domain, the Wellness Token prioritises preventive care and encourages citizens to acquire long-term healthy habits.

3. Compulsory growth pressure: On debts and compound interest

None of the nine systems proposed has an interest mechanism built into it. Therefore, compulsory growth is not a part of these motivation systems.

4. Unrelenting wealth concentration: The never-ending story of the poor versus the super-rich

Poverty is caused as much by lack of appropriate savings tools as by lack of income. A widely held prejudice that the poor do not have the desire or capacity to save is false; it turns out that the demand for secure and convenient saving services is often stronger among the poor than the demand for credit services.[8] This has been confirmed numerous times by empirical evidence, particularly from studies in the field of micro-finance.[9] Natural Savings provides a better savings instrument than any savings account, and it is able to deal with very small sums.

---

7   James Stodder (2009) and (2000).

8   See, e.g. Daryl Collins *et al.* (2009).

9   Beatriz Armendariz de Aghion and Jonathan Morduch, 'Microfinance: Where Do We Stand?', in Goodhart (2004), pp.135-148; and Graham A. N. Wright, 'A Critical Review of Savings Services in Africa and Elsewhere', working paper, (1999), 35 pages.

5. Devaluation of social capital: Why competition tends to overwhelm cooperative behaviour

Systems like Doraland, Wellness Tokens, Natural Savings, Torekes, Biwa Kippu, and Civics provide environments for people who otherwise would never meet to work together on projects that develop their gifts and the health and strength of their community. If people are given a powerful voice on which projects are chosen, these systems can rebuild and strengthen social capital over time.

* * *

Another way to understand what an economic ecosystem would look like is to imagine what would currently be different if some of the solutions we are proposing had been well established before the 2007-2008 crisis. The C3 system would have reduced the level of unemployment resulting from the crisis. Civics would have empowered municipal governments to address their social and environmental challenges even with shrinking bank-debt money budgets. Together they would have provided an effective choice of tools to generate healthy local and regional economies.

Five years after the start of the crisis, there is much that local communities can do to dampen its effects and to address austerity measures. The Doraland Foundation, city-generated Torekes and Civics systems all demonstrate ways to mobilise local human resources and make a significant difference without burdening city finances. In the event of a euro or dollar crisis, the role of the TRC in preserving a global web of vital trade would become obvious. It could, for instance, rescue us from the biggest and broadest global trade disruption in human history if a dollar crisis were to occur.

All nine innovative systems could also interact with the thousands of local and social currency experiments already under way around the world. The pioneers who started this movement should be recognised and honoured. They have started at grassroots level a massive education and learning process about monetary literacy that could become essential for informed decision-making in the 21st century.

Chapter IX

Beyond the Limits to Growth?

We should be cutting lies instead of trees.
– Jerry Martien, *Salvage This*[1]

Exactly forty years ago, the first Report for the Club of Rome, *The Limits to Growth,* was published.[2] It provided the first scientific demonstration that by remaining on our current development path, critical limits in raw materials, pollution and food production would be experienced during the first two decades of the 21st century.

The Limits to Growth has been the launch pad for a growing awareness of how the biosphere constrains the economy as an open system. Using a methodology drawn from systems dynamics, novel at that time, computer simulations of hundreds of interacting variables were produced to support its claims and recommendations. *The Limits to Growth* was highly praised for legitimising a new paradigm, Ecological Economics. It also attracted a lot of criticism, especially from believers in the Traditional Economics paradigm, who rejected it as a doomsday scenario.

---

1 Quoted by Paul Hawken (2007), p.27.

2 Meadows *et al.* (1972).

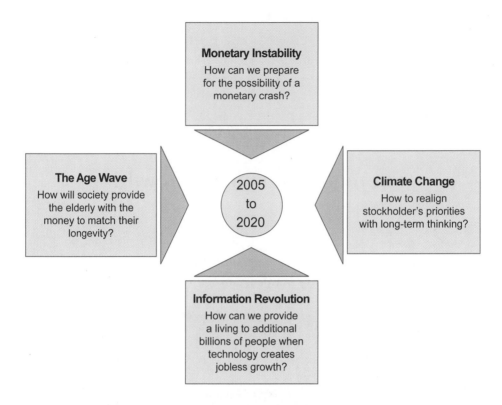

Figure 9.1: Convergence of four megatrends, each with a 'money question' that cannot be resolved within the existing monetary paradigm.

Thirteen years ago, one of the authors of the present Report published *The Future of Money.*[3] The core argument was that four megatrends – the information revolution, climate change, monetary instability and an ageing population would converge to create unprecedented challenges before 2020 (see Figure 9.1).

Each megatrend was summed up in a money question, as follows:

- How can society provide the elderly with the money to match their longevity?

- How can we provide jobs for billions of people when technologies create jobless growth?

- How can we realign corporate financial interests with the longer-term thinking that society needs?

- How can we prepare for a global financial crash?

---

3   The German edition was published thirteen years ago, the English edition two years later. Bernard Lietaer, *Das Geld der Zukunft: Über die destruktive Wirkung des existierenden Geldsystems und die Entwicklung von Komplementärwährungen* (1999) and *The Future of Money: Creating New Wealth, Work, and a Wiser World* (2001).

Addressing these issues, so *The Future of Money* argued, would force a redesign of the monetary system before 2020, because a monopoly of a single currency created by bank debt could not possibly allow citizens, businesses and governments to develop workable solutions. Only by opening up the possibility of a plurality of exchange means could we overcome the obstacles that we are facing in the 21st century.

In a sense, *The Future of Money* focused on the need to re-think money in order to answer the questions formulated by *The Limits to Growth*. Essentially this was because the conventional principle of creating money through interest-bearing bank credit has a *systemic growth obligation* built into it – not even necessarily out of ideological choice (although this can also be present as an additional factor), but out of sheer mechanical necessity. Therefore, seeking to counteract all the deleterious effects of economic growth without questioning the omnipresent monetary tool that drives this growth, could not work. But getting to the solution requires us to find a way to see some way around the monetary blind spot that we identified in Chapter II.

An economy based on several currency systems running in parallel would actually not be new. In reality, it would be the recovery of an ancient idea. In Dynastic Egypt and the Central Middle Ages in Western Europe – to name two examples – such an idea was considered totally obvious. As Jean Houston put it elegantly: "The icons of old are the codings of tomorrow. And tomorrow holds the promise of recovery of forgotten wisdom."[4]

Still, the assimilation into common sense today of such an old idea requires that it be heard, understood, accepted and internalised. This is a very ambitious goal, as some learning will be needed on almost everyone's part.

For today's elites, particularly financial elites, revisiting the classic works of Arnold Toynbee[5] or more recently the writing of Jared Diamond,[6] might be useful. Toynbee is the economic historian who demonstrated that the collapse of 21 different civilisations could be attributed to just two causes: too much concentration of wealth and an elite that, confronted with changing circumstances, remains unwilling to shift its priorities until it is too late. Diamond focuses on environmental degradation as a proximate cause for the collapse of civilisations. We are currently pushing the limits on all three causes, at the same time!

Being part of an elite is no real protection in a collapsing civilisation. Is the advent of a monetary ecology, even if it implies some losses compared to the *status quo*, not a suitable terrain for compromise?

---

4   Jean Houston, *Life Force: The Psychohistorical Recovery of the Self* (1993), p.13.

5   Toynbee (1939). For a mercifully abridged version, see Toynbee (1960).

6   Jared Diamond (2005).

Box 9.1 – A Terrain for Compromise?

Is there a terrain of compromise that might also be acceptable to the protagonists of the financial system? Anyone enjoying the privilege of a monopoly will tend to fight to retain it. Legitimising non-financial incentive systems will therefore not be an easy path for the financial system, and even harder to accept for some central banks. However, in contrast to the Chicago Plan, what is proposed here keeps the core of the banking system's business model intact. Interest in a Chicago Plan reincarnated under the name of 'Modern Money Theory' (MMT) is now spreading, even at the grassroots level. Just one example: a public conference entitled 'the MMT Summit' was held in Rimini, Italy, on 24-26 February 2012. It attracted several thousand participants![7]

When assessed in terms of its societal consequences, maintaining the monetary *status quo* and the Official Paradigm seems increasingly irresponsible, perhaps untenably so. European countries have been financially cornered into dismantling social safety nets that took generations to build, and into retracting the promises made to people who contributed throughout their entire working lives to a pension and health care system. Governments will also be obliged to privatise cultural heirlooms that have, in many cases, been public property for centuries or even millennia. Most regrettably, universal austerity will render them totally unable to exert the leadership required for the kinds of investment needed to avoid runaway climate change.

The Fiat Currency Paradigm makes it clear that our money system is an 18th century legacy information system, rendered quite convoluted and sclerotic by 300 hundred years of use and abuse. How will we explain to our children and grandchildren that thanks to the technological means available in a new Information Age, we were able to update all our information systems except our monetary system? Who will take responsibility for telling them that we sacrificed the planetary biosphere in order to keep our monetary system operational for one more decade?

Thomas Friedman's op-ed piece from the *New York Times*, previously mentioned in Chapter VI, concludes: "Capitalism and free markets are the best engines for generating growth and relieving poverty – provided they are balanced with meaningful transparency, regulation and oversight. We lost that balance in the last decade. If we don't get it back – and there is now a tidal wave of money resisting that – we will have another crisis. And, if that happens, the cry for justice could turn ugly. Free advice to the financial services industry: Stick to being bulls. Stop being pigs." [8]

For the rest of us, a bit more learning may also be the best first step for the immediate future.

- For anybody trained in economics, the required mental switch is to look at the paradigm used in the teachings they have received, and compare it with the approach used in this Report. The Ecological Economics paradigm – in contrast with the Traditional Economics still widely taught in universities – allows to re-think the role of money within an open-system economy

---

7   See a 2-minute video about the atmosphere at the summit: *bit.ly/TPlink49*. An analysis of the intellectual content is available at *http://dandelionsalad.wordpress.com ~ bit.ly/TPlink50*

8   Thomas Friedman, 'Did you hear the one about the bankers?' *op. cit.*

that uses up natural and human resources, throws off waste, and needs to feed and protect a growing and ageing population.[9] Endless growth is impossible without terminal harm to natural, social and, eventually, even narrowly defined economic capital. However, "sustainable abundance"[10] is also available, and quite different. It requires devising a differentiated monetary system in which specific means of exchange target urgently required activities. It is not the first time in history that worldview changes have been needed in order to forestall catastrophe. Sometimes they happen in time; but more often they do not, as Jared Diamond has shown. In the present case, we have no excuse for ignorance. The evidence, the concepts, the analytical tools and pilot experiments are all openly available.

- For the scientific community, there are two domains where quality data exists to test our core theoretical framework empirically. These two domains are the electrical distribution networks and the banking system. We can measure the real-life resilience of a sufficiently diverse and interconnected network flow system versus that of one in which efficiency is the only criterion. The data, however, remain in the hands of organisations that consider them to be confidential. People with access to the data would be performing an enlightened and immensely beneficial task were they to make them publicly available, if necessary in a manner which protects the anonymity of the individual institutions involved. Or they could use these data to test for themselves the theory whose technical and mathematical content are available in Appendix D.

- For the population at large, perhaps the most important learning needed is to grasp non-linearity, and specifically to integrate the difference between linear and exponential growth. Although this does not appear particularly difficult to achieve at first sight, this challenge should not be underestimated. When a scientist such as Lovelock admits "I find to my personal horror that I have not been immune to naïveté about exponential functions", it would appear that our brains have difficulty in assimilating such concepts. We are now dealing with a world with increasingly non-linear challenges. There are thresholds or 'tipping points' beyond which catastrophic events become highly likely, something which climate scientists, and experts on debt are warning us about, validly, and with increasing urgency.

Exponential growth in population, greenhouse gas emissions or cumulated deficits is mathematically incompatible with sustainability, however the term is defined. However, there also exist 'good' non-linearities in the form of dampening mechanisms that can *slow down* growth when and where needed, and stabilise otherwise explosive

---

9   These two aspects – growing population, ageing population – are not necessarily mutually exclusive. The population of the planet as a whole is still growing quite strongly, whereas in the so-called "developed" world the "age wave" is imminent and, in fact, already starting to come in.

10 See Lietaer (2001) pp.17-30.

dynamics. This is what logarithmic or self-slowing growth makes possible. Judicious steering of our current economy requires a subtle combination of positive and negative feedback mechanisms. A monetary ecology is one of the centrepieces of such a combination. Some of the complementary motivation systems described in Chapters VII and VIII offer counter-cyclical stabilisation. Combining several of them may create an economy in which a *global reduction* in environmentally and socially harmful activities is matched with a *local build-up* of ecologically and socially beneficial ones. Sustainable abundance is not generalised poverty – on the contrary, it is generalised prosperity on the basis of a plurality of means of exchange allowing people to gain more awareness and control over their social lives, and over their interactions with the rest of the biosphere.

Suggesting several domains of learning to many people sounds like an unusually ambitious aim. However Chapter VII showed that some of the necessary innovations are already working in practice. Citizens, NGOs, businesses and political decision-makers are already using the concept of a monetary ecology, simply by creating it. Fortunately for all of us, these courageous pioneers are following Sophocles' centuries-old advice: "One must learn by doing the thing; for though you think you know it, you have no certainty, until you try."

Recent monetary history demonstrates that those who officially manage the system are also concerned. The EU sovereign debt crisis and the associated euro crisis clearly have their roots in the functioning of the current monetary system. Faced with the threat of a eurozone breakdown, European governments are scrambling to combine bailouts, commitments to future bailouts and extreme austerity measures to 'save' the monetary system in its present form. *This is exactly what will not succeed* simply because the crisis is only the latest symptom of the same underlying structural flaw.

Whenever someone considers the possibility of a euro breakup, the only option that seems to be debated is a return to the old national currencies. One popular definition of insanity comes to mind: "doing the same thing over and over again, and expecting different results".

Not enough has been learned yet at the official level, while a 'blessed unrest' ripples through citizens and NGOs on the planet. Is humanity suicidal, as sociobiologist Edward O. Wilson claims in one chapter of his book *The Future of Life*?[11] We do not believe so. However, if the forces behind the current *status quo* believe it can continue to do 'business as usual' for one more round and continue to make money out of a failing system – they may well send *all of us* tumbling into the abyss of a collective demise.

---

11 Edward O. Wilson, *The Future of Life* (2002).

We need to collectively usher in a new age of monetary and societal experimentation, and this requires us to accept new knowledge and experience in areas where it was previously unheard-of. 'Thinking outside the box' of conventional monetary arrangements may have to become the new common sense – not out of a taste for 'newness' *per se,* for anarchy, or for new age ideology, but simply because our future welfare depends on it.

Ultimately, our plea for a monetary ecology is a call for a new mode of economic governance. The aim is to allow two types of economy to coexist peacefully: on the one hand, the mainstream economy will continue to use conventional money in the competitive economy and, on the other hand, the rebirth of a cooperative economy will see regions, cities, neighbourhoods, NGOs and grass-roots citizens' organisations develop the full potential of their projects without needing to depend on the supply of bank-debt currency.

Most crucially, we need to revisit our *monetary governance*. This is a highly unusual question in the current framework. Democratic governance is a weak spot for all monetary systems, be it the official one, or the ongoing complementary experimental systems. Due to our monetary 'blind spot', we are used to leaving governance of the monetary system to an opaque and highly centralised set of institutions. We can hardly envisage what the democratic management of a plurality of currencies might look like. This may be the most crucial unresolved organisational question we need to deal with, if we are serious about sustainability.

Friedrich Hayek (quoted in Chapter IV) showed remarkable vision when he concluded that, "What is now urgently required is not the construction of a new system, but the prompt removal of all the legal obstacles which have for two thousand years blocked the way for an evolution which is bound to throw up beneficial results which we cannot now foresee."[12]

Actually, many of the beneficial results of these complementary systems *can* now be foreseen. Each community, business group or geographical area can begin something at its own scale, if it feels so inspired. What matters is to be able to learn from each other's experiences. What works? And even more usefully: what failed and why? We need a learning movement that anyone can join. The relevant technologies for communicating this learning are also, for the first time, available on a planetary level.

On the website *www.money-sustainability.net* (formally a part of this Report) we invite public input on how to deal with the matters presented in this Report. The potential number of issues worthy of attention and debate is infinite. They can be as rich as life itself. Here are just four examples of topics well worth some attention:

---

12 See *http://mises.org ~ bit.ly/TPlink51* p.133-134.

- What initiatives or experiments can be started now to help the government and citizens of Greece deal with their country's economic collapse? Why could Greece not stay within the eurozone for its international transactions (tourism, shipping, exports and imports), while allowing its cities to start Civics systems to replace the vanishing governmental social support mechanisms? Would this not help reduce the Greek central government's budget deficit while giving a breath of hope to the millions affected by savage cuts in jobs and vital social programmes?

- How can we address horrendous youth unemployment,[13] in countries like Spain (45% official youth unemployment), Slovakia (33.6%), Lithuania (33.2%), Ireland (29.8%), Portugal (28.7%) and Italy (27.7%)? Why not implement C3 systems at the regional level? Wanting 'regional development' while using only the euro has been shown to be an economic oxymoron, a contradiction in terms.[14]

- Why not mobilise the European Investment Fund for launching C3 systems? Several billion euros are available through the JEREMIE program ('Joint European Resources for Micro to Medium-sized Enterprises'),[15] if a 2010 administrative decision to make these funds available only for SMEs starting brand-new activities backed by a formal business plan is reversed. How many SMEs in today's economic environment are able to start brand-new activities, when they are dying like flies from not getting paid on time for their existing sales? As a consequence, most of these JEREMIE funds will expire unused in 2015. How can such administrative blockages be lifted?

- Much of our approach to education still involves preparing children for an industrial world that no longer exists. Why not experiment with systems such as the Doraland that considers everyone a potential teacher and learner? How might learning multiply with mutual-learning approaches, in and out of school?[16] With an infinite number of domains requiring learning in a world of ever-accelerating change, should we not use all of our collective intelligence, well beyond the mechanisms and horizons encouraged by our out-of-date industrial-age structures?

We are facing the greatest challenges ever to be faced by humanity. We know that we must switch to a post-carbon economy, and swiftly, if we are to avoid disaster. We know that this is technologically possible, but that it can be implemented within the time available only with massive government support and funding – something

---

13 *http://ec.europa.eu ~ bit.ly/TPlink52*

14 Documentation about the arguments for a regional development strategy has been provided in: Kennedy & Lietaer *(*2004); Lietaer & Kennedy (2008); Lietaer & Kennedy (2010).

15 See *www.eif.org ~ bit.ly/TPlink53*. The data available as of January 2012 date back to the 2nd quarter of 2011.

16 Anne Querrien, *L'école mutuelle: Une pédagogie trop efficace?* (2005).

which reined-in budgets in conventional money will not allow for at least the next decade. At the same time, we face caring for a booming greying population that will no longer be contributing to the economic base, but will need to rely on social support programmes that are now under frontal attack. We face all this with shrinking economies, under brutal compulsion by an anonymous 'financial market' to reduce enormous public debts, bloated by the cost of the 2007-8 banking meltdown and its immediate economic consequences.

The stakes are unprecedentedly high. But the possibilities for creative solutions are also near at hand – solutions that do not further strain public budgets, that have already demonstrated their effectiveness in practice, that can turn populations from hopeless rage to fruitful engagement within their communities, and that can preserve corporate profits, but not at the expense of social and environmental health. We still have a fighting chance to give birth to a sustainable world that works for everyone...

Is this scenario pie-in-the-sky? Are we offering just one more miraculous panacea? We do not think so. We have never claimed that a monetary ecosystem would be *sufficient* to address the challenges of today. We hope to have shown, however, that rethinking our money system is a *necessary* part of any solution. This is the core message of this Report.

Our sincere hope is that as the world of the old economy breaks down, the seeds of a new and more humane economy may be given a chance to emerge. "There is a rabbinical teaching that if the world is ending and the Messiah arrives, you first plant a tree; and then see if the story is true. Islam has a similar teaching that tells its adherents that if they have a palm cutting in their hand on Judgement Day, plant the cutting."[17]

---

17 Hawken (2007) p.4.

Appendices

The following appendices are available online at
www.money-sustainability.net and at *www.triarchypress.com/missinglink*

A: A Primer about Money

B: Climate Change

C: Mapping Paradigms

D: Complex Flow Networks

E: A Chinese Insight

F: Wealth Concentration

G: Kondratieff and the 'long wave'

Acknowledgements

Brussels, May 2012

This Report is the result of two waves of efforts. The first wave, from 2001 to 2004, involved an international working group of 15 experts. It resulted in a German-language publication in 2005.[18] The current Report is the product of a second wave of work from 2010 to 2012. It required an autopsy of the 2007-8 financial crash, and the lessons we should draw from it. It also made possible a number of theoretical updates from recent peer-reviewed publications.

This report has been substantially enriched with suggestions by academic colleagues from various backgrounds. It was not possible to reference all of them in footnotes, for which we apologise. The responsibility for any remaining errors and omissions rests with the co-authors.

Given the mixed linguistic background of the authors, the editing for this work has been laborious. We want to express our gratitude to a group of important women who made this publishable version possible. Among them, Jacqui Dunne has delivered much of the initial heavy language lifting. Gwendolyn Hallsmith contributed many substantial ideas for Chapters II and VII. Sherry Cox has contributed clarity to all chapters. Last but not least, Stephanie Taché managed to incorporate a feminine sensitivity to what would otherwise be a heavier Report. The illustrations were produced with help from Thibault d'Ursel. Finally, Andrew Carey and Alison Melvin from Triarchy Press helped publish this book in record time, without compromising on quality.

Our gratitude also to the thousands of pioneers who have already initiated monetary experiments on their own scale! What they are learning – by doing – is more important for humanity than they may realise themselves.

---

18 Stefan Brunnhuber and Harald Klimenta, *Wie wir wirtschaften werden: Szenarien und Gestaltungsmöglichkeiten für zukunftsfähige Finanzmärkte* (2005).

About the Authors

Bernard LIETAER has been active in money systems for 35 years in an unusual variety of functions. While at the Central Bank in Belgium he co-designed and implemented the convergence mechanism (ECU) to the single European currency system and served as President of Belgium's Electronic Payment System. He was General Manager and Currency Trader for the Gaia Hedge Funds, when *Business Week* identified him in 1990 as the world's top trader. He is currently Research Fellow at the University of California, Berkeley, and Visiting Professor at the Finance University in Moscow. He is the author of fifteen books relating to monetary and financial issues. *www.lietaer.com*

Christian ARNSPERGER received his PhD in economics from the Université Catholique de Louvain. He is a Senior Research Fellow with the Belgian National Science Foundation (F.R.S-FNRS) and a Professor in Economics at the Université Catholique de Louvain. He specialises in the epistemology of economics; the existential underpinnings of economic rationality; the link between economy, natural resources and the environment; the link between money and sustainability; and the transition to a green economy. He is the author of six books and numerous articles in academic journals. *www.eco-transitions.blogspot.com*

Sally GOERNER is the Director of Triangle Center for the Study of Complex Systems, President of the Integral Science Institute, and Economic Development Coordinator for the Greater Pittsboro Community Development Corporation. She has advanced degrees in engineering, systems physics (MS, PhD) and psychology (PhD/ABD), and is the author of 5 books, including *After the Clockwork Universe* and *The New Science of Sustainability*. She is one of the leaders of the international movement to integrate the findings of 'intricacy' research and apply them to human systems from economics to urban planning. *www.integralscienceinstitute.org/about_ISI.html*

Stefan BRUNNHUBER has two PhDs, one from Medical school (MA, MD, Dr. med. habil.) and studied socioeconomics (Dr. rer. Soc.) with Lord Ralf Dahrendorf . He is vice-chairman of the European Institute of Medicine and has multiple international Visiting Professorships. Former Visiting Fellow at the C. G. Jung Institute in Zurich, he is currently Medical Director and Chief Medical Officer at the hospital for integral psychiatry in Saxonia, Germany. He has written and delivered over 300 publications and presentations and is a member of the European Academy of Sciences and Arts and the Austrian Chapter of the Club of Rome. *www.stefan.brunnhuber.de*

About the Club of Rome

The **Club of Rome**, an affiliation of individual members and over thirty associations all over the world, is unique. The network of Club members and their institutions is extensive. It draws on all sectors and disciplines, including senior individuals from the banking and financial sectors, scientists, academics, technologists, social scientists and philosophers. Many are world renowned, Nobel recipients and exceptional personalities. The members of the Club of Rome work on a wide variety of issues relevant to the future of humankind.

The mission of the Club of Rome is to undertake forward-looking analysis and assessments for the betterment of humanity and to provide a range of options and ways forward towards a happier, more contented, resilient and sustainable planet. For more information please visit *www.clubofrome.org*

The **Club of Rome EU Chapter** is an independent, Brussels-based, non-profit Association. It is registered under Belgian law, and affiliated with the Club of Rome. It aims to build bridges between the institutions of the European Union, their constituencies and the Club of Rome as a leading think-tank at world level. Its mission is to act as a catalyst of reflection on sustainable development in Europe and at the global level.

Its specific aims are:

- To identify the most crucial sustainability problems facing European society; to analyse them in the global context and to reflect on alternative future solutions for a sustainable society, including the elaboration of specific scenarios for the future of the European continent.
- To initiate and facilitate cutting-edge research in which the major theme is the development of ground-breaking concepts for globally sustainable development and for the specific contributions that Europe can make.
- To organise a societal discourse on the implementation of European policies for sustainable development in a global context, involving key public authorities and private sector decision-makers, the media as well as the public at large.

For more information please visit *www.clubofrome.at/cor-eu*

Bibliography

Edward Abbey: *The Second Rape of the West* (Chicago: Playboy Enterprises, 1975)

Paul S. Adler and Seok-Woo Kwon, "Social Capital: Prospects for a New Concept", *Academy of Management Review*, vol. 27 (2002), pp. 17-40

Dan Ariely, *Predictably Irrational: The Hidden Forces That Shape Our Decisions* (New York: Harper Perennial, 2009).

Máni Arnarson, Þorbjörn Kristjánsson, Atli Bjarnason, Harald Sverdrup and Kristín Vala Ragnarsdóttir, *Icelandic Economic Collapse: A Systems Analysis Perspective on Financial, Social and World System Links* (Reykjavik: Reykjavik University, 2011)

Christian Arnsperger, *Full-Spectrum Economics: Towards an Inclusive and Emancipatory Social Science* (London: Routledge, 2010a)

Christian Arnsperger, "Monnaie, dette et croissance sans prospérité: Portée et limites du 'tournant jacksonnien'", *Etopia*, No. 8, December 2010(b)

Kenneth J. Arrow, "Uncertainty and the Welfare Economics of Medical Care", *American Economic Review*, vol. 53(1963), no. 5, pp. 941–73

Cecilia Åslund, Bengt Starrin and Kent W. Nilsson, "Social Capital in Relation to Depression, Musculoskeletal Pain, and Psychosomatic Symptoms: A Cross-Sectional Study of a Large Population-Based Cohort of Swedish Adolescents", *BMC Public Health*, vol. 10 (2010), issue 715

Anthony B. Atkinson and S. Morelli, "An Inequality Database For 25 Countries, 1911-2010", Discussion Paper (Geneva: International Labor Office, 2010)

Jacques Attali, *Tous ruinés dans dix ans? Dette publique: la dernière chance* (Paris: Fayard, 2010).

Kenny Ausubel, *Nature's Operating Instructions* (San Francisco: Sierra Club Books, 2004)

Sunny J. Auyang, *Foundations of Complex-System Theories in Economics, Evolutionary Biology, and Statistical Physics* (Cambridge: Cambridge University Press, 1998)

Robert Axelrod, *The Evolution of Cooperation* (New York: Basic Books, 1984)

Robert Axelrod and Michael D. Cohen, *Harnessing Complexity: Organizational Implications of a Scientific Frontier* (New York: Basic Books, 2000)

Belén Balanya, Ann Doherty, Olivier Hoedeman, Adam Ma'anit and Erik Wesselius, *Europe Inc.: Regional and Global Restructuring and the Rise of Corporate Power*, new edition (London: Pluto Press, 2003)

Edward Barbier, *A Global Green New Deal: Rethinking Economic Recovery* (Cambridge: Cambridge University Press, 2010)

Francesca Bastagli, Working paper, 60, 12/2009 From social net to social policy? The role of conditional cash transfer in welfare state development in Latin America, 2009, UNDP

Michael Baumgart and William McDonough, *Cradle to Cradle: Re-Making the Way We Make Things* (New York: Farrar, Strauss & Giroux, 2002)

Eric Beinhocker, *The Origin of Wealth: Evolution, Complexity and the Radical Remaking of Economics* (Boston: Harvard Business School Press, 2006)

H. C. Binswanger, *Geld und Natur: Das wirtschaftliche Wachstum zwischen Ökonomie und Ökologie* (Stuttgart: Weitbrecht, 1991)

Olivier J. Blanchard and Mark W. Watson, "Are Business Cycles All Alike?", NBER Chapters, in Robert J. Gordon (ed.), *The American Business Cycle: Continuity and Change* (Cambridge: National Bureau of Economic Research, 1987), pp. 123-180

Adrian Blundell-Wignall and Paul Atkinson, "Thinking Beyond Basel III: Necessary Solutions for Capital and Liquidity", *Financial Markets Trends*, vol. 2 (2010), issue 1, pp. 9-33

M. Borgdorff, K. Floyd and J. Broekmans, (2002) "Interventions to Reduce Tuberculosis Mortality and Transmission in Low- and Middle-income Countries", *Bulletin of the World Health Organisation*, 80(3), 217-227

H. R. Fox Bourne, *The Romance of Trade* (London: Cassell, 1876)

Bridges, C., Thompson, W., Meltzer, M., Reeve, G., Talamonti, W., Cox, N., Lilac, H., Hall, H., Klimov, A. and Fukuda, K. (2000) "Effectiveness and Cost-benefit of Influenza Vaccination of Healthy Working Adults", *Journal of the American Medical Association*, 284(13), 1655-1663

Stefan Brunnhuber and Harald Klimenta, *Wie wir wirtschaften werden: Szenarien und Gestaltungsmöglichkeiten für zukunftsfähige Finanzmärkte* (Frankfurt/ Wien: Überreuter Redline Wirtschaft, 2005).

Zbigniew Brzezinski, *The Choice: Global Domination or Global Leadership* (New York: Basic Books, 2004)

James Buchan, *Frozen Desire: the Meaning of Money* (New York: Farrar Straus Giroux, 1997)

Adrian Buckley, *Financial Crisis: Causes, Context and Consequences* (Harlow: Pearson, 2011)

Carole B. Burgoyne and Stephen E. G. Lea, "Money Is Material", *Science* 314 (17 November 2006), pp. 1091-1092

Gerard Caprio and Daniela Klingebiel, "Bank Insolvencies: Cross-Country Experience", Policy Research Working Paper no. 1620 (Washington, DC: World Bank, Policy and Research Department, 1996)

Molly Scott Cato, *Green Economics: An Introduction to Theory, Policy and Practice* (London: Earthscan, 2009)

Stephen G. Cecchetti, Madhusudan S. Mohanty and Fabrizio Zampolli, "The Future of Public Debt: Prospects and Implications", BIS Working Paper #300 (Basel: Bank for International Settlements, March 2010)

Eric Chaisson, "Non-equilibrium Thermodynamics in an Energy-Rich Universe", in A. Kleidon and R.D. Lorenz (eds), *Non-Equilibrium Thermodynamics and the Production of Entropy: Life, Earth, and Beyond* (Berlin/New York: Springer, 2005), pp. 21-33

L. Chapman, "Meta Evaluation of Worksite Health Promotion Economic Return Studies" *The Art of Health Promotion*, 6(6), (2003)

James Coleman, *Foundations of Social Theory* (Cambridge: Harvard University Press, 1990)

Committee on Capitalizing on Social Science and Behavioral Research to Improve the Public's Health, (2000) Institute of Medicine

Daryl Collins, Jonathan Morduch, Stuart Rutherford and Orlanda Ruthven, *Portfolios of the Poor: How the World's Poor Live on $2 a Day* (Princeton: Princeton University Press, 2009)

Robert Costanza, "Changing Visions of Humans' Place in the World and the Need for an Ecological Economics" (2003), in Fullbrook (2004)

D. Cutler and R. Zechhauser, *Insurance Markets and Adverse Selection: A Handbook for Health Economists* (1998)

Predrag Cvitanovic, *Introduction to Universality in Chaos* (Bristol: Adam Hilger, 1984)

Alain Dagher, "Shopping Centers in the Brain", *Neuron*, vol. 53 (2007), pp.7-8

Aiguo Dai, "Drought under Global Warming: A Review", *Climate Change*, Volume 2, Issue 1 (Jan/Feb 2011)

Herman E. Daly and John B. Cobb, *For the Common Good: Redirecting the Economy Toward Community, the Environment, and a Sustainable Future* (Boston: Beacon Press, 1989)

Herman Daly, *Beyond Growth: The Economics of Sustainable Development* (Boston: Beacon Press, 1996)

Herman Daly and Joshua Farley, *Ecological Economics*, second edition (New York: Island Press, 2011)

Paul Davidson, *Money and the Real World* (London: Macmillan, 1978)

Philippe Derudder and André-Jacques Holbecq, *La dette publique, une affaire rentable*, (Paris: éditions Yves Michel, 2008)

Roderick Dewar, "Information Theory Explanation of the Fluctuation Theorem, Maximum Entropy Production and Self-Organized Criticality in Non-Equilibrium Stationary States", *Journal of Physics A: Math. Gen. 36 #3* (2003), pp. 631-641

Jared Diamond, *Collapse: How Societies Choose to Fail or Succeed* (New York: Viking, 2005)

Walter Dolde, "The Use of Foreign Exchange and Interest Rate Risk Management in Large Firms", Working Paper #93-042 (Storra: University of Connecticut School of Business Administration, 1993), pp.18-19

Peter T. Doran and Maggie Kendall Zimmerman, "Examining the Scientific Consensus on Climate Change", *EOS, Transactions, American Geophysical Union*, Vol. 90, No 3, January 2009

Rüdiger Dornbusch, Yung Chul Park and Stijn Claessens, "Contagion: How It Spreads and How It Can Be Stopped", *World Bank Research Observer*, Vol. 15, issue 2 (August 2000), pp. 177-197

Richard Duncan, *The Dollar Crisis: Causes, Consequences, Cures* (Singapore: Wiley, 2003)

Elizabeth W. Dunn, Lara B. Aknin and Michael I. Norton, "Spending Money on Others Promotes Happiness", *Science* 319 (21 March 2008), pp. 1687-1688

Arthur S. Eddington, *The Nature of the Physical World* (New York: Macmillan, 1928)

Barry Eichengreen and K. Mitchener, "The Great Depression as a Credit Boom Gone Wrong", BIS Working Paper No. 137 (Basel: Bank for International Settlements, 2003)

Charles Eisenstein, *Sacred Economics: Money, Gift, and Society in the Age of Transition* (Berkeley: Evolver Editions, 2011)

J. C. Erfurt, A. Foote and M.A. Heirich, "The Cost Effectiveness of Worksite Health Programmes for Hypertension Control, Weight Loss, Smoking Cessation, and Exercise", *Personnel Psychology*, 45, (1992)

Niall Ferguson, *The Cash Nexus: Money and Power in the Modern World, 1700-2000* (New York: Perseus Books, 2001)

Irving Fisher, *100% Money: Designed to Keep Checking Banks 100% Liquid; to Prevent Inflation and Deflation; Largely to Cure or Prevent Depression; and to Wipe Out Much of the National Debt*, (New York: Adelphi, 1935)

John Follain, "Hard-Up Italy Sells Islands and Palaces", *Sunday Times* (London), 7 April, 2010, p.24

Jerôme Fourel, "Wall Street et ses bonus: $135.500.000.000 pour 2010", *Le Monde*, 7 February, 2011 (*http://finance.blog.lemonde/2011/02/*).

J. Frankel and A. Rose, "Currency Crashes in Emerging Markets: an Empirical Treatment", *Journal of International Economics*, vol. 4 (1996), pp.351-366

Milton Friedman, "The Case for Flexible Exchange Rates", *Essays in Positive Economics* (Chicago: University of Chicago Press, 1953)

Milton Friedman, "The Role of Monetary Policy", *American Economic Review*, vol. 68 (1968), pp.1-17

Milton Friedman and Anna Jacobson Schwartz, *A Monetary History of the United States, 1867-1960* (Princeton: Princeton University Press, 1993)

Francis Fukuyama, *Trust: Social Virtues and the Creation of Prosperity* (New York, Free Press: 1995).

Edward Fullbrook (ed.), *The Crisis in Economics: The Post-Autistic Economics Movement – The First 600 Days* (London: Routledge, 2003)

Edward Fullbrook (ed.), *A Guide to What's Wrong With Economics* (London: Anthem, 2004)

John Kenneth Galbraith, *Money: Whence It Came, Where It Went* (Boston: Houghton Muffin Co., 1975)

Nicholas Georgescu-Roegen, *Analytical Economics* (Cambridge, Mass.: Harvard University Press, 1966)

Nicholas Georgescu-Roegen, *The Entropy Law and the Economic Process* (Cambridge, Mass.: Harvard University Press, 1971)

Jamshid Gharajedaghi, *Systems Thinking: Managing Chaos and Complexity* (Boston: Butterworth & Heineman, 1999)

Orio Giarini, "Science and Economy: The Case of Uncertainty and Disequilibrium", *Cadmus*, Vol I, No.2 (April 2011)

Global Trends 2015 (Washington, D.C.: Central Intelligence Agency, April 2007)

Wynne Godley and T. Francis Cripps, *Macroeconomics* (Oxford: Oxford University Press, 1983)

Wynne Godley and Marc Lavoie, *Monetary Economics: An Integrated Approach to Credit, Money, Income, Production and Wealth* (London: Palgrave-MacMillan, 2007)

Sally J. Goerner, *After the Clockwork Universe: The Emerging Science and Culture of Integral Society* (Edinburgh: Floris Press, 1999)

Sally J. Goerner, Robert G. Dyck and Dorothy Lagerroos, *The New Science of Sustainability: Building a Foundation for Great Change*, (Chapel Hill, NC: Triangle Center for Complex Systems, 2008)

Sally Goerner, Bernard Lietaer and Robert Ulanowicz, "Quantifying economic sustainability: Implications for free-enterprise theory, policy and practice", *Ecological Economics*, 2009, Vol. 69(1), pp.76-81

R. Z. Goetzel, T. R. Juday and R. J. Ozminkowski, "What's the ROI? A Systematic Review of Return on Investment (ROI) Studies of Corporate Health and Productivity Management Initiatives", *AWHP Worksite Health*, 6, 12-21 (1999)

Ian Gondriaan, *How to Stop Deflation* (London: Search Publishing, 1932)

Charles E. Goodhart, *Money, Information and Uncertainty* (Cambridge: MIT Press, 1996)

C. Goodhart (ed.), *Financial Development and Economic Growth: Explaining the Links* (Basingstoke: Palgrave-Macmillan, 2004)

John Gowdy and Jon D. Erikson, "The Approach of Ecological Economics", *Cambridge Journal of Economics*, Vol. 29 (2005), pp.207-222

Benjamin Graham, *Storage and Stability* (New York: McGraw Hill, 1937)

Benjamin Graham, *World Commodities and World Currency* (New York: McGraw Hill, 1944)

Thomas Greco, *The End of Money and the Future of Civilization* (White River Junction: Chelsea Green, 2009)

Edward Griffin, *The Creature From Jekyll Island: A Second Look at the Federal Reserve* (Appleton, WI: American Opinion Publishing, 1994)

Alexander Grimme, *Vom Reichtum sozialer Beziehungen: Zum Verhältnis von Gemeinschaft und Sozialkapital* (Marburg: Tectum Verlag, 2009)

St Clare Grondona *Economic Stability is Attainable* (London: Hutchinson Benham Ltd, 1975)

Benedetto Gui and Robert Sugden (eds), *Economics and Social Interaction: Accounting for Interpersonal Relations* (Cambridge: Cambridge University Press, 2005)

Bilal Habib, Ambar Narayan, Sergio Olivieri and Carolina Sanchez-Paramo, "Assessing Ex Ante the Poverty and Distributional Impact of the Global Crisis in a Developing Country: A Micro-Simulation Approach With Application to Bangladesh", Policy Research Working Paper #5238 (Washington, DC: World Bank, 2010)

Andrew Haldane and Robert May, "Systemic Risk in Banking Ecosystems", *Nature*, vol. 469 (20 January 2011), pp.351-355

Gwendolyn Hallsmith, *The Key to Sustainable Cities: Meeting Human Needs, Transforming Community Systems* (Gabriola Island: New Society Publishers, 2004)

Gwendolyn Hallsmith and Bernard Lietaer, *Creating Wealth: Growing Local Economies with Local Currencies* (Gabriola Island: New Society Publishers, 2011)

Lyda Judson Hanifan, "The Rural School Community Center", *Annals of the American Academy of Political and Social Science,* no. 67 (1916)

Elmer Harmon, *Commodity Reserve Currency* (New York: Columbia University Press, 1959)

Albert Hart (Columbia University), Nicholas Kaldor (King's College, Cambridge) and Jan Tinbergen (Netherlands School of Economics): *The Case for an International Reserve Currency* (Geneva: presented on 2/17/1964 Document UNCTAD 64-03482)

Paul Hawken, *Blessed Unrest* (New York: Viking, 2007)

Friedrich Hayek, *Denationalization of Money* (London: Institute of Economic Affairs, 1976) online at *http://mises.org/books/denationalisation.pdf*

Richard Heinberg, *The End of Growth: Adapting to Our New Economic Reality* (Gabriola Island: New Society Publishers, 2011)

Hazel Henderson, *The Politics of the Solar Age: Alternatives to Economics* (New York: Doubleday, 1981)

Hazel Henderson: *Paradigms in Progress: Life beyond Economics* (Indianapolis: Knowledge Systems Inc., 1991)

Hazel Henderson: *Creating Alternative Futures* (Sterling, VA: Kumarian Press, 1996a)

Hazel Henderson: *Building a Win-Win World: Life beyond Economic Warfare* (San Francisco: Berrett Koehler, 1996b)

Hazel Henderson *Ethical Markets: Growing the Green Economy* (White River Junction, VT: Chelsea Green Publishing Co., 2006)

Hazel Henderson, *Real Economies and the Illusion of Abstraction* (London: Network for Sustainable Financial Markets, 2010)

Hazel Henderson, *Green Transition Scoreboard 2012* (St Augustin, FL: Ethical Markets, 2012)

P. F. Henshaw, "Linking Economics and Natural Systems Physics", 20 March, 2009 online at *www.synapse9.com*

Jean Houston, *Life Force: The Psychohistorical Recovery of the Self* (Wheaton: Theosophical Publishing House, 1993)

Joseph Huber and James Robertson, *Creating New Money: A Monetary Reform for the Information Age* (London: New Economics Foundation, 2001)

Marek Hudon and Bernard Lietaer, "Natural Savings: A New Microsavings Product for Inflationary Environments – How to Save Forests with Savings For and By the Poor?", *Savings and Development*, vol. 4 (2006), pp. 357-381

Lewis Hyde, *The Gift: Imagination and the Erotic Life of Property* (New York: Vintage, 1983)

In Larger Freedom: Towards Development, Security and Human Rights for All, 2005 report for the United Nations 60th-anniversary summit

Bruna Ingrao and Giorgio Israel, *The Invisible Hand* (Cambridge: MIT Press, 1990)

Mitchell Innes, "What is Money?", *Banking Law Journal*, vol. 30 (1913), no. 5, pp. 377-408

Tim Jackson, *Prosperity Without Growth: Economics For a Finite Planet* (London: Earthscan, 2009)

Sarah James and Tobjörn Lahti, *The Natural Step for Communities: How Cities and Towns Can Change to Sustainable Practices* (Gabriola Island: New Society Publishers, 2004)

W.S. Jevons, *Money and the Mechanism of Exchange* (New York: D. Appleton & Co., 1875)

Robert Wood Johnson Foundation, *Service Credit Banking Project Site Summaries* (University of Maryland: Centre of Aging, 1990)

C. Jones, "Preventing System Failure", *Central Banking*, vol. 21 (2010), pp. 69-75

Nicholas Kaldor, *The Scourge of Monetarism* (London: Oxford University Press, 1985)

Graziela L. Kaminsky and Carmen M. Reinhart, "The Twin Crisis: The Causes of Banking and Balance of Payment Problems", *American Economic Review*, vol. 89, no. 3 (1999), pp.473-500

George Kaufman, "Banking and Currency Crises and Systemic Risk: Lessons From Recent Events", *Economic Perspectives: A Review from the Federal Reserve Bank of Chicago*, No. 3 (2000)

I. Kawachi, B. P. Kennedy, K. Lochner and D. Prothrow-Stith, "Social Capital, Income Inequality and Mortality", *American Journal of Public Health*, vol. 87 (1997), no. 9, pp. 1491-1498

J. P. Keeler, "Empirical Evidence on the Austrian Business Cycle Theory", *Review of Austrian Economics*, vol.14 (2001), pp. 331-351

Margrit Kennedy, *Interest- and Inflation-Free Money* (Philadelphia: New Society Publishers, 1995)

Margrit Kennedy and Bernard Lietaer, *Regionalwaehrungen: Neue Wege zu nachhaltigem Wohlstand* (Munich: Riemann Verlag, 2004)

John Maynard Keynes, *The General Theory of Employment, Interest and Money* (New York: Macmillan, 1936)

John Maynard Keynes, *The Collected Writings, Vol XI: Economic Articles and Academic Correspondence*, ed. Donald Moggridge (London/ Cambridge: Macmillan/ Cambridge University Press, 1983)

Matthew J. Kiernan, *Investing in a Sustainable World* (New York: Amacom, 2009)

Charles P. Kindleberger, *Manias, Panics, and Crashes: A History of Financial Crises*, 5th edition (Basingstoke: Palgrave Macmillan, 2005)

Brooks King-Casa, Damon Tomlin, Cedric Anen, Colin F. Camerer, Steven R. Quartz and P. Read Montague, "Getting to Know You: Reputation and Trusting in a Two-Person Economic Exchange", *Science*, 308 (1 April 2005), pp.78-83

Naomi Klein, *No Logo: Taking Aim at the Brand Bullies* (New York: Picador, 2000)

Georg Friedrich Knapp, *The State Theory of Money* (New York: Augustus Kelley, 1973) [1924]

N. Kondratieff, "Die langen Wellen der Konjunktur" *Archiv für Sozialwissenschaft und Sozialpolitik* 1926

M. Kosfeld, "Economic networks in the laboratory: A survey", *Review of Network Economics*, vol. 3, no. 1 (2004), pp. 20–41

Thomas Kuhn, *The Structure of Scientific Revolutions* (Chicago: University of Chicago Press, 1965)

Luc Laevan and Fabian Valencia, "Resolution of Banking Crises: The Good, the Bad, and the Ugly", IMF Working Paper 10/146 (Washington: International Monetary Fund), 2010, p.4. (*bit.ly/TPlink55*)

Erwin Laszlo, *The Systems View of the World: A Holistic Vision for our Time* (Creskill: Hampton Press, 1996)

Serge Latouche, "Minuswachstum: Die falsche Kritik der Alternativökonomen", *Le Monde Diplomatique*, deutsche Ausgabe, November 2004 (*bit.ly/TPlink56*)

Serge Latouche, *L'invention de l'économie* (Paris: Albin Michel, 2005).

J. H. Lawton and R. M. May, *Extinction Rates* (Oxford: Oxford University Press, 1995)

S.G. Lea, R.M. Tarpy and P. Webley, *The Individual in the Economy: A Textbook for Economic Psychology* (Cambridge: Cambridge University Press, 1987)

Y. Leitner, "Financial Networks: Contagion, Commitment, and Private Sector Bailouts", *Journal of Finance* vol. 60, no. 6 (2005), pp. 2925–2953

Christian Léonard, *Croissance contre santé: Quelle responsabilisation du malade?* (Charleroi: Couleur Livres, 2008)

Abba Lerner, "Functional Finance and the Federal Debt", *Social Research*, vol. 10 (1943), pp. 38-51

Abba Lerner, "Money as a Creature of the State", *American Economic Review*, vol. 37 (1947), no. 2, p. 313

Claude Lévi-Strauss, *Les structures élémentaires de la parenté* (Paris: Presses Universitaires de France, 1949)

Yaojun Li, Mike Savage and Andrew Pickles, "Social Capital and Social Exclusion in England and Wales (1972-1999)", *British Journal of Sociology*, vol. 54, no. 4 (2003), pp. 497-526

C.H. Lia, P. Fernald, J. Gertler, Lynnette M Neufeld, "Role of cash in conditional cash transfer programmes for child health, growth, and development: an analysis of Mexico's Oportunidades", *Lancet* 2008, 371: 828–37

Bernard Lietaer, *Mysterium Geld: Emotionale Bedeutung und Wirkungsweise eines Tabus* (Munich: Riemann Verlag, 2000)

Bernard Lietaer, The *Future of Money: Creating New Wealth, Work and a Wiser World* (London: Random House, 2001)

Bernard Lietaer and Stephen De Meulenaere, "Sustaining Cultural Vitality in a Globalizing World: the Balinese Example", *International Journal for Social Economics*, Vol. 30, issue 9 (2003), pp.967-984

Bernard Lietaer, "A World in Balance", *Reflections (Journal of the Society for Organizational Learning – SoL)*, vol. 4, no. 4 (2003)

Bernard Lietaer & Margrit Kennedy: *Monnaies Regionales: De nouvelles voies vers une prosperité durable* (Paris: Editions Leopold Mayer, 2008)

Bernard Lietaer, *Au Coeur de la Monnaie* (Paris: Editions Yves Michel, 2011)

Bernard Lietaer and Stephen Belgin, *New Money for a New World* (Boulder: Qiterra Press, 2011)

George Loewenstein, Scott Rick and Jonathan D. Cohen, "Neuroeconomics", *Annual Review of Psychology*, vol. 59 (2008), pp. 647-672

John Maloney (ed.), *Debts and Deficits: An Historical Perspective* (Cheltenham: Edward Elgar, 1998)

Gregory Mankiw, *Macroeconomics* (New York: Worth Publishers, 2003)

Marcel Mauss, *Essai sur le don* (Paris: Presses Universitaires de France, 1920)

Campbell McConnell and Stanley Bruce, *Macroeconomics: Principles, Problems and Policies* (New York: McGraw Hill, 2008)

Donella H. Meadows, Dennis L. Meadows, Jorgen Randers and William W. Behrens III, *The Limits to Growth* (New York: Universe Books, 1972)

Donella H. Meadows, Jorgen Randers and Dennis L. Meadows, *Limits to Growth: the 30-Year Update* (White River Junction: Chelsea Green, 2004)

Enzo Minigione, *Urban Poverty and the Underclass – A Reader* (Oxford: Blackwell, 1996)

Hyman Minsky, *Stabilizing an Unstable Economy* (New Haven: Yale University Press, 1986)

Philip Mirowski, *More Heat than Light: Economics as Social Physics, Physics as Nature's Economics* (Cambridge: Cambridge University Press, 1989)

Frederic Mishkin, *The Economics of Money, Banking and Financial Markets* (New York: Addison Wesley, 2007)

Basil Moore, *Horizontalists and Verticalists: The Macroeconomics of Credit Money* (Cambridge: Cambridge University Press, 1988)

Warren Mosler, *Soft Currency Economics* (1995)

Warren Mosler, "Full Employment and Price Stability", *Journal of Post-Keynesian Economics,* vol. 20 (Winter 1997-1998), pp. 167-182

Warren Mosler, *Seven Deadly Innocent Frauds of Economic Policy* and *Soft Currency Economics* (2010), available on *www.warrenmosler.com*

L. Nefiodow, *Der fünfte Kondratieff: Strategien zum Strukturwandel in Wirtschaft und Gesellschaft* (Wiesbaden: Gabler, 1991)

L. Nefiodow, *Die Informationgesellschaft: Arbeitsplatzvernichtung oder Arbeitsplatzgewinne?* (Munich: IFO-Schnelldienst #12, April 1994)

L.A. Nefiodow, *Der Sechste Kondratieff* (Sankt Augustin: Rhein-Sieg-Verlag, 2001)

Friedrich Nietzsche, *Thus Spoke Zarathustra,* translated by Adrian del Caro and edited by Robert Pippin (Cambridge: Cambridge University Press, 2006)

Martin A. Novak, Akira Sasaki, Christine Taylor and Drew Fudenberg, "Emergence of Cooperation and Evolutionary Stability in Infinite Populations", *Nature* 428 (8 April 2004), pp. 646-650

Patrick O'Brien and Philip Hunt, "The Rise of the Fiscal State in England, 1485-1815", *Historical Research*, vol. 66 (1993), pp. 129-176

Office of the Inspector-General, City of Chicago, *An Analysis of the City's Parking Meter Lease,* September 2009

Naomi Oreskes and Erik M. Conway, *Merchants of Doubt: How a Handful of Scientists Obscured the Truth On Issues From Tobacco Smoke to Global Warming* (New York: Bloomsbury, 2010)

Paul Ormerod, *The Death of Economics* (New York: Wiley, 1994)

Elinor Ostrom, *Governing the Commons: The Evolution of Institutions for Collective Action* (Cambridge: Cambridge University Press, 1990).

Elinor Ostrom and Toh-Kyung Ahn (eds), *Foundations of Social Capital* (Cheltenham: Edward Elgar, 2003)

Greg Palast, *The Best Democracy Money Can Buy: An Investigative Reporter Exposes the Truth About Globalization, Corporate Cons and High-Finance Fraudsters* (London: Plume, 2003)

René Passet, *L'Économique et le vivant* (Paris: Bibliothèque Payot, 1979)

C. Paxson C. and N. Schady, "Does Money Matter? The Effects of Cash Transfers on Child Health and Development in Rural Ecuador", *World Bank Policy Research Working Paper* 4226, May 2007

David Pearce and Edward Barbier, *Blueprint For a Sustainable Economy* (London: Earthscan, 2000)

John Perkins, *Confessions of an Economic Hit Man* (San Francisco: Berrett Koehler, 2004).

Peter G. Petersen, "Gray Dawn: The Global Aging Crisis", *Foreign Affairs* (January-February 1999)

Ann Pettifor, *The Coming First-World Debt Crisis* (London: Palgrave-Macmillan, 2006).

Karl Polanyi, *The Great Transformation: The Political and Economic Origins of Our Time* (New York: Beacon Press, 1944)

D. R. Powell, Characteristics of Successful Health Programmes *Employee Benefits Journal*, 15-21 (1999)

Friedrich Preisigke, *Girowesen im Griechischen Ägypten, enthaltend Korngiro, Geldgiro, Girobanknotariat mit Einschluß des Archivwesens* (Strasburg: Schlesier & Schweikhardt, 1910; reprinted by Hildesheim, New York: Georg Olms, 1971)

Nomi Prins, *It Takes a Pillage: Behind the Bailouts, Bonuses, and Backroom Deals from Washington to Wall Street* (New York: Wiley, 2009)

Robert D. Putnam, Robert Leonardi and Raffaella Y. Nanetti, *Making Democracy Work: Civic Traditions in Modern Italy* (Princeton, NJ: Princeton University Press, 1994)

Robert D. Putnam, *Bowling Alone: The Collapse and Revival of American Community* (New York: Simon and Schuster, 2000)

Anne Querrien, *L'école mutuelle: Une pédagogie trop efficace?* (Paris: Seuil, 2005).

Franz J. Radermacher, *Balance or Destruction: Eco-Social Market Economy as the Key to Global Sustainable Development* (Vienna: Ökosoziales Forum Europa, 2004)

John Rawls, *A Theory of Justice* (Cambridge: Harvard University Press, 1971)

Uwe E. Reinhardt, "Can Efficiency in Health Care Be Left to the Market?", *Journal of Health Politics, Policy and Law*, vol. 26(2001), no. 5, pp. 967–92

Carmen M. Reinhart, Graciela Kaminsky and Carlos Vegh, "When It Rains, It Pours: Procyclical Capital Flows and Macroeconomic Policies", in *NBER Macroeconomics Annual* (Cambridge: National Bureau of Economic Research, 2004), pp. 11-53

Carmen M. Reinhart and Kenneth S. Rogoff, "The Aftermath of Financial Crises", *American Economic Review*, Vol. 99 (May 2009a), pp.466-472

Carmen M. Reinhart and Kenneth S. Rogoff, *This Time is Different: Eight Centuries of Financial Folly*, (Princeton, NJ: Princeton University Press, 2009b)

Adrienne Rich, "Natural Resources", *The Dream of a Common Language – Poems* (New York: W.W. Norton, 1993)

James Robertson and John Bunzl, *Monetary Reform: Making It Happen* (London: International Simultaneous Policy Organisation, 2003)

James Robertson, *Future Money: Breakdown or Breakthrough* (Totnes: Green Books, 2012).

François Roddier, *Le pain, le levain et les gènes* (Paris: Parole Editions, 2009)

Gerry Rodgers, Charles G. Gore and Jose B. Figueiredo (eds), *Social Exclusion: Rhetoric, Reality, Responses* (Geneva: International Institute of Labour Studies, 1995)

Joseph Romm, "Desertification: the Next Dustbowl", *Nature* 478 (27 October, 2011)

M. Rothschild and J. E. Stiglitz, "Equilibrium in Competitive Insurance Markets: An Essay on the Economics of Imperfect Information", *Quarterly Journal of Economics*, 90, 629-650 1976)

David Rotman, "Praying for Energy Miracle", *Technology Review*, March/April 2011

Stephen Rousseas, *Post-Keynesian Monetary Economics* (Armonk: M.E. Sharpe, 1986)

C. J. Ruhm, *Macroeconomic Conditions, Health and Government Policy* (University of Michigan: Gerald R. Ford School of Public Policy, National Poverty Center, 2006)

Jacques Sapir, *Faut il sortir de l'Euro?* (Paris: Seuil, 2011)

Detlev S. Schlichter, *Paper Money Collapse: The Folly of Elastic Money and the Coming Monetary Breakdown* (Hoboken: Wiley, 2011)

Juliet B. Schor, *Plenitude: The New Economics of True Wealth* (New York: Penguin, 2010)

Joseph A. Schumpeter, *Capitalism, Socialism and Democracy* (London: Routledge, 1942)

Frank Schweitzer, Giorgio Fagiolo, Didier Sornette, Fernando Vega-Redondo and Douglas R. White, "Economic Networks: The New Challenges", *Science*, vol. 325 (2009a), pp. 422-425

Frank Schweitzer, Giorgio Fagiolo, Didier Sornette, Fernando Vega-Redondo and Douglas R. White, "Economic Networks: What Do We Know and What Do We Need to Know?", *Advances in Complex Systems,* vol. 12, no 4 (2009b), pp. 407-422

Kenneth Scot, *Counterfeiting in Colonial America* (Philadelphia: University of Pennsylvania Press, 2000)

Peter M. Senge, *The Necessary Revolution: How Individuals and Organizations Are Working Together to Create a Sustainable World* (Boston: Nicholas Brealey, 2008)

G. Seyfang and K. Smith, *The Time of our Lives: Using time banking for neighbourhood renewal and community capacity building* (London: New Economics Foundation, 2002)

Adam Smith: *The Wealth of Nations,* Cannan Edition (New York: The Modern Library, 2000) [1776]

Andrew Ross Sorkin, *Too Big to Fail* (London: Penguin Books, 2010)

George Soros, *The Alchemy of Finance* (London: George Weidenfeld & Nicolson Ltd, 1987)

Joseph Stiglitz, *Globalization and Its Discontents* (New York: Norton, 2002)

Joseph Stiglitz, "Of the 1%, by the 1%, for the 1%", *Vanity Fair,* May 2011

James Stodder, "Reciprocal Exchange Networks: Implications for Macroeconomic Stability", paper presented at the International Electronic and Electrical Engineering (IEEE), and the Engineering Management Society (EMS), Albuquerque, New Mexico, August 2000

James Stodder, "Complementary Credit Networks and Macroeconomic Stability: Switzerland's Wirtschaftring", *Journal of Economic Behavior and Organization*, vol. 72 (2009), pp. 79-95

Federico Sturzenegger and Jeromin Zettelmeyer, *Debt Defaults and Lessons from a Decade of Crises* (Cambridge: MIT Press, 2006)

The Earth Charter Community Action Tool, *www.earthcat.org*

The Financial Crisis Inquiry Report: Final Report of the National Commission of the Financial and Economic Crisis in the United States (Public Affairs, 2011)

The Global Economic Crisis: Assessing Vulnerability With a Poverty Lens (Washington, D.C.: World Bank, 2009) [*www.siteresources.worldbank.org ~ bit.ly/TPlink35*]

'The Real Housewives of Wall Street', *Rolling Stone*, 4 Nov 2011, *www.rollingstone.com ~ bit.ly/ TPlink54*

Harding Tibbs, 'Sustainability', *Deeper News,* (Global Business Network), Vol. 3, no.1, January 1999

Towards Sustainable Development (Paris: OECD, 2000)

Arnold Toynbee, *A Study of History, Vols. I to VI* (Oxford: Oxford University Press, 1939) and *Vols. I to X* (1960)

Robert Ulanowicz and B. M. Hannon, "Life and the Production of Entropy", *Proceedings of the Royal Society of London B,* Vol. 232 (1987), pp.181-192

Robert Ulanowicz, *A Third Window: Natural Foundations for Life* (Oxford and New York: Oxford University Press, 2008)

Robert E. Ulanowicz, Sally J. Goerner, Bernard Lietaer and Rocio Gomez, "Quantifying Sustainability: Resilience, Efficiency and the Return of Information Theory", *Ecological Complexity*, Vol. 6 (2009), pp.27-36

U.S. Health (2005) National Center for Health Statistics, Department of Health and Human Services, No: 2005-1232.

Anton R. Valukas, *Lehman Brothers Inc. Chapter 11 Proceedings Examiner's Report* (2010),

Kathleen D. Vohs, Nicole L. Mead and Miranda R. Goode, "The Psychological Consequences of Money", *Science* 314 (17 November 2006), pp.1154-1156

Ludwig von Mises, *Human Action: A Treatise on Economics* (New Haven: Yale University Press, 1949)

Léon Walras, *Éléments d'économie pure* (Paris: Guillaumin, 1874)

E. U. von Weizsäcker, A. B. Lovins and L. H. Lovins, *Factor Four: Doubling Wealth – Halving Resource Use* (London: Earthscan, 1997)

Ken Wilber, *Sex, Ecology, Spirituality: The Spirit of Evolution* (Boston: Shambhala, 1995)

Edward O. Wilson, *The Future of Life* (New York: Knopf, 2002)

World Commission on the Environment and Development, *Our Common Future* (Oxford: Oxford University Press, 1989)

L. Randall Wray, *Money and Credit in Capitalist Economies: The Endogenous Money Approach* (Aldershot: Edward Elgar, 1990)

L. Randall Wray, *Understanding Modern Money: The Key to Full Employment and Price Stability* (Cheltenham: Edward Elgar, 1998)

Graham A. N. Wright, "A Critical Review of Savings Services in Africa and Elsewhere", working paper, (Nairobi: MicroSave, 1999)

Stephen Zarlenga, *The Lost Science of Money* (American Money Institute, 2002)

Also available from Triarchy Press

People Money: The Promise of Regional Currencies

Bernard Lietaer, Margrit Kennedy and John Rogers

ISBN:978-1-908009-760

People Money is a handbook for anyone who wants to develop a regional currency and for anyone who wants to learn how regional currencies can transform the lives and well-being of local communities. Find out how they can sustain businesses, how local authorities can participate in their success and why supporting regional currencies is of vital importance to the future of any community, region or country.

People Money begins with the blind spot identified here in *Money and Sustainability* – the 'blind spot' that means we can only see one kind of money: national currencies. It presents regional currencies as a powerful tool for localisation policies, explains the key characteristics of regional money systems and describes Banco Palmas in Brazil and WIR Bank in Switzerland – two leading examples of effective regional money systems.

The core of the book – a section entitled Regional Currencies in Practice – profiles the diverse global movement of local currency systems, from business-to-business exchange systems to LETS, Time Bank and Transition Town currencies. It explores the approaches used by the most effective local currency organisers and sets out a design methodology – the ORDER process – for new systems, followed by portraits of leading systems from around the world.

It continues with portraits of agencies that research, develop and support local currencies such as IRTA, STRO, QOIN, Community Forge and the German Regional Money Association.

The book ends with 'Future Positive', a summary of lessons learned, recommendations for action and brief portraits of the Bristol Pound (to be launched in 2012) and the Nanto (launch due in 2013) – both being supported by local authorities.

Regional currencies featured in the book include:

The Business Exchange, Scotland ~ Community Connect Trade, USA

RES, Belgium ~ puntoTRANSacciones, El Salvador

Brixton Pound, England ~ Talente Tauschkreis Vorarlberg, Austria

Equal Dollars, USA ~ BerkShares, USA

Chiemgauer, Germany ~ SOL Violette, France

Ithaca HOURS, USA ~ Blaengarw Time Centre, Wales

Community Exchange System, South Africa ~ Dane County Time Bank, USA

> *"Regional currencies transform a central aspect of today's economic difficulties into a central part of their solution for tomorrow. It is time to provide these new instruments with the start-up support they need to enable them to unfold their potential for good. This support must come not only from enthusiastic initiators, farsighted politicians and willing participants in the regions but also from central banks, which not only tolerate them but give protection and support, as they do in Brazil and Uruguay."*

www.triarchypress.com

About Triarchy Press

Good books and bright ideas about organisations and society

Triarchy Press is a small, independent publisher of the best new thinking about organisations and society – and practical applications of that thinking.

Our authors bridge the gap between academic research and practical experience and write about praxis: ideas in action. Those authors include:

Thought leaders in Design and Systems Thinking like Russ Ackoff and John Seddon

Experts in Cultural Theory and Complexity like Don Michael and Michael Thompson

Forward thinkers like Gerard Fairtlough, Bernard Lietaer, Jay Ogilvy and International Future Forum's Graham Leicester.

Visit **www.triarchypress.com** to find out more about their books and explore the Idioticon for examples of their thinking and ideas.